Near-Death Experiences

Near-death experiences (NDEs) fascinate everyone, from theologians to sociologists and neuroscientists. This ground breaking book introduces the phenomenon of NDEs, their personal impact and the dominant scientific explanations. Taking a strikingly original cross-cultural approach and incorporating new medical research, *Near-Death Experiences* combines new theories of mind and body with contemporary research into how the brain functions.

Ornella Corazza analyses dualist models of mind and body, discussing the main features of NDEs as reported by many people who have experienced them. She studies the use of ketamine to reveal how central characteristics of NDEs can be chemically induced without being close to death. This evidence challenges the conventional 'survivalist hypothesis', according to which the near-death experience is a proof of the existence of an afterlife.

This remarkable book concludes that we need to move towards a more integrated view of body and soul, in order to understand what human life is and also what it can be.

Ornella Corazza is a Fellow in the Department of the Study of Religions at SOAS, the University of London. In 2004–5 she was a member of the 21st Century, Centre of Excellence (COE) program on the 'Construction of Death and Life Studies concerning Culture and Value of Life' at the University of Tokyo.

Near-Death Experiences

Exploring the Mind–Body Connection

Ornella Corazza

Routledge
Taylor & Francis Group

LONDON AND NEW YORK

First published 2008 by Routledge

2 Park Square, Milton Park, Abingdon, Oxon. OX14 4RN

Simultaneously published in the USA and Canada
by Routledge
270 Madison Ave, New York, NY 100016

Routledge is an imprint of the Taylor & Francis Group, an informa business

© 2008 Ornella Corazza

Typeset in Times NR MT by Graphicraft Limited, Hong Kong
Printed and bound in Great Britain by TJ International Ltd,
Padstow, Cornwall

British Library Cataloguing in Publication Data
A catalogue record for this book is available from the British Library

Library of Congress Cataloging in Publication Data
Corazza, Ornella.
  Near-death experiences : exploring the mind-body connection /
  Ornella Corazza.
    p. cm.
  Includes bibliographical references and index.
  1. Near-death experiences.   I. Title.
  BF1045.N4C67 2008
  133.901′3–dc22
  2008000555

ISBN10 0-415-45519-7 (hbk)
ISBN10 0-415-45520-0 (pbk)
ISBN10 0-203-92890-3 (ebk)

ISBN13 978-0-415-45519-0 (hbk)
ISBN13 978-0-415-45520-6 (pbk)
ISBN13 978-0-203-92890-5 (ebk)

In memory of two marvellous teachers, Laura Huxley (1911–2007) and Yasuo Yuasa (1925–2005).

Contents

Foreword

Through her experiential knowledge of the near-death experience, Ornella Corazza brings us, in a convincing and logical way, a deeper understanding of the relation between body and soul, pointing out that the spirituality of the senses and the sensuality of the spirit are one during our lifetime.

Laura Archera Huxley
Los Angeles
September 2007

Acknowledgments

The completion of this book was a fascinating and arduous journey, which would not have been possible without meeting many people who provided me with plenty of encouragement and numerous inspiring discussions. Amongst these, special thanks go to Cosimo Zene, who helped this project at every step with his criticism, charm and sense of humour. I owe a special gratitude to Peter and Elizabeth Fenwick, who introduced me to the field of near-death studies and who stimulated my critical thinking during our numerous meetings in both London and Tokyo. My sincere appreciation also goes to Paul Badham and Karl Jansen, for supporting me with valuable guidance and profound insights. I also owe a debt to Susumu Shimazono who made it possible for me to take part in his 21st Century COE program on the 'Construction of Death and Life Studies' at the University of Tokyo, one of my most life-changing experiences. There I met friends and scholars who were of great help and inspiration, especially Allan Kellehear, Yasuo Yuasa, Hiroshi Motoyama, Carl Becker and Yoshi Honda.

I should also like to thank The Japan Foundation and The Great Britain Sasakawa Foundation for the generous funding that made my research in Japan possible.

My editor Lesley Riddle and the rest of the team at Routledge made the process of revising for publication both constructive and pleasant, despite all the challenges of writing a book in my third language. I also benefited from Paul Marshall's vigilant eye and useful suggestions.

Several other scholars and friends contributed to this work: Fabrizio Schifano, Shigenori Nagatomo, Lucia Dolce, David Lorimer, Cherie Sutherland, David Fontana, Rupert Sheldrake, Chris French, James Robinson, Fulvia Cariglia, Giuseppe Festa, David Luke and Sidney Chang.

I should also like to acknowledge the help of those who agreed to be interviewed for this project and the Religious Experience Research Centre at the University of Wales, Lampeter, for supporting me with invaluable material, which made much of this book possible.

To my family, for their love and support, I reserve a very special gratitude.

Finally, a thought of gratitude goes to the memories of two marvellous teachers, Laura Huxley and Yasuo Yuasa, who taught me so much about the possibility of a deep harmony between body, mind and spirit during our lifetime, which will continue to inspire my work to an indefinite degree.

Ornella Corazza
London
May 2008

List of abbreviations

CCS   Center for Consciousness Studies
DBV   death-bed vision
EEG   electroencephalogram
ESP   extra-sensory perception
fMRI   functional magnetic resonance imaging
IANDS   International Association for Near-Death Studies
MEG   magnetic encephalography
NBE   near-birth experience
NCC   neural correlates of consciousness
NDE   near-death experience
NDEr   near-death experiencer
OBE   out-of-body experience
PET   positron emission tomography

Introduction

Life is a fascinating journey and at some stage or another each one of us will ask questions such as 'Who are we?', 'Is there life after death?', 'Does God exist?' My aim in this book is to address these questions by stressing the vital importance of physicality, and to emphasize that we not only have bodies, we *are* our bodies. As William Blake put it: 'Man has no Body distinct from his Soul: for that called Body is a portion of Soul discerned by the five senses, the chief inlets of Soul in this age,' a statement that could fittingly be printed in every page of this book. We live in a time in which, on the one hand, there is a growing scientific consensus on the unity of mind and brain and on consciousness as a product of brain activity, while, on the other, the dualistic theories that separate mind and brain (and the implications that this separation has for our understanding of what it means to be human) remain deeply embedded in our culture, and appear to be supported by recent research into the experiences of those who claim to have been outside their bodies either during a close encounter with death (so-called 'near-death experiences' or NDEs) or through the ingestion of dissociative drugs.

In this book I challenge both these approaches and propose in their place a non-dualist, non-reductionist view of NDEs that is strongly influenced by an Eastern – particularly Japanese – theory of the mind–body relationship that rejects any version of dualism. The work of Yasuo Yuasa, of Tetsuro Watsuji and of Hiroshi Ichikawa, among many others, serves to further our understanding of what it means to be human and encompass both our psycho-physiological and our inter-personal activities. This work regards the human body as not limited by the skin but as extending far beyond its physical boundaries. Our use of tools creates a semi-definite body-space around us, while our visual and tactile perception extends this dimension still further until it reaches the immensity of space. Within such a wider understanding of embodiment, near-death or dissociative experience and the sensation of being outside one's body no longer challenge what it means to be human, because being human is seen as identified with this holistic understanding of the body and of the universe that contains it.

My starting point is necessarily an examination of the mind–body problem, and of the solutions to this problem proposed by those engaged in the contemporary study of consciousness. Such an examination necessarily leads us to secular questions such as 'Who are we?', 'What are we made of?' In my view, our Western societies may – thanks to modern scientific discoveries – know a great deal about the human body and its functions, but there is little or no physical understanding of the mind. The dualist view is that mind and body are two distinct forms of consciousness, with the mind serving as an immaterial 'something' that resides within the material body. However, the idea that mind and body are two distinct forms of consciousness has various negative implications for our everyday life, the most insidious of which is probably that although the body determines our presence in the world, it also tends to 'escape' from our conscious experience in the sense that the mind is largely out of touch with the body's physical processes and regards them as controlled by the unconscious autonomic nervous system. This dichotomy between body and mind is sometimes referred to as the 'absent body' theory, which is not in fact shared by all cultures. A radically different approach prevails in Eastern traditions, religions and philosophies, which see the mind as an embodied phenomenon.

The problem with this Eastern approach is of course that it is challenged in various ways by near-death studies, which first came to prominence in the late 1960s with the work of Elizabeth Kübler-Ross, of Christophe Hampe, of Michael Sabom and of Ian Stevenson, and culminated in the publication by Raymond Moody's *Life after Life* in 1975. The main features of the NDE, namely clinical death, movement through a darkness or tunnel, entering other realms, encountering deceased loved ones and other entities, visions of the Light, telepathic communication with God, a life review, and a perception of separation from the physical body, will all be considered in the course of the book, as will the exponential increase in reported NDEs over the past decades, largely thanks to improved resuscitation techniques that enable increasing numbers of people to survive brief periods of clinical death. One of the most impressive features of the NDE is the lasting after-effect that it has upon those who experience it, and another is that it allows us to compare the experience with the images of the afterlife that occur in Western and Eastern mythology. However, a number of aspects of NDEs as reported are open to challenge, as will also be made clear.

Some of this challenge arises from the cultural differences in approaches to the mind–body relationship mentioned earlier. For example, do Japanese patients who experience NDEs report the same experiences as Westerners? We now have the results of the first small research study on NDEs in Japan, and these results enable me to undertake an analysis of the complex phenomenon of the NDE from a cross-cultural perspective, and to attempt to answer the question whether or not NDEs are universal experiences. Do they, for example, have common features across cultures and religions, and if so, what are they? Further light on these questions is thrown by the extraordinary experiences of Hiroshi Motoyama, a Japanese man whose ability to exit his body at will through the practice of meditation I have investigated.

A further piece of research relevant to questions on the mind–body problem that I have undertaken focuses upon a group of recreational users of ketamine, an anaesthic that is sometimes used as a drug in clubs and other non-clinical settings and that is said to facilitate out-of-body experiences (OBEs). How do these chemically facilitated experiences compare with the spontaneous OBE experienced in NDEs? I shall attempt to answer this question, illustrating my conclusions with some intensely personal accounts by some members of my sample of ketamine users who have courageously taken the drug in an attempt to experience the afterlife. Were they really able to talk to God and to deceased loved ones? Or were their hallucinations simply a consequence of the action of the drug? The answers put forward in the book depend in large measure upon what is known of the neurophysiological responses of individuals to near-death experiences, and also upon comparisons between the 36 accounts of dissociative experiences induced by ketamine that I have collected in the course of my research. They also draw upon the 36 accounts of NDEs collected by Peter Fenwick, consultant neuropsychiatrist at the Maudsley Hospital, University of London, and pioneer researcher into near-death experiences (data on the latter group are also available in the Religious Experience Research Centre Archive at the University of Wales in Lampeter). One of the conclusions that I consider can be drawn from these comparisons is that some NDE features, such as the vision of the Light, the meetings with others, and the arrival at a 'point of no return', are less likely to happen during a ketamine experience. There are various possible explanations for this, but in general the findings call into question Karl Jansen's much publicized but anecdotal observations that NDE and ketamine experiences are sometimes difficult to distinguish from each other. It is appropriate to remind ourselves that unlike NDEs (though these obviously carry risks of a different kind!), the ingestion of ketamine outside controlled clinical settings carries a number of serious health risks.

No study of NDEs would be complete without a discussion of the explanations for the NDE advanced respectively by biologists and psychoanalysts in support of the idea that NDEs are a defense mechanism of the dying brain, and those put forward by commentators who favor transcendental theories in support of the view that during the NDE an immaterial mind becomes separated from the physical body and journeys briefly to what is said to be the afterlife. However, for reasons that will become clear in the book, neither of these approaches seems adequate to me as an explanation of the experiences reported by those who encounter the phenomenon of temporary death.

In their place I suggest that the non-dualist and non-reductionist concept of embodiment advanced by Eastern commentators that focuses upon both psychophysiological and interrelational sets of activities – i.e. on the phenomenological relevance to NDEs of space (or 'place'; Japanese: *Basho*) – during transcendence is more helpful in furthering our understanding of these states. This concept depends particularly upon Yasuo Yuasa's innovative theories of the human body, which argue that the human organism can be conceptualized as an energy system characterized by multi-layered information circuits. His theories reflect a holistic view of the human body in terms of which the function of the mind is not only related to the brain but also to the rest of the body. Such a view represents a new and important approach relevant to both Eastern and Western theories of mind–body as well as to contemporary brain research. As I hope to make clear, it points us towards a new and improved understanding not only of what human beings are, but of what they can become.

Enjoy the journey!

The mind–body connection[1]

> Man has no Body distinct from his Soul: for that called Body is a portion of Soul discerned by the five senses, the chief inlets of Soul in this age.
>
> (William Blake)

Life is a fascinating journey and at some stage or another each one of us will ask questions such as 'Who are we?', 'Is there life after death?', 'Does God exist?' To address these questions in all their complexity, we would need to consider the relationship between humans and the universe, their more immediate natural and inanimate environment, between individual persons and other individuals, and groups, and whole societies; between individuals living now and in past times; the cultural traditions of their own societies and other societies. And this of course is an enormous topic of enquiry. However, what I propose to discuss in this chapter is more limited: what we are in relation to our own minds and bodies – or, seeing that there is no single word, let us use it in a hyphenated form – our own mind–bodies? So what are we in relation to our mind–body? What are we in relation to this total organism in which we live? (Huxley 1992). From a common-sense point of view, there is no problem at all. Most of the time, as we go about our everyday activities, we experience such transparency between the mental and the somatic aspects of our being that we are not led to reflect on their differences. For us, it is just natural and immediate to be who we are, without feeling the necessity to reduce ourselves either to mind (or soul) or body. Let me give you an example. Right now my mind wants to write this sentence and my fingers move across the keyboard and make the words appear on the computer screen. This action may seem natural and unproblematic to most of us; however, the moment we start thinking about it in greater detail, the problems start. If I wish to write this sentence, I simply type it. But who is the 'I' who does the typing?

It is obvious to me that it is not exclusively the 'I' who is sitting here thinking about it, the 'I' who writes it, because I do not have the faintest idea how my fingers can type! All I know is that I expressed the wish to write this sentence, whereupon something within me set to work a number of little muscles in perfect harmony so as to produce this movement in my right arm and fingers.

Similarly, we can ask ourselves, how did we form in the womb of our mothers? How did we grow up? How did we learn to walk, or to talk? Or more 'simply', how does our heart beat? How do we breathe? How do we digest our food? Just to mention some of the few imponderables – we don't have the faintest idea. All these actions are left to an ineffable deeper intelligence, which is far greater than our thinking self. The question then arises: 'How are we connected to it?' This enquiry requires some historical analysis.

What are we made of?

Since the seventeenth century, especially with the influential philosophy of René Descartes (1596–1650), we have been taught to conceive of ourselves as composed of two classes of substances: an immaterial mind and a physical body. Descartes, a devout Catholic, prepared the way for his conception of the mind–body relationship with his famous Latin dictum *cogito ergo sum* ('I think therefore I am').[2] With this, he identified the thinking 'I' as the soul, and confined it within a physical body, as made explicit in the following statement:

> I knew that I was a substance, the whole essence or nature of which is to think, and for its existence there is no need of any place, nor does it depend on any material thing; so that this 'me', that is to say, the soul by which I am what I am, is entirely distinct from the body, and is even more easy to know than is the latter; and even if the body were not, the soul would not cease to be what it is.[3]

The tendency to separate the mind from the body can be traced back to the Hippocratic *Corpus* (ca 400 BC). Hippocrates and his students were primarily concerned with the introduction of the first elements of clinical practice such as observation, palpation, diagnosis and prognosis. But at the same time they attempted to disregard all the 'irrational' and 'magical' methods used by traditional folk-healers along with their ancient knowledge of the human body. In Hippocrates' treatise on epilepsy, ironically entitled *On the Sacred Disease*, we read:

> I do not believe that the so-called Sacred Disease is any more divine or sacred than any other disease, but that on the contrary, just as other diseases have a nature and a definite cause, so does this one, too, have a nature and a cause . . . It is my opinion that those who first called this disease sacred were that sort of people that we now call 'magi'. These

magicians are vagabonds and charlatans, pretending to be holy and wise, and pretending to more knowledge than they have.

(Scheper-Hughes and Lock 1987: 9)

The distinction between body and mind is even more explicit in the German language, where two different words are used to describe the body (*Leib* and *Körper*). *Der Leib* refers to the animated body, while *der Körper* refers to the objective, exterior and institutionalized body (Turner 1992: 9). Gilbert Ryle mockingly called the idea of the physical body inhabited by the non-physical mind 'the ghost in the machine', a phrase which has nowadays entered into common use (see, for instance, Blackmore 2003).

Descartes' separation of body and mind has to be put into the context where it belongs. As Mary Midgley has pointed out:

In Descartes' time, their separation was intended as quarantine to separate the new, burgeoning science of physics from views on the other, more general attempt to separate Reason from Feelings and establish Reason as the dominant partner, Feeling being essentially part of the body.

(Midgley, in Lorimer 2004: 173)

The argument that we need to attempt a reconciliation between reason and emotion has largely been supported by Antonio Damasio, who has drawn on his experience with neurological patients affected by brain damage to present a new theory of emotion that emphasizes its inseparable dependence on reason (Damasio 1994). According to Damasio, Descartes' error was

the abyssal separation between body and mind, between the sizable, dimensional, mechanically operated, indefinitely divisible body stuff, on the other hand, the unsizable, undimensional, un-pushpullable, nondivisible mind stuff; the suggestion that reasoning, and moral judgement, and the suffering that comes from physical pain or emotional upheaval might exist separately from the body. Specifically: the separation of the most refined operations from the structure and operation of a biological organism.

(ibid.: 249–50)

As we have just seen, Descartes' idea of a disembodied mind also goes against our ordinary experience, which seems to present us with a transparency, not an opposition, between body and mind. Metaphorically speaking, if we think of the ocean, the seventeenth-century idea of the mind and body relationship is like the one between the water and the sand: they never become one. On the contrary, from a common-sense point of view, the relationship between mind and body is like that between the water and the salt. As Kasulis

has pointed out: 'Unlike the sand, the salt surrenders its crystalline structure to dissolve completely into the water' (2004: 15).

The spirituality of the material body

In order to find a link between mind and body, Descartes was able to identify a physical point in the body through which the immaterial mind could
actually operate to effect changes in the physical world. He believed the pineal
gland,[4] located between the left and the right brain, made this function even
more likely. He understood the process as follows:

> Although the soul is joined with the entire body, there is one part of the
> body [the pineal] in which it exercises its function more than elsewhere
> . . . [the pineal] is so suspended between the passages containing animal
> spirits (guiding reason and carrying sensation and movement) that it can
> be moved by them; and it carries this motion on to the soul. Then con-
> versely, the bodily machine is so constituted that whenever the gland
> is moved in one way or another by the soul, or for that matter by
> any other cause, it pushes the animal spirits, which surround it to the
> pores of the brain.
>
> (Descartes 1954: 357)

It is important to point out that the recognition of mind–body unity was
also the departure point for Descartes' philosophy, as emerges clearly in *The
Passions of the Soul*. For instance, he wrote:

> I am not only lodged in my body as a pilot in a vessel . . . I am besides
> so intimately conjoined, and as it were intermixed with it, that my mind
> and body compose a certain unity. For if this were not the case, I should
> not feel pain when my body is hurt.
>
> (Descartes 1937: 135)

With this statement he explicitly recognized that the soul could not simply
be reduced to that abstract 'something' confined within a physical body. As
I will argue in greater detail in the following section, this more integrated
conception of mind-in-the-body has been increasingly recognized today in
the so-called 'new science of consciousness' (see, for instance, Damasio 1994).
As Yuasa observed, 'it has taken three hundred years . . . to return to the
bon sens behind Descartes' theory' (1987: 193).

The absent body

Far from being a mere philosophical speculation, the seventeenth-century
separation of body and mind had an enormous influence not only on the

new developments of mechanistic paradigms of science, but also in generating a gradual process of desacralization, objectification and exploitation of all nonhuman nature (Metzner 1999). The phenomenon has been well described by Rupert Sheldrake in his *Natural Grace*:

> The soul, the animate principle, was withdrawn from the whole universe and also from the body. The world was deanimated and was effectively regarded as an automatic machine with no soul, no spontaneous life, and no purpose of its own, animals and plants became inanimate machines, and so did the human body. The only part of the material world that was not entirely mechanical was a small region of the human brain, the pineal gland, where the rational conscious mind of man somehow interacted with the machinery of the nerves. The old view was not that the soul was in the body, but that the body was in the soul. Now the soul survived only inside our heads.
>
> (Sheldrake, in Sheldrake and Fox 1996: 15)

Although this is not the topic of this book, it will be informative to remember that the idea that nature is alive is not only part of the world-view of many other cultures, such as shamanistic societies (Eliade 1964; Metzner 1999), but it was an 'old view' of our own ancestors in pre-industrial societies. Aristotle, for instance, postulated that animals, plants as well as the Earth (or 'Gaia', its ancient Greek name) and the entire universe were believed to have a soul.

This strange course of events has also resulted in a disembodied and desacralized vision of our everyday life. Caught up in the frenetic rhythms of our daily activities, rapid communication and transportation, we feel very much dissociated from our spiritual nature and that of the world around us. As a result, mind and body have become two different forms of consciousness, two different lives that we live. I believe we need very sincerely to keep a connection. We not only have, but we *are* our bodies. According to Drew Leder, dualism allowed us to develop a kind of mechanistic conception of the body and its functions, according to which there is no interaction or at least no significant interaction between mind and body (Leder 1998: 117). Consequently, we tend to perceive the body as a sort of machine, as 'something' that is different from ourselves. This phenomenon is also known as that of the 'absent body' (ibid.). Never before have we spent so much money on beauty treatments and products, rejuvenation remedies, and so on, pretending to be younger and smarter. I was a model in Milan and London for some years, and I am convinced more than ever that real beauty comes from the spirituality of the material body. As Yasuo Yuasa has observed:

> It seems that the more affluent the world has become materially, the poorer it has become spiritually: contemporary civilization is on the verge of

losing its spiritual wealth. But, isn't the most truly important thing for human beings the act of enhancing one's own mind and heart, while nurturing the soul which harmonizes with others?

(Yuasa 1993: 36)

Healing the split

This 'unholy' way of life is now coming to an end. The twenty-first century has already shown the symptoms of a new revolutionary change, in which science, spirituality and the sense of the sacred are coming together in the so-called 'new science of consciousness'. We rapidly are developing a certain consensus philosophy, which strongly moves away from the mind and body dichotomy. This new tendency is partially influenced by an Eastern view of conceiving the mind–body, which rejects any kind of dualism (see, for instance, Yuasa 1993; Nagatomo 1992). According to Yuasa, the mind–body relationship today has become a 'new problem':

the problem has changed from the disjunctive mind-body dualism ('Cartesian dualism') to a dualism of mind-body correlativity. Following this model of mind-body correlativity it is possible to study the body in its physiological functions and its various organs by dividing the whole into numerous parts in light of anatomical classification.

(Yuasa 1993: 41)

Yuasa warns that this classification is not possible for the mind:

Although the mind is usually believed to be in the brain, the function of the mind is not only related to the brain but also influences the functions of all the organs in the whole body. Consequently, when we take mind-body correlativity as our standpoint, the reductionist attitude, which first divides the whole into parts and then understands it as the sum of its parts, is clearly insufficient. For this reason, a holistic standpoint is advocated today which takes note of the holistic function of the mind/body.

(ibid.: 41–2)

According to this approach, although mind and body may be *conceptually* distinguishable from some perspectives, they are not assumed to be ontologically distinct (ibid.). A useful metaphor to explain this concept is that of the Japanese *shimenawa*. The *shimenawa* is a sacred robe, which indicates the presence of a certain *kami*,[5] or divinity. Usually it is hung on a tree. Nevertheless, it is interesting to observe how, for the Japanese, this does not mean that a certain *kami* ('divinity') inhabits the tree, but rather that the tree itself is a *kami*. The same thing could be said about the mind–body relationship. This does not mean that an immaterial soul (mind) inhabits a physical body, or/and that it can be placed in some part of the brain, but rather the physical body is the soul.

Toward an Eastern theory of the mind–body

The originality of this Eastern view consists in the fact that mind–body unity ('oneness') is conceived as an *achievement* rather than an essential relation, which can be reached through physical practice (Yuasa 1993). This implies a form of knowing which is strictly corporeal and that can be developed through 'self-cultivation' (in Japanese, *shugy-o*). Pragmatically speaking, the process of self-cultivation is fundamental at any stage of our existence. We cultivate a plant in order to let it grow; we educate our children in order to let them be good adults, so we 'cultivate' our minds in order to let them be in harmony with our bodies. According to Yasuo Yuasa, one of the greatest theorists of the body in the contemporary period, personal 'cultivation' is the philosophical foundation of Eastern theories, where the mind–body relations represent not only a way of 'thinking' about the world, but also a mode of 'being' in the world. In other words, we could say that self-cultivation is a valid method of overcoming dualism through *praxis*. For instance, a famous *renga* poet, Shinkei conceived the 'training' and the 'diligence' in composing *waka* poetry as follows:

> Whatever the way [of practice], shouldn't one's mind change greatly through training (*keiko*) and diligence? If so, no matter how much one is exposed to sacred teaching and books, attainment is not his unless he knows for himself what is cold to be cold, what is hot to be hot.

The phrase 'to know for himself what is cold to be cold, what is hot to be hot' is a common Zen expression meaning that cultivation can only be understood by personal experiencing with the whole body–mind. This fundamentally means that true knowledge cannot be obtained simply by means of theoretical thinking, but only through 'bodily recognition or realization', which means through the utilization of one's total mind and body. This can be seen as a way to 'learn with the body', not only with the brain (Yuasa 1987).

In other terms, the practice of self-cultivation is designed as a form of personal growth that accompanies the spiritual development, or the enlightenment of the person. Accordingly, everyone can become enlightened when the entire mind–body is completely dissolved to the point that there is no hint of ego-consciousness at work. At this stage, thought and action, when they are engaged, are no longer two distinct, competing factors in the being of a person; instead, they reach a level of oneness.

Let me quote an example, the performance of a master in martial arts. To reach a high performance in martial arts means to achieve a state of body–mind oneness (as the Japanese idiom suggests) where one can move the body freely without intending it. Zen monk Takuan Soho, who lived nearly five hundred years ago, curiously suggested that our mental attitude should be trained in a *bushi* way (Takuan 1986). He said that a person who becomes stagnant in certain thoughts, stiffened on pondering on something (what he called a 'delusory' or 'unbalanced' mind) is like the swordsman, who is unable to execute his techniques because he is captivated by the movement of his opponent's sword, or his opponent's movements, in short, by the changing situation. On the contrary, a skilled swordsman acts in a state in which the mind flows freely in all directions, forward, backward, right and left, as he wishes without becoming stagnant. He called this an 'original' or 'right' mind, as if to say that at the center of these movements lies an 'immovable wisdom' or 'state of no-mind'. At such a time, the mind 'fills' the body and it expands unlimited in order to reach the optimal performance. In his words:

> If one puts his mind in the action of his opponent's body, his mind will be taken by the action of his opponent's body. If he puts his mind in his opponent's sword, his mind will be taken over by that sword. If he puts his mind in thoughts of his opponent's intention to strike him, his mind will be taken over by thoughts of his opponent's intention to strike him. If he puts his mind in his own sword, his mind will be taken by his own sword. If he puts his mind in his own intention of not being struck, his mind will be taken by his intention of not being struck . . . What this means is that there is no place to put the mind . . . If you put it in your right hand, it will be taken by the right hand and your body will lack its functioning. If you put your mind in the eye, it will be taken by the eye, and your body will lack its functioning. If you put your mind in your right foot, your body will lack its functioning. No matter where you put it, if you put the mind in one place, the rest of your body will lack its functioning.
>
> (Takuan 1986: 30)

It comes naturally to ask the question: 'Where shall the mind go then?' Following Takuan, the correct answer is 'anywhere'. The mind should be able to move freely in all parts of the body. 'In this way, when it enters our hand, it will realize the hand's function. When it enters the foot, it will realize the foot's function. When it enters your eye, it will realize the eye's function' (ibid.: 31). In other words, the 'right mind' is like water, whereas the 'confused mind' is like a cube of ice: 'when ice is melted, it becomes water and flows everywhere' (ibid.: 32).

The interconnected universe

The non-dualist view of mind–body opens up a new way of conceiving our being as part of a network of interconnections with other beings and the entire cosmos. Watsuji (1889–1960) called this network of interconnections a state of 'between-ness' (or *aidagara*), which for him was the most important aspect of a human being. But what does it mean to exist in a 'state of between-ness'? From an etymological point of view, the term 'between' (*aida*) signifies a spatial distance separating thing and thing. So our 'between-ness' implies that we always exist within a given 'life-space', which is characterized by a large set of interrelationships (or 'personal context'). In *Climates*, Watsuji defines between-ness as 'the extension of [embodied] subjective' to underline that to exist in space is the primordial fact, the primordial significance of human beings.[6] According to Yuasa, the state of 'between-ness' has to be understood in physical terms. A very well-known example that Watsuji gave is that of the intimate relation between a mother and her baby, or that between friends. He wrote, 'That one wishes to visit a friend implies she intends to draw near to the friend's body. If she goes to visit a friend who is at some distance by streetcar, then her body moves in the friend's direction, attracted by the power between them that draws them together' (Watsuji 1996: 62). In other words, for Watsuji, the relationship between two people is not only psychological (or 'mind based'), but also somatic (or grounded in the 'physical body'). Space for him was the most crucial fact in the life of a person, rather than the conscious subject as it emerged from Cartesianism.

The idea that we are all interconnected is also increasingly supported by science. For instance, recent evidence has emerged from brain imaging studies, carried out by a team of researchers in Hawaii, where they asked a group of 11 healers who claimed to be able to heal at a distance to choose a person with whom they felt a special connection and whom they thought they could heal. This subject was placed in an fMRI scanner and isolated from all forms of sensory contact from the healers. Random episodes of healing energy and no energy were given so there was no way that the subjects in the scanner could know when they were receiving healing energy. Significant differences were found between the experimental (send) and control (no send) conditions. There was less than approximately one chance in 10,000 that the results could be explained by chance happenings ($p = 0.00127$) (Achterberg *et al.* 2005). Even stronger evidence has emerged from the accounts of people who have a particular kind of transcendental experience that Paul Marshall classified as 'universal mystical experience because it is 'suggestive of contact with the universe as a whole' (1992: 63). Before analysing this phenomenon in greater detail in terms of the near-death experience (NDE), I would like to take a fresh look at the epistemology of consciousness.

The new science of consciousness

At the beginning of a new millennium, it is rather surprising that the mind–body connection is again a hot topic of research from a multidisciplinary

point of view (Chalmers 1996; Velmas 1996; Blackmore 2003). As Stuart
Hameroff has pointed out, the recent interest has been confirmed by the
'boom' in new books, articles and international symposiums on the subject
(Hameroff *et al*. 1996; 1997; 1999). For instance, since 1994 a major debate
has been held every two years in Tucson at the Center for Consciousness
Studies, University of Arizona, where scientists and researchers from various backgrounds meet to discuss the 'new science of consciousness'. The
discussion is mainly about what David Chalmers originally called the 'hard
problem' of consciousness (Chalmers 1996). But what is the 'hard problem'?
The answer varies considerably from investigator to investigator, but a consensus seems to have emerged that the 'hard problem' refers to the problem
of how *subjective experience* associated with cognitive or mental events
arises from the *objective* activity of brain cells.

In many ways, the hard problem of consciousness is just another name
for the classic mind–body problem. According to Susan Blackmore: 'What
makes the problem of consciousness somewhat different from other versions
of the mind-body problem is the modern context' (2003: 9). While theories
of consciousness proliferate, the question remains: 'What is consciousness?'
Although consciousness is one of the most familiar and intimate aspects that
each one of us possesses, it also remains a poorly understood phenomenon.
Francisco Varela defined consciousness as a sort of 'bag term' in which we
throw anything we don't understand yet (1996: 23), while Daniel Dennett
described it as 'the last surviving mystery' (1991: 21). I would like to focus
now on the origins of this contemporary debate.

The origins of consciousness studies

The contemporary approach to consciousness was initially developed at
the beginning of the last century, particularly by those who followed the
Husserlian phenomenological tradition, such as Martin Heidegger, Maurice
Merleau-Ponty, among others. Edmund Husserl (1859–1938) had taken a
different and new approach to the understanding of the mind–body relationship
in order to overcome dualism. He observed:

> I cannot shut myself up within the realm of science. All my knowledge
> about the world, even my scientific knowledge, is gained from my own
> peculiar point of view, or from some experience of the world without
> which the symbols of science would be meaningless. The whole uni-
> verse of science is built upon the world as directly experienced. If we
> want to subject science itself to rigorous scrutiny and arrive at a precise
> assessment of its meaning and scope, we must begin to reawaken the
> basic experience of the world of which science is the second order of
> expression. Science has not and never will have, by its nature, the same

significance *qua* form of being as the world which we perceive, for the simple reason that it is a rationale or explanation of that world.

(Husserl, in Merleau-Ponty 1962)

Such an approach produced a distinction between an 'objective' body, which can be identified with its anatomical description and the *lived* body, which lives through and sustains the act of perception.

According to Gallagher (1997), the distinction between 'subjective' (lived) body and 'objective' body is best understood not as one between two different bodies, but as a way of perceiving the same body.

The phenomenological notion of the *lived* body brought a lot of common sense into the debate on our existence, where lived-body–environment became a unitary structure devoid of a sharp separation between the human organism and the surrounding world. In Heidegger's words, the lived body is a *'mode of being-in-the-world'* (Heidegger 1962).

Phenomenological thinking was also taken up by the Kyoto School in Japan, initiated by Nishida Kitarō and carried on by Nishitani Keiji and other members. It was later developed in the works of scholars such as Yasuo Yuasa and Hiroshi Ichikawa (Ichikawa 1979; Yuasa 1993).

For several reasons, phenomenology did not become the dominant mainstream approach in Western societies, where the Cartesian legacy is still influential. According to Yasuo Yuasa, this is because: (1) phenomenology has limited its investigation to a universal or normal state of consciousness, with no significant attention paid to the study of altered states of consciousness (ASC), such as meditation or mystical states of consciousnesses; (2) it did not emphasize a *dynamic* perspective of consciousness, assuming instead that the connection between body–mind was constant and not developed or cultivated during the life of an individual; and (3) finally, it largely stressed a 'temporal' dimension of human existence, rather than a spatial dimension, or an integration between the two (Yuasa 1993).

Phenomenology has recently been re-evaluated in cognitive science (Varela 1996; Thompson 2001; Depraz *et al.* 2003), where its latest offshoot is called neurophenomenology (Varela 1996). This can be defined as a style of research that aims to incorporate the first-person lived experience with the brain dynamics of consciousness. In a paper entitled 'Neurophenomenology: a methodological remedy for the hard problem', Francisco Varela wrote:

Neurophenomenology is the name I am using here to designate a quest to marry modern cognitive science and a disciplined approach to human experience, thus placing myself in the lineage of the continental tradition of phenomenology. My claim is that the so-called hard problem . . . can only be addressed productively by gathering a research community armed with new pragmatic tools enabling them to develop a science of consciousness.

(1996: 330)

In other words, according to Varela, Chalmers' 'hard problem' cannot be solved by 'piecemeal' studies of neuronal correlates of experience but requires a strict method for rediscovering the primacy of lived experience. Anyone following this method must cultivate the skills of stabilising and deepening their capacity for attentive bracketing and intuition, and for describing what they find.

Varela describes the basic working hypothesis of neurophenomenology as follows: 'phenomenological accounts of the structure of experience and their counterparts in cognitive science relate to each other through reciprocal constraints' (ibid.: 343). So the findings of a disciplined first-person approach should be an integral part of the validation of a neurobiological proposal.

Varela was very critical of the attitude of the dominant 'philosophy of mind' to 'just-take-a-look' with regards to human experience, where this is conceived as a pure cognitive or mental event. 'The mental', says Varela, 'does not have any obvious manner to investigate itself, and we are left with a clear logical conclusion but in a pragmatic and methodological limbo' (ibid.: 334). The point is well expressed by Searle:

> Much of the bankruptcy of most work in the philosophy of mind . . . over the past fifty years . . . has come from a persistent failure to recognize and come to terms with the fact that the ontology of the mental is an irreducibly first-person ontology . . . there is, in short, no way for us to picture subjectivity as a part of our world view because, so to speak, the subjectivity in question is the picturing.
>
> (1992: 95–8)

In agreement with Searle, Heidegger (1889–1976) argued that in order to experience the *Dasein* (or 'being here'), we need to move from an *ontic* perspective (the aspect of being upon which the philosophy of mind has concentrated) towards the *ontological* one (what Searle calls 'first-person ontology').

From a neurophenomenological point of view, the claim that all states of mind are generated by brain states and electro-stimulation does not invalidate the world outside ourselves nor does it prevent us from looking at and seeing what we choose. The argument has been well summarized by Parvizi and Damasio (2001), who specified that neuroscience needs to explain both 'how the brain engenders the mental patterns we experience as the images of an object (the *noema* in phenomenological terms)', and 'how, in parallel . . . the brain also creates a sense of self in the act of knowing . . . how each of us has a sense of "me" . . . how we sense that the images in our minds are shaped in our particular perspective and belong to our individual organism (Parvizi and Damasio 2001: 136–7). In phenomenological terms, the last question addresses a (pre-)*noetic* quality of consciousness, in particular, the noetic aspect of the 'ipseity', or the minimal subjective sense of 'I-ness' in experience, which is constitutive of a 'minimal' or 'core self', as contrasted with a 'narrative' or 'autobiographical' self (Gallagher 2003). The pre-noetic level of consciousness is fundamentally linked to the bodily processes of life regulation, emotion and affect, such that all cognition and intentional action are emotive (Panksepp 1998; Damasio 1999). For instance, I look at a fashion magazine with a friend of mine. We both look at the same model posing with a pink hat. By doing so we both activate certain neural activities in our brains, but when I look at this figure, I can recall that I have the same hat and that this was a present from my boyfriend on my last birthday. Now, such an acknowledgment generates a sense of 'me', which makes my experience rather different from that of my friend. This has been called by Damasio the 'sense of knowing' (1999: 82–106). In his view, this is a fundamental component of a 'core consciousness', or that part of consciousness which is always present in the nowness of the experience and it is disconnected from both past or future, which belongs to an 'extended consciousness'. On the contrary, the latter lies at the foundation of the former and provides us with an identity and offers us an awareness of the lived life and anticipation of the future, in the here and now. In other words 'extended consciousness is everything core consciousness is, only bigger and better, and it does nothing but grow across evolution and across the lifetime of experience of each individual' (ibid.: 196). This is supported by Damasio's observation of neurological patients who presented with an impairment of extended consciousness, but whose core consciousness remained untouched. By contrast, impairments that begin with core consciousness may demolish the entire edifice of consciousness and thus are not an independent variety of consciousness.

Is consciousness a field?

A further innovative contribution to the phenomenology of consciousness was made about a century ago by William James (1842–1910). In his Gifford Lectures of 1901–02, which were later published as *The Varieties of Religious Experience* (1902), he states that humans have 'fields of consciousness', so as to indicate that the unbroken, ever-changing flow of ideas, perceptions, feelings, and emotions that make up our lives, are going far beyond our narrow conception of the self. This is to say that our consciousness is simply a kind of filtering down, some form of what Richard Maurice Bucke first called 'cosmic consciousness' (Bucke 1901).

With the words 'fields of consciousness', well ahead of both his time and ours, I believe William James seized upon the mechanism essential to the understanding of consciousness, as an 'extended' phenomenon. More recently, Rupert Sheldrake has formulated a theory of the 'extended mind' (Sheldrake 2003; Sheldrake and Smart 2005). In his book *The Sense of Being Stared at and Other Aspects of the Extended Mind* (2003), he suggests that minds are not confined to the insides of our heads, but stretch out beyond them. The images we experience as we look around us are just where they seem to be. He wrote: 'If you feel the pressure of your bottom on a chair, this sensation is located inside the head and not where they seem to be. By contrast, I suggest that these feelings are just where they seem to be' (ibid.: 281). He gives the example of an amoeba, well known as a representative unicellular organism, which moves about by sending out projections into the world around it:

> In all other animals, amoeboid cells are vital for our survival. The most extreme example of amoeboid cells is the nerves. Some nerve cells have enormously elongated pseudopod-like projections, which serve as the nerve fibers that conduct nerve impulses. These pseudopodia, called axons, can be several feet in length, such as those that connect the sciatic nerve with our toes. As axons grow, they send out many thin, hair-like projections (called *filopodia*) that explore the area around the tip of the growing axon. Nerve cells have many axons, some of which project out toward the surface of other nerve cells, forming a network of interconnection. It is no coincidence that the mind is rooted in networks of nerve cells, with pseudopod-like axons stretching out far beyond the main part of the cell body. The mind in turn is capable of sending out mental pseudopodia into the world beyond the body, and it is forming networks of interconnections with other minds.
>
> (ibid.: 264)

He went a step further observing that: 'If there is an outwards movement of the mind to touch that which is perceived, then perhaps we can affect things or people just by looking at them. Can we test this? Can we affect people just by looking at them?' (Sheldrake and Fox 1996: 78). Sheldrake has called this phenomenon 'the sense of being stared at'. He observed that 'when we look at anything, fields of perception link us to what we see. Hence we might affect things or people just by looking at them'. The sense of being stared at provides us with evidence for this (Sheldrake 2003: 170). In previous publications, he suggested that the extensions of the mind take place through what he called 'morphic fields':

> I became convinced that living organisms were organized by fields when I was doing research on plants. How do plants grow from simple embryos inside seeds into foxgloves, sequoias, or bamboos? How do leaves,

flowers, and fruits take up their characteristic forms? These questions are about what biologists call morphogenesis, the coming into being of form (from Greek morphe = form; genesis = coming into being).

The naïve answer is to say that everything is genetically programmed. Somehow each developing plant or animal follows the instructions coded in its genes. Nevertheless, since the 20s many biologists who have studied the development of plants and animals have been convinced that in addition to the genes, there must be organizing fields within the developing organism, called 'morphogenetic fields'. These fields contain, as it were, invisible plans or blueprints for the various organs and for the organism as a whole.

(ibid.: 276)

According to Sheldrake (2003), the contrast between brain theory and 'field' theory is clearest in the case of 'phantom limbs'.[7] Sheldrake comments: 'I suggest that phantom limbs are fields of the missing limbs', while the conventional theory says that they are in the brain (ibid.: 281). The British biologist is currently studying the implications of morphogenetic fields for various phenomena, such as telepathy (Sheldrake and Smart 2005).

These theories represent a new development in consciousness studies, but they do not reject dualism completely, for they accept some kind of duality between mind and body. I would like to suggest here that the term 'extended body', rather than 'extended mind' may be more appropriate to describe the phenomenon. Such a notion probably originated with the work of Edward Hall, when he observed that the most characteristic feature of human beings is their capacity to develop corporeal extensions. In *The Hidden Dimension*, he wrote:

Man is an organism with an extraordinary past. He is distinguished from the other animals by virtue of the fact that he has elaborated what I have termed *extensions* of the organism. By developing his extensions, man has been able to improve or specialize various functions. The computer is an extension of part of his brain, the telephone is an extension of the voice, the wheel extends the legs and feet. Language extends experience in time and space while writing extends language. Man has elaborated his extensions to such a degree that we are apt to forget that his humanness is rooted in his animal nature.

(1969: 3)

In a way, the theory that the body could extend in space can be further traced back to the 1950s work of Weston La Barre. In his book entitled *The Human Animal* (1955), he argues that men and women have accelerated their evolutionary process by shifting evolution from their bodies to their extensions. As he put it: 'The real evolutionary unit now is not man's mere body; it is all-mankind's-brains-together-with-all-the-extrabodily-materials-that-come-under-the-manipulation-of-their-hands' (ibid.: 91). He called this ongoing process 'evolution-by-prosthesis', which has the function to enhance our evolutionary variation:

> The evolution-by-prosthesis is uniquely human and uniquely freed from the slowness of reproduction and of evolutionary variation into blind alleys from which there is no retreat. Man with tools as his projected body and machines the prosthetic creatures of his hands, is not merely a promising animal biologically: he makes every other animal wholly obsolete, except as they serve *his* purposes of prosthetic metabolism, locomotion, manufacture of materials and of biological medicine. This new kind of human evolution is fully proved in the positive sense by man's conquest of reality.
>
> (ibid.: 92)

In other words, for La Barre, tools and machines are not only useful, but they have an additional advantage in evolutionary terms. This view supports many aspects of Ichikawa's theory of the extended body ('Body-space') by arguing in favour of both a 'semi-definite body-space' (*junkōseiteki shintai kūkan*) and an 'indefinitely varying body-space' (*fukakuteki na kahenteki shintai kūkan*). La Barre wrote:

> It is an error to suppose that a spider's web is in this sense a tool. For, besides being instinctive (a genetically given function), the spider web is merely an autoplastic extension into space of its own-living substance or metaplasm. No more is a bird's nest a 'tool' since neither insight nor tuition and neither memory nor experience plays any part in this instinctual activity.
>
> (ibid.: 90)

The evolution-by-prosthesis is not only a new kind of evolution, but it has greatly accelerated evolution itself:

> It took millions and millions of years from fish to whale to evolve a warm-blooded marine mammal: but man evolved submarines from dream to actuality in a mere few centuries and at no genetic price in physical specialization.
>
> (ibid.: 91)

So it was for the human dream of flying. An airplane for La Barre has a strong evolutionary meaning because it 'is part of a larger kinaesthetic and functional self; it is a larger ownership of reality by the questing ego of life. And airplanes are biologically cheap' (ibid.: 91). In an age of technological discoveries, the notion of an extended body is becoming increasingly important. Not only does the concept enable us to glimpse a bit of a new worldview by giving a better understanding of what a human being is, but also about what it can be. The concept of corporeal extensions will be further developed later on in this book. I would like to carry on the ongoing discussion on the origins of contemporary study of consciousness.

Consciousness study: a manic depressive cycle?

After the contributions of Husserlian phenomenologists in Europe and William James in the United States, there was a period of relative silence. Then, interest in consciousness came back again strongly in the 1970s. In an interview for an Italian radio programme, neuroscientist Francisco Varela defined this process as a sort of 'manic depressive cycle' (Varela 2001). He commented:

> In the 70's the centre of the scientific interest was cognition and we were not allowed, and I repeat, allowed, to talk about consciousness. Consciousness was something mystical, of pertinence to the philosophers more than a scientific argument . . . and then suddenly was born what today is called the science of consciousness and it is very important to talk about it and to ask what part of our brain makes possible the existence of experience, the existence of a phenomenological world.[8]

This renewed interest in the study of consciousness becomes very strong when we once again start asking 'What is it like to be a bat?', in the words of Thomas Nagel (1974), or right to the point 'What does it mean to be someone?', 'What does it mean to have an experience?', 'What is it like to be' a bat or a human being and how do things look when one is a bat or a human being? The 'what it is like to be' issue expresses, in other words, the *subjective* character of an experience. The fact that an organism has a 'conscious' experience means basically that there is some quality of being of that organism. As Nagel puts it, when we say that another organism is conscious, we mean that 'there is something it is like *to be* that organism . . . something it is like to be *for* the organism' (1974: 436); 'the essence of the belief that bats have experience is that there is something that is like to be a bat' (ibid.: 438).

Near-death studies

A further challenge to consciousness studies emerged from the investigations on experiences reported from persons at or near the point of death and also contributed to renewed interest in the question of consciousness in a very unique way. This will be the main topic of discussion in the next chapters.

2

Journeys in the afterlife

When Pope John Paul II died in 2005, he was buried in Rome with 12 golden coins in his pocket. I don't know why this treasure was left with him, but certainly this act reflects an ancient Greek-Roman belief according to which the departed souls need to pay an *obolus* (or a coin) to Charon, the ferry-man of Hades, to cross the River Acheron. If not, the spirit is condemned to wander the deserted shore without refuge. Dante Alighieri incorporated this fascinating myth into his *The Divine Comedy*. At the beginning of his visionary journey to the underworld, Dante meets Charon who asks him to leave the Hades because he was still living. In the third Canto of *Inferno*, we can read about their encounter:

> As I looked onwards, I saw people on the bank of a great river, at which I said: 'Master [Dante to Virgil], now let me understand who these are, and what custom makes them so ready to cross over, as I can see by the dim light.' And he to me: 'The thing will be told you, when we halt our steps, on the sad strand of Acheron.' Then, fearing that my words might have offended him, I stopped myself from speaking, with eyes ashamed and downcast, till we had reached the flood. And see, an old man, with white hoary locks, came towards us in a boat, shouting: 'Woe to you, wicked spirits! Never hope to see heaven: I come to carry you to the other shore, into eternal darkness, into fire and ice. And you, who are there, a living spirit, depart from those who are dead.' But when he saw that I did not depart, he said: 'By other ways, by other means of passage, you will cross to the shore: a quicker boat must carry you.' And my guide said to him: 'Charon, do not vex yourself: it is willed there, where what is willed is done: ask no more.' Then the bearded mouth, of the ferryman of the livid marsh, who had wheels of flame round his eyes, was stilled.
>
> (Dante, *Inferno*, Canto III: 70–99)

The idea of placing coins, jewels, or other goods, in the graves of loved ones is a cross-cultural phenomenon. It does not matter how valuable these treasures are, but what matters is that the departing soul has some kind of security for its journey in the afterlife. For instance, in Japan, the corpses are dressed in a white, light cotton kimono and a light gown-like jacket with other traveling outfits such as straw sandals, walking stick, bamboo hat, and so on, and a bag containing six coins is also added. As in ancient Greece and Rome, in Japan, they believe these coins will help the departing soul to cross the river. Even more interestingly, in the case of cremation, the metal coins are replaced with six paper coins. This is because the paper coins 'go' with the soul, rather than being left in this world after cremation.[1] Similarly, the Chinese place jade, pearls and gold leaf in the corpse's mouth. The Twana Indians of the American north-west sea border region also buried their loved ones in their canoes, although they also did it in trees. Sometimes the Arctic tribes and the Scandinavians set their dead adrift at sea, highlighting that a journey was undertaken (Hickman 2002). All these examples are suggestive of a belief that death is not the end of life but the beginning of a new journey. Evidence in this sense has emerged from the accounts of those who survived in life-threatening circumstances. Since the 1970s, a growing number of studies have shown that people who nearly died, or were even considered clinically dead for a period of time, were able to describe a mysterious journey in the afterlife. For some scientists, these claims are mere hallucinations induced by a dying brain, or by drugs, which do not deserve particular attention beyond that which might be given to an ordinary dream. For others, these might be the 'scientific' proof of an afterlife.

Myths of the afterlife journeys

The first evidence of a journey in the afterlife in ancient literature is probably that of *Er*, narrated by Plato (427–347 BC) more than two thousand years ago. In Book 10 of his *Republic*, he tells the story of a soldier (Er), who was killed in battle and then came back to life:

> He [Er] said that when he left his body he travelled in company with many others till they came to a wonderful place, where there were, close to each other, two gaping chasms in the earth, and opposite and above them two other chasms in the sky. Between the chasms sat Judges, who, having delivered judgement, ordered the just to take the right-hand road that led up to the sky, and fastened the badge of their judgement in front of them, while they ordered the unjust, who carried the badges of all that they had done behind them, to take the left-hand road that led downwards. When Er came before them, they said that he was to be a messenger to men about the other world, and ordered him to listen to and watch all that went on in that place.
>
> (Plato 1925: 394)

Similarly, Eastern thought has been no less drawn into the belief that some can experience an afterlife. A classic example is *The Tibetan Book of the Dead*, where the *Bardo* state (or the intermediate state between life and death) describes the nature of the 'mind' immediately after death. Another less popular example, but despite this, a no less interesting one, is the myth of creation of the Japanese islands, which will be narrated in Chapter 3.

The origin of near-death studies

The first more formal studies of near-death-related phenomena developed in the late 1800s, when the Swiss geologist, Albert von St Gallen Heim (1849–1937), who was a mountain climber, had a profound mystical experience, having fallen down a mountain:

> What I felt in five to ten seconds could not be described in ten times that length of time. All my thoughts and ideas were coherent and very clear, and in no way susceptible, as are dreams, to obliteration. First of all I took in the possibilities of my fate and said to myself: 'The crag point over which I will soon be thrown evidently falls off below me as a steep wall since I have not been able to see the ground at the base of it. It matters a great deal whether or not snow is still lying at the base of the cliff wall. If this is the case, the snow will have melted from the wall and formed a border around the base. If I fall on the border of snow I may come out of this with my life, but if there is no more snow down there, I am certain to fall on rubble and at this velocity death will be quite inevitable. If, when I strike, I am not dead or unconscious I must instantly seize my small flask of spirits of vinegar and put some drops from it on my tongue. I do not want to let go of my alpenstock; perhaps it can still be of use to me.' Hence I kept it tightly in my hand. I thought of taking off my glasses and throwing them away so that splinters from them might not injure my eyes, but I was so thrown and swung about that I could not muster the power to move my hands for this purpose. A set of thoughts and ideas then ensued concerning those left behind. I said to myself that upon landing below I ought, indifferent to whether or not I were seriously injured, to call immediately to my companions out of affection for them to say, 'I'm all right!' Then my brother and three friends could sufficiently recover from their shock so as to accomplish the fairly difficult descent to me. My next thought was that I would not be able to give my beginning university lecture that had been announced for five days later. I considered how the news of my death would arrive for my loved ones and I consoled them in my thoughts. Then I saw my whole past life take place in many images, as though on a stage at some distance from me. I saw myself as the chief character in the performance. Everything was transfigured as though by a heavenly

light and everything was beautiful without grief, without anxiety and without pain. The memory of very tragic experiences I had had was clear but not saddening. I felt no conflict or strife; conflict had been transmuted into love. Elevated and harmonious thoughts dominated and united the individual images, and like magnificent music a divine calm swept through my soul. I became ever more surrounded by a splendid blue heaven with delicate roseate and violet cloudlets. I swept into it painlessly and softly and I saw that now I was falling freely through the air and that under me a snowfield lay waiting. Objective observations, thoughts, and subjective feelings were simultaneous. Then I heard a dull thud and my fall was over.[7]

This profound experience stimulated his interest in finding out whether other people had reported similar events in their lives. It was not a difficult search. In a short period of time, Heim was able to collect a large number of accounts from war soldiers wounded in battles, masons and roofers who had fallen from heights, workers who survived disasters in mountain projects and railway accidents, and fishermen who had nearly drowned, and, above all, Alpine climbers, like him, who had survived near-death situations. He presented his findings in a paper given at the Swiss Alpine Club in 1892. Heim reported that 95 per cent of the cases he collected were strikingly similar. He came to the conclusion that some accidents were much more 'horrible and cruel' for observers than for the victims.

Further studies were made on 'death-bed visions' (DBV), which emerged from the observers of the last moments of the dying, rather than from individuals who recovered from a situation of temporary death. DBVs present strong similarities to near-death accounts. The phenomenon was largely investigated by Ernesto Bozzano (1862–1943), an Italian psychical researcher and a strong defender of the concept of survival of bodily death, whose work is almost forgotten today. His survival model is based on what he called the phenomenon of 'bilocation', a term he used for the phantom limb sensations experienced by amputees, autoscopy, out-of-body and near-death experiences, and a variety of luminous or cloud-like emanations that clairvoyants claimed left the body at the moment of death that he thought of 'decisive importance' to the argument for the survival of death (Alvarado 2005). He believed these phenomena indicated the existence of an 'etheric body' within the somatic body that may exit the physical body during its life (Bozzano 1934: 8). The interest Bozzano showed in survival after-death later continued with Sir William Barrett, a member of the Society for Psychical Research. In collaboration with his wife, Barrett collected numerous accounts of dying persons who reported the presence of deceased relatives, or religious figures, who were assisting them during the process of dying (Barrett 1986). However, the most extensive investigation into DBV was carried out in 1961 by Karlis Osis and Erlendur Haraldsson. Their work was initially published as a pilot study *Death bed Observations of Physicians and Nurses* (1961), and later as a book entitled *At the Hour of Death* (1977), where they provided an examination of a detailed questionnaire from two thousand doctors and nurses about the experiences of their dying patients in the US and in India. They came to the conclusion that 10 per cent of patients, who were conscious in the last hour before dying, experienced vivid visions; 52 per cent of these visions represented dead persons who were known to the patients; 28 per cent were of living persons; and 20 per cent were of religious figures (Osis and Haraldsson 1977). Other interesting results emerged from a study by Russell Noyes and Donald Slymen in 1971, who interviewed 186 survivors of serious illness or accidents. The researchers were able to identify recurrent patterns and they divided them into three stages: (1) the first stage is the phase of resistance, which is characterized by the fear of dying and the struggle for life; (2) the second stage is a 'life review', during which the person relives important events, or their entire life; and (3) the final stage is a period of transcendence, during which the dying experience a mystical rapture and a sense of union with a cosmic consciousness (Noyes and Slymen 1971).

Stanislav Grof and Joan Halifax carried out research with dying patients with cancer. In their book *The Human Encounter with Death* (1977), they argued that the passage from life to death could be seen as a 'rite of passage'. Elizabeth Kübler-Ross also studied the cases of many terminally ill patients, some of whom recovered from nearly fatal experiences. In her book, *On Death and Dying* published in 1969, she came to the conclusion that death is simply like 'the butterfly coming out of a cocoon'. Some of her patients described how 'someone' was there to help them during this transition from life to 'death'. This figure was sometimes identified as a deceased family member or friends, an angel or a spirit being.

In 1975, German Lutheran minister Johann Christophe Hampe was working on similar studies on dying people and on victims of accidents, which were later published in English in 1979 under the title *To Die is Gain*. In his book, Hampe attempts to illustrate the experience of death as lived 'from within'. He came to the conclusion that, far from being anticipated with fear and dread, death should be experienced as a *gain*. The presence of some commonalities in the accounts he collected made him conclude that these experiences were something more than dreams and hallucinations. He wrote:

> If dying is not oppression, my knowledge that I am going to die will no longer oppress me. Instead of making me feel melancholy it will expand and deepen me . . . My loneliness is broken because these experiences strengthen my belief in the continuance of an indestructible core in me and my fellow men.

> (Hampe 1979: 134–5)

As has been argued, Hampe's study is particularly important in the field because 'it represents the very first attempt from within the context of theology to investigate the phenomenon that only later became known as the "near-death experience"' (Fox 2003: 55).

There was some popular excitement as a result of these early reports on life after death, which for some people seemed to provide evidence for an afterlife, while for many scientists these were (and, for some, still are) studies of little value. The situation developed enormously when medical science became more successful in terms of its ability to resuscitate those individuals who might otherwise have died from heart attacks, automobile accidents, and other physical trauma. Some of these patients came forward to tell of having met deceased friends and relatives, guardian angels, or beings of light in other dimensions or realms of existence before returning to their bodies. It was at this time that Raymond Moody brought the phenomenon to the attention of the general public and coined the term 'near-death experience' (NDE) (Moody 1975). Moody interviewed 50 people who were considered clinically dead by their doctors and then had recovered. He published his findings in a book *Life after Life* (1975), among other publications.

What happens during an NDE?

During the winter of 1971, 18-year-old Mr L. nearly died because of a virus known as the 'Asian flu', that made him seriously ill:

> After being in bed for a couple of days, I lost consciousness and experienced myself being drawn down a long tunnel, at the end of which was a very bright (but not dazzling) white Light. The experience was absolutely sublime, and engendered within me feelings of indescribable peace and joy, the likes of which I had never before known. When I emerged from the tunnel, I found myself in the presence of a powerful spirit-being who radiated Light from himself, and who seemed to be the source of the Light all around me. I seemed to be in a beautiful landscape, with majestic mountains, sweeping valleys and forests. The entity communicated certain information to me about the purpose for my being in incarnation, and he spoke of various future events in my life (many of which have already come to pass). To my dismay he also told me that I would have to return to my body in order to fulfil the purpose of my life – and very shortly afterwards, I gradually regained body consciousness. The experience was far more real, vibrant and intense than any which I had ever had in the physical world – it was a fourth-dimensional rather than a three-dimensional experience. Since that profound experience, I have never had any fear of death, and actually look forward to it, having had a brief glimpse of a higher state of existence outside of the human body. Many sceptical psychologists who have never had an NDE

dismiss them as hallucinations or fantasies. However, my own experience demonstrates that this is not so; *for the spirit-being who communicated with me while I was out of my body continues to do so*, as a number of my friends can testify, having themselves experienced his presence very tangibly on numerous occasions. Had my NDE merely been a halluci-nation, the Being of Light would also have been unreal, and would therefore not be able to manifest clearly in the 'real' physical world. His *continuing* objective manifestations, however, clearly demonstrate that my NDE was not just a hallucination and cannot be explained in purely material terms; it has a basis in spiritual reality.

Following Raymond Moody in his *Life after Life* (1975), the most common elements of a near-death experience are: (1) the difficulty of expressing in words an experience of such a nature, or *ineffability*; (2) the feeling of dying; (3) moving through darkness or a tunnel, a cave, a cylinder, a valley; (4) the sense of joy, love, and peace; (5) encountering the presence of deceased loved ones and other entities; (6) visions of beings of lights, guardian spirits, and so on – communication with these beings occurs without words, by the power of mere thought; (7) the perception of separation of the physical body, or out-of-body experience; (8) a life review, or a panoramic view of the proper life, or specific events that had happened in life; (9) many people reported hearing certain sounds, some of these were described as unpleasant (such as noise, buzzing, ringing sounds); and, finally, (10) the decision of conscious return.

It is very important to note that often an NDE does not incorporate all or even most of these features. As Moody confirmed: 'I have found no one person who reports every single component of the composite experience' (1975: 23). There is a continuing debate about what the diagnostic criteria for an NDE might be. Moreover, the sequence in which they occur can vary a great deal from person to person:

> The order in which a dying person goes through the various stages . . . may vary from that given in my 'theoretical model'. To give one exam-ple, various persons have reported seeing the 'being of light' before, or at the same time, they left their physical bodies, and not as in the 'model', some time afterward.
>
> (ibid.: 24)

Bruce Greyson systematically divided all the main elements of the NDE into four sub-groups and presented them in a 16-point questionnaire, known as the 'Greyson NDE Scale' (Greyson 1983). These are: affective (sense of joy, peace, etc.); cognitive (alteration in thought processes and sense of time); transcendental (mystical experience); and paranormal (OBE, ESP, etc.). He hypothesized that circumstances around the time of the NDE determined the type of the experience.

Such a theory in part contradicts Kenneth Ring's view that NDEs are not independent of the precipitating event, but they are always the same. In his book called *Life at Death: A Scientific Investigation of the Near-Death Experience* (1980), Ring published the results of his investigation on 102 individuals who had been near to death. Some 48 per cent of them reported an NDE and, of these, 60 per cent claimed that the near-death experience had brought them a sense of peace and well-being; 37 per cent reported a separation of consciousness from the physical body; 23 per cent mentioned the process of entering a dark tunnel; 16 per cent said that they had seen a bright light; and 10 per cent claimed that they had entered the light (Ring 1980).

According to the evidence that he provided, Ring classified the parts of the experience into five main stages:

1 *Peace and well-being.* This was reported by 60 per cent of those who claimed an experience similar to an NDE. Although the majority of NDEs are blissful experiences, some of them can also be frightening events (see, for instance, Greyson and Bush 1992). The latter can be divided into three different groups. The first group is represented by those experiences, which phenomenologically appear to be similar to the positive one, but are perceived as negative. The second group include hellish experiences and meetings with demon entities. They may involve torture and suffering. The third category is characterized by a sense of loneliness or featurelessness (French 2005a), or the sense that nothing is real, which carries with it a deeply unpleasant feeling (states referred to by psychiatrists as derealization and depersonalization).

2 *A sense of bodily separation.* This represents the out-of-body experience, which was reported by 37 per cent of the participants in Ring's study (Ring 1980). This is the experience during which a person is able to perceive the world from a location outside his or her physical body.

3 *Entering the darkness.* This experience, also known as the 'tunnel effect', was reported by 23 per cent per cent in Ring's study (ibid.). Usually, it was described before or after the experience. As will be discussed at length later, in recent years the phenomenology of the 'tunnel effect' has become a highly controversial field of investigation. Following Allan Kellehear, the 'tunnel' is frequently used to describe apparent traveling through a period of darkness, which seems to be a cross-cultural phenomenon. According to him, the tunnel has to be confined 'to societies where historic religions are dominant – perhaps because the tunnel-shape is more frequently encountered in such societies and it is thus more readily to hand as a way of describing the sensation of moving rapidly through a darkness' (Kellehear 1996: 188). As will be argued later on in this study, the argument has also some interesting neuro-scientific implications.

4 *Seeing a brilliant light.* The next stage is the meeting with the Light, which is often described as being God, or another spiritual entity. According

to Ring, this vision is not very frequent among those who reported an NDE. He suggested that only 16 per cent had this kind of experience (Ring 1980). A person I interviewed in Tokyo gave me the following account:

> The light was very bright and emanating warmth. I could easily stand the heat. It was like facing God. We spoke. I cannot remember what he said, but I remember that I couldn't lie. It is hard to describe, I never experienced such an intensity of feeling.

Another respondent said:

> I had been taken into hospital with a porphyria attack and was told that I had been out of it for a week or more. However, I do recall very vividly this lovely emerald green grass in this avenue of soft beautiful trees, I was walking down, and thinking how warm and cosy I felt, all the pain had gone. There was this bright, in fact, very bright light at the end of the avenue and I thought to myself, if I keep walking towards that light I will never have those dreadful pains again and I will be comfortable and happy. Then I thought, ah, but if I do walk on I will never see David grow up, I will never know what it's like to hold and cuddle him again. David was my 2-year-old child and he was so precious to me as I had lost my first child. So even though I felt quite sad to leave, I decided to turn around and walk back. The next thing I remember was a nurse standing over me saying, 'Hello Mrs. Farrow (my name at that time), how are you feeling? We thought we had lost you.'

Curiously, regardless of the intensity of the described experience, the person was not able to remember the content of the message given by the Light. This seems to be a common phenomenon among those who reported a similar kind of experience.

5 *Entering the Light*. Nearly 10 per cent of those who met the light had the feeling of entering another realm or dimension of reality. Various spiritual beings were sometimes met in these alternative realms. These could be relatives and friends as well as unknown beings. Some kind of border, or point of no return, was also described. Symbolically speaking, to cross it means to accept death and thus to die, as emerges from the following account:

> I found myself going through a very dark tunnel with a beautiful light at the end. I went towards this light. I remember being totally at peace. I had no pain whatsoever, just this feeling of total calm. When I reached the light I could see a stream. On the other side of this stream there were many people, some of whom I recognized. The colours in this place were extraordinary, nothing could

describe them. I went towards the edge of the stream but there was no bridge for me to cross over to the people waiting for me. Then I was back. The pain returned and I had to have an emergency operation because of peritonitis. I was told my heart had stopped for a brief second, which could account for my experience. I must admit I used to be very afraid of dying, but I can now say that it does not hold the same fear as it once did.

Kenneth Ring is also co-author of another study with blind people who self-reported an NDE or OBE (Ring and Cooper 1997). The team came to the conclusion that participants were able to identify colors and they became depressed after these experiences because of their return to blindness. Other researchers consider this finding highly controversial and claimed that it requires careful replication under rigorous scientific conditions (see, for instance, French 2005).

How common is an NDE?

In 1982, an extensive survey conducted by George Gallup (Gallup 1982) found that eight million Americans (5 per cent of the adult population) confirmed that they had had a near-death experience. In 1992, a new Gallup poll revealed that around 13 million Americans claimed to have undergone at least one NDE. Numerous other surveys have been conducted. According to Ring (1980), 43 per cent, and according to Sabom (1982), 48 per cent of adults who found themselves in life-threatening circumstances had an NDE. The score seems to be higher among children (85 per cent) (Morse 1994). Paul Badham has suggested that these results gain stronger values when related to the frequency of spiritual experiences among the population in general. For instance, David Hay, a former Director of the Alister Hardy Religious Experience Research Centre has stated that 76 per cent of the population in Britain in 2001 described having 'an awareness of a transcendental reality' (in Badham 2005a: 202). This evidence has been supported by another study carried out at the Department of the Study of Religions at SOAS, University of London. Olga Pupynin and Simon Brodbeck carried out an original piece of research called 'Religious Experience in London'. They asked passers-by in Trafalgar Square, 'What kind of things have made you feel most sublime?' They collected a wide range of replies ranging from 'being in love', to 'the beauty of nature', to knowing 'God was present'. Then the participants were asked: 'Have you ever had an experience which you could categorize as sacred, religious, spiritual, ecstatic, paranormal, or mystical?' The researchers were amazed to find out that 65 per cent of those interviewed had had an experience, which could be defined 'as religious, spiritual, ecstatic, sacred, paranormal or mystical' (Pupynin and Brodbeck 2001).

While statistics and accounts of NDE proliferate, at present there may be no proven trait that can accurately predict who will have an NDE (Greyson 1993). These seem to happen with similar frequency and content to people of both genders and of all ages, races, levels of education, socio-economic backgrounds, spiritual/religious affiliations (or non-affiliation), sexual orientations, and precipitating circumstances (illness, accident, suicide, medical procedure, etc.) (Osis and Haraldsson 1977; Ring 1980; Gabbard *et al.* 1981; Pasricha and Stevenson 1986; Roberts and Owen 1988; Blackmore 1996a). As has already been discussed,[8] the oldest recorded account of travel in the afterlife can be dated to more than two thousand years ago.

Does the NDE occur only in people close to death?

Some interesting questions now arise. One of these is whether an NDE occurs only in those close to death. According to current evidence, the answer is clearly no. NDEs can occur in many other situations, such as in people who were extremely tired, during rapid acceleration during training of fighter pilots (Whinnery and Whinnery 1990), during electro-stimulation of the temporal lobe (Persinger 1983; 1987), after prolonged isolation and sensory deprivation (Comer *et al.* 1967), occasionally while carrying out everyday activities, while dreaming, by people who have taken certain drugs, such as the dissociative anesthetic ketamine (Jansen 1989) and dimethyltryptamine (DMT) (Strassman 2001).

In addition to these, similar experiences have been described as a result of shamanic (Eliade 1964; Harner 1980) or meditative practices (see, for instance, Becker 1993), where these experiences do not seem to be as unusual as they are in our Western countries. Charles Tart tells us the story of a student excitedly rushing to his *roshi* (master) to describe a vision of gods bowing down to him and the feelings of ecstasy that occurred during his meditation. The *roshi* asks him if he remembered to keep his attention fixed on the rise and fall of his belly in breathing during the vision, as per the meditation instructions, and when the student says no (who would care about the rise and fall of the belly during such a vision?), the *roshi* reprimands the student for allowing himself to be distracted! (Tart 1975: 83).

NDE and children

We currently know that children of any age can have an NDE (Morse 1990; Sutherland 1995). Very young children, as soon as they are able to speak, have reported NDEs they had as infants or in the process of being born. One of these was Mark Botts, who had an NDE at the age of 9 months. His story emerged in a study that was carried out by Kenneth Ring and Evelyn Valarino (2000). At that time, the little boy was suffering from severe bronchiolitis, which caused a full cardiopulmonary arrest. It apparently took more than 40 minutes for doctors to revive him, and afterwards he was in a coma for a further three months. A trachea tube, which prevented him speaking, remained in place until he was aged 3. And then another two years passed before, one day totally out of the blue he surprised his parents by talking about 'when he had died'. He described how, during his experience, he left his body and crawled through a dark tunnel into a bright golden light where he was greeted warmly by some 'white clouded figures'. He then glided down a golden road until suddenly a being, whom he understood to be God, appeared in front of him. They conversed telepathically until Mark was told he had to return to his body. He was told: 'You have a purpose in life, and when you fulfil it, you can come back and visit me again someday.' Interestingly, while out of body Mark saw things that could be subsequently verified. He observed the doctors and nurses working on him, and then he watched as his grandmother tried to find his mother who was 'at least a hundred yards away through many corridors, rooms and doors'. As Mark's mother said, in response to the cynicism she faced when talking about Mark's experience, 'How can you *not* believe when he can tell you where you stood, when it's impossible to see you? How can you not believe him when the things he said, happened?' (ibid.: 108–12).

NDEs of children are particularly interesting because of the innocence of their accounts. Morse and Perry carried out one of the first studies on the experiences of a group of 12 children who had survived the resuscitation process (Morse and Perry 1992). The results were very astonishing. Eight out of 12 reported the experience of leaving their bodies and traveling in other realms. These experiences seemed to be very similar to NDE in adults. However, some differences emerged from later studies. One of these was carried out by Peter and Elizabeth Fenwick who found out that children are more likely to include descriptions of a very concrete Heaven, peopled by angels, Jesus figures and golden gates. 'There was a big window and I saw Jesus with two child angels either side floating down to me', said one of their interviewees (Fenwick and Fenwick 1995: 175). According to the Fenwicks, these differences may arise: 'because a child's intellectual and perceptual world is simpler than that of an adult' (ibid.: 82). Interestingly, the researchers observed that 'the younger they are, the less likely they are to see their experience as spiritual or mystical, or to feel that it made them more religious' (ibid.: 82).

OBEs are also very common among children. Mrs H. Pelling remembers very clearly the out-of-body experience she had when she was 6 years old. At that time she was very ill in hospital after an operation for peritonitis. She said:

> My recollections are of being up in the corner of the ceiling at the end of the ward, completely encompassed in this most brilliant light with an ecstatic feeling of warmth and comfort, looking down at myself in bed,

with the vicar and ward sister kneeling at my bedside in prayer giving me the last rites (so I was told years later). I can still see it all as clearly now, all these years later. I remember the doctor saying to my mother on later visits, 'It was a miracle, she had the will to live.'

(ibid.: 180)

In the same way as described by adults, for her the Light was 'brilliant', the feelings of warmth and comfort all-enveloping. Another interesting peculiarity of children's experiences is when they have apparently been greeted by relatives whom they did not personally know, but whom they later recognized. Paul and Linda Badham in their *Immortality or Extinction?* (1982) mentioned one of these singular cases, which they found in a weekly paper called *Pulse*, where a GP, Dr Thomas Smith, wrote a review about the case of a little girl who had an NDE and met her grandfather's mother, of whom she had had no previous knowledge. Later on she was able to recognize her in a photograph at her uncle's home without having met her before (Thomas Smith, 'Called back from the dead', in *Pulse*, 10 July 1980).

Another very exceptional case is that of Hannah, which was reported by Cherie Sutherland in her *Children of the Light* (1995). Hannah has had four near-death experiences in her life, two of them in early childhood, one as a teenager and another, aged 20, during childbirth. She said:

I was born a Jew in Germany, probably some time in late 1937 but as I have no papers and all the people connected with me are dead, I have no way of proving it. My first experience happened when I was 3 or 4 years old. I remember being taken out of my house by my father and a soldier who sent us to the other side of the road. I looked back and saw my mother being held by a group of neighbours. She was yelling at the soldier who told her to be silent. I was afraid and started crying. My mother continued to scream at the soldier so he stepped up to her and hit her in the head with his rifle. As she was lying on the ground an SS officer went over to her, stood with one foot on her body and shot her in the head with his pistol.

I screamed. He turned, raised the pistol and pointed it at me. I turned to run and was shot in the back. I experienced a shock, and pain that nearly took the top of my head off. Then I heard music. I can't describe it in earthly terms. I was in darkness. Then the darkness changed into a passage and then it was light and peaceful, like being in a big smile. I heard voices and they were like a caress, but I didn't understand what was being said. In the light I could feel someone else's tears and I saw 'beings'. I then saw one who I remembered seeing at another time. I tried to reach out to him. Tears were in his eyes and his thoughts came clearly to me, 'You cannot touch us.' At that moment the pain started again and then I must have slipped into a state of sleep or unconsciousness.

Upon regaining consciousness some time later, Hannah realized she had been taken to the nuns, who were looking after her. She was afraid because she'd heard terrible things about nuns and Christians. Doctors examined her back, then strapped her to a table and one of them gave her a drink that made her feel dizzy and sick. He then began to operate on her back. She said:

> I faded out. It was blue-black then a roaring black, then once again there was peace. This time there was no music, no lullaby. I saw two people I knew but I don't remember their relationship, and I also saw three 'beings'. The third 'being' then sent me a message of hope, love and caring. He sent me messages of a future without pain.
>
> (ibid.: 142–5)

As Sutherland reported, Hannah assumed she then returned to her body, because later, while strapped in splints, she remembers the building being on fire. She said, 'I was rescued by being thrown out the window.' Before the end of the war Hannah was taken to New Zealand as an orphan. Her next NDE occurred when she was about 15 in a bicycle accident when she hit a truck. This time she had no awareness of any darkness or pain but, while out-of-body, observed the people who were gathered around her. She said, 'I floated quite happily, watching myself and them for a very long time.'

Five years later, aged 20, while afflicted with pneumonia and heavily pregnant, she was rushed to hospital in labour. Her child was born 'in a great hurry'. She said, 'I could see her, myself, and the doctors and nurses and then I travelled through the tunnel until I was presented with the choice of rest or going back.' The next thing she knew, she was in intensive care; and three days later her daughter died.

According to Sutherland:

> In view of her many tragic life experiences it might seem surprising that Hannah did not choose 'rest' during her NDE. However, as a child she had seen her 'light being' guardian again – her 'friend of the tears' – and his message of hope had left her feeling she was not on her own, and that there *was* a future without pain.
>
> (Sutherland 2007)

There is a growing amount of evidence that children who have had an NDE take a different path in life. Atwater, who interviewed more than 250 NDE children, reported that the after-effects of an NDE can last more than 20 or 30 years (Atwater 2003). The argument has been extensively researched by Sutherland (1995) who came to the conclusion that the 'children of the light' may feel different from their friends and they may be more intuitive. She also suggested that some of them may be 'less afraid of death, have more vivid dreams, and are more likely to have an out-of-body experience and precognitive episodes. The experience may also influence career choices' (ibid.: 40). In the case of Donna (the little girl mentioned above), she had various precognitive dreams. She dreamed for four nights in a row that her grandfather died only a few days before this actually happened. In the dream, her grandfather went to the family grave plot and cleaned the spot on the stone where his name would be engraved. Then he sat at the grave site and talked to his grandson who had died previously in an automobile accident. In the dreams she couldn't hear what he was saying. She told her mother the story about each episode and somehow she knew he was going to die. He died of a massive heart attack just a few days after her fourth dream. After the grandfather's death, Donna's mother read his journal. He wrote of sweeping leaves off the grave site and talking to his grandson on the very days that Donna dreamed it (Morse 1990).

Cardiac arrest studies

Some scientists have studied the NDE in terms of current scientific knowledge using new brain mapping technologies. One of these studies was carried out on cardiac arrest survivors by Peter Fenwick, a neuropsychiatrist at the Institute of Psychiatry in London, and by Sam Parnia, a clinical research Fellow at Southampton General Hospital (Parnia et al. 2001). The group interviewed all survivors (63 individuals) of cardiac arrests that had happened at the Southampton hospital during a period of one year, within one week of their arrest. Seven of them (11 per cent) reported some sort of memories from the period while they were unconscious. These were examined by using a semi-structured questionnaire known as the 'Greyson NDE Scale' (Greyson 1983). Results were quite interesting. Four patients (6 per cent) exceeded the score of seven and thus their reports were accepted as compatible with an NDE. All four sensed a point of no return, three of them reported seeing a bright light, and feelings of peace, pleasantness and joy. 'Two of the four saw deceased relatives, entered a new domain, felt that time had speeded up, lost awareness of their bodies, experienced harmony and had heightened senses' (Parnia et al. 2001: 152). Two of the three remaining patients had some memories, which could be addressed on the Greyson NDE Scale (Greyson 1983), but these were not enough to pass the criterion. The third one had confused memories (Parnia et al. 2001: 153). In this study no out-of-body experience was reported.

Another investigation was carried out in the Netherlands by Pim van Lommel and his colleagues Ruud van Wees, Vincent Meyers and Ingrid Elfferich (van Lommel et al. 2001). They interviewed 344 cardiac arrest survivors in ten different Dutch hospitals; 62 of them (18 per cent) reported some recollection of the time of clinical death. Of these patients, 21 (6 per cent) had a superficial NDE and 41 (12 per cent) had a core experience. These results are very similar to those reported at the Southampton General Hospital (Parnia *et al.* 2001). While commenting on their research results published in *The Lancet* (December 2001), Pim van Lommel and his colleagues asked the following question: 'How could a clear consciousness outside one's body be experienced at the moment that the brain no longer functions during a period of clinical death with flat EEG?' (van Lommel *et al.* 2001). In a commentary on this article, Chris French, Professor of Psychology at Goldsmiths College, University of London, replied: 'The truth is that nobody knows when the NDEs reported by these patients actually occurred. Was it really during the period of flat EEG or might they have occurred as the patients rapidly entered or gradually recovered from this state?' (French 2001: 2010). However, according to Sam Parnia and Peter Fenwick: 'It is unlikely that the NDE arises either when the cortical modules are failing, that is, during the process of becoming unconscious, or when the cortical modules are coming back on line, that is when consciousness is returning' (Parnia *et al.* 2001: 154). They concluded that a possible alternative is that the near-death experiences occur during 'unconsciousness':

> This is a surprising conclusion, because when the brain is so dysfunc-tional that the patient is deeply comatose, the cerebral structures which underpin subjective experience and memory must be severely impaired. Complex experiences such as are reported in the NDE should not arise or be retained in memory. Such patients would be expected to have no subjective experience (as was the case in 88.8% of patients in this study) or at best a confusional state if some brain function is retained. Even if the unconscious brain is flooded by neurotransmitters, this should not produce clear, lucid, remembered experiences, as those cerebral modules which generate conscious experience and underpin memory are impaired by cerebral anoxia. The fact that in a cardiac arrest loss of cortical function precedes the rapid loss of brainstem activity lends further support to this view.
>
> (ibid.: 154)

Some of the above observations carry within them an implicit belief in the complete efficacy of the EEG as a mirror of cerebral activity. It is possible that in the future, the EEG may be seen as a rather primitive measure and that more advanced methods may reveal considerable and complex activity during some periods currently described as 'flat line EEG'.[9] In this context, it is of interest to note that the phenomenon known as 'night terrors' arises during four well-defined stages of sleep, known as non-REM (NREM) (Rechtschaffen and Kales 1968), when there is relatively little EEG activity, and not during REM sleep (Hobson *et al.* 2000; Solms 2000). One variety of night terrors involves semi-awaking with the belief that one is in a space with no coordinates and no time, or buried alive, which leads the person to scream very loudly (Hobson *et al.* 2000; Jansen 2001). The similarities between the space with no coordinates and no time is reminiscent of a negative near-death experience of hell.[10]

It is of interest to note that the mind, or the minds of some people, appears to be able to experience states which are described as similar to this, while the EEG is relatively bland, as occurs during stage four sleep. The belief that complex mental activity such as dreams only occurs during REM sleep has been disproved in recent years. Evidence of this has been provided by Mark Solms (2000), Professor at the Royal London Hospital, who observed that dreams can also be activated by a variety of non-REM triggers:

> The paradigmatic assumption that REM sleep is the physiological equivalent of dreaming is in need of fundamental revision. A mounting body of evidence suggests that dreaming and REM sleep are dissociable states, and that dreaming is controlled by forebrain mechanisms. Recent neuropsychological, radiological and pharmacological findings suggest that the cholinergic brainstem mechanisms which control the REM state can only generate the psychological phenomena of dreaming through the mediation of a second, probably dopaminergic, forebrain mechanism. The latter mechanism (and thus dreaming itself) can also be activated by a variety of non-REM triggers.
>
> (Solms 2000: 127)

Encounters with angels and other beings

Mrs C. remembers with clarity the experience she had when 30 years ago she survived a nearly fatal pneumonia:

> A feeling of great calm came over me for the first time in weeks and I gradually became aware that a number of my dead relatives [my father, aunties and uncles] had gathered around the bottom of my bed. I recognized them all even though they appeared not to have faces. There was a strong light on top of as well as inside the head of each of them. They were smiling at me and beckoning me to come with them. At first, I thought how nice and peaceful it would be to join them, but suddenly I became very frightened. I was greatly concerned for the welfare of my children in my absence and felt I could not leave them to the care of social services or my mother-in-law, who I did not like. She had not proved herself to be a very caring or loving woman to her own sons so I knew the children would not be loved as I loved them. At this point, I fought against the decision to join my relatives and shouted out loudly, 'I can't come with you, I have to stay for the children, I can't come yet.' With that, they disappeared but I was by then too afraid to relax again in case they came back and was not able to resist them . . . I truly believe

I did experience this event and don't believe I was hallucinating. I have repeated the story on many occasions since and the account never varies, as it is imprinted indelibly in my mind forever.

As in this case, near-death accounts often include claims of having met deceased relatives, friends, religious figures or unknown beings, who come to help during the dying process. All those who reported these experiences are absolutely sure that what happened was a real experience and not a mere hallucination.

In some particular cases, these 'others' are beings who supposedly died at the same moment and who become companions on the journey in the after-life, as in the case of Timothy Wyllie, who had the following experience:

I died. It was for me quite incontrovertible, although I didn't fully under-stand what it all meant until I came across the researches of Drs. Moody and Elizabeth Kübler-Ross some years later. Here's what hap-pened. My body just broke down. I had walking pneumonia; my back had given out and I was terminally exhausted from attempting to hold together a disintegrating situation. If I managed three or four hours of sleep a night, I reckoned myself ahead of the game. No holidays. No weekends. Constantly having to prop myself up; put on a good face; encourage a wilting and depressed crew of about 50 people to yet greater efforts. One evening I collapsed. My body would go no further. The donkey could be beaten no more. I dragged myself back from our First Avenue monster to the relative place of our house on East 48th Avenue to the relative peace of our house on East 49th Street and drew one final bath. I knew I was finished but I had little idea of what lay in store for me. Within moments of stretching out in the bath, I found myself, to my utter amazement, hovering somewhere out in space, my body clearly visible in the bath far down below me. The next thing I knew I seemed to be in a valley as real and solid as any landscape I have seen in my travels. A monorail car was sweeping down towards me on a single, shin-ing curve of metal. Then, mysteriously, I was inside the monorail cabin together with nine or ten other people. I can see them today in my mind's eye; opposite me sat a black man playing a trumpet with great beauty. Somehow at that moment I knew we were all dying at the same time. A voice came to me over what I took to be a speaker-system, although it may well have been directly into my mind. It was very clear and lucid and quite the most loving voice I have ever heard. 'You are dying,' the Voice confirmed to me, 'but we wish you to make a choice. You can indeed pass on to what awaits you on the other side . . .' At this point I was given to see my body very casually sinking under the water of my bath somewhere below me. A simple and painless death. '. . . or you can choose to return to your life. We wish you to know, however, that you have completed what you came to do.' The Voice was utterly without attitude, wholly kind and considerate and with no bias whatsoever as to which option I might choose. I thought for a moment with a crystal clarity I have never since experienced, and knew in my heart I desired to return to the world.

(Wyllie 1984: 7–8)

It was at this stage that Timothy met two angels:

On announcing my decision, there was an expression of delight so profound the monorail cabin dissolved around me, leaving me, once again, suspended in space, this time before a seemingly endless wall of angelic Beings. Such music and singing welled around me as I have never conceived, or perceived, before or since. I disintegrated into the overwhelming beauty of the sounds. The next sensation was becoming aware I was standing on the edge of a vast, very flat plain. Beside, and slightly behind me stood two tall Beings dressed in white, or simply creatures of light – I could see clearly, since my attention focused on what lay in the center of the plain. It was an immense structure I can liken only to an extraordinary elaborate and beautiful offshore oil rig. It shone with gold and silver and had at each corner the faces of people and animals. Somehow it was in constant movement, yet in itself, it did not move. Intuitively I knew at that moment I was seeing the same structure Ezekiel describes with such elegance, although I find it difficult to retain the image now in my imagination. I was led into this enormous place and taken to a bright lit room where I was gently laid out on a flat surface similar to an operating table. Beings clustered around me, murmuring soft encouragement. Some apparatus appeared and I have a dim recollection of being hooked up to it. There was a moment of intense pain, except it was not truly pain. It wasn't quite shock either but some combination of both sensations. I felt as if in some way my blood had been completely changed, as if all the tired old vital fluids had been switched in one infinitely rapid moment. I recall that after the 'operation' I was taken 'somewhere'. I am still, to this day, rather embarrassed to admit I believe it was heaven. I have no conscious recollection of this last journey, my only clue being a strange sense of familiarity with a description of 'heaven' I came upon some years later in Robert Monroe's book *Journeys Out of the Body*.

(ibid.: 10)

Timothy's experience had also a very deep healing effect:

The next thing I was aware of was descending gently again to my body still propped in the bath, the water now cool. When I got out to dry myself off I found myself completely healed, my back straightened and the thick phlegm in my lungs gone. From being terminally ill I found myself fully restored and stronger than ever.

(ibid.: 10)

Religious figures are also encountered. As will be argued in the next chapter in greater detail, sometimes these visions are culturally dependent. For instance, a Christian will be more likely to meet Jesus, while a Buddhist will meet Amida, a Hindu will meet Yama, the King of Death, while non-believer will meet an unidentified 'Being of Light'. Usually, these figures fulfil the same function of welcoming the person to a new realm of existence, independent of their culture. As Paul Badham observed: 'As in all religious experiences what is "encountered" is described in the language of specific religious traditions, but that does not exclude the possibility that the under-lying reality may be the same in all cases' (Badham 1990).

But this is not always the case. Sutherland reported several cases in which the NDErs specifically noticed how some aspects of their near-death visions were very different from what they were encouraged to assume from their religious background. The story of little Daniel is one of these. One day, he shocked his mum when at the age of 4 he told her that Jesus didn't look like illustrations she was showing him in a religious book:

This 4-year-old was telling me that this picture and the picture on the wall were totally wrong, that Jesus didn't like look like that at all. As he explained it, Jesus had a black flowing cape. And then he drew him, he always used to draw him with a black flowing cape.

(Sutherland 1995: 99)

Life review

In 1979, Allan Pring was undergoing a surgical operation, during which he thought he died. He saw a replay of events of his life, which started from his early childhood and included many occurrences that he had completely forgotten. He said:

On Monday 6 August the preparation for surgery was routine and I lost consciousness within seconds of being injected with an anaesthetic. All perfectly normal. But the manner in which I regained consciousness was anything but normal. Instead of slowly coming round in a drowsy and somewhat befuddled state in a hospital ward I awoke as if from a deep and refreshing sleep and I was instantly and acutely aware of my situation. Without any anxiety or distress, I knew that I was dead, or rather that I had gone through the process of dying and was now in a differ-ent state of reality. The place that I was in cannot be described because it was a state of nothingness. There was nothing to see because there was no light; there was nothing to feel because there was no substance. Although I no longer considered that I had a physical body, nevertheless I felt as if I were floating in a vast empty space, very relaxed and waiting. Then I experienced the review of my life, which extended from my early childhood and included many occurrences that I had completely forgotten. My life passed before me in a momentary flash but it was entire, even my thoughts were included. Some of the contents caused me to be ashamed but there were one or two I had forgotten about of which I felt quite pleased. All in all, I knew that I could have lived a much better life but it could have been a lot worse. Be that as it may, I knew that it was all over now and there was no going back. There was one most peculiar feature of this life review and it is very difficult to describe, let alone explain. Although it took but a moment to complete, literally a flash, there was still time to stop and wonder over separate incidents. This was the first instance of distortion of time that I experienced but it was the beginning of my belief that the answers to many of the questions that are posed by NDEs lie in a better understanding of the nature of time and what we term reality.

(Fenwick and Fenwick 1995: 113–14)

As in many other cases of life review, Mr Pring did not feel he had been judged except by himself. As Peter and Elizabeth Fenwick, who originally reported the case of Mr Pring, observed:

He was absolutely convinced that he was dead and that everything that he experienced was real. The event was still very vivid in his memory as if it happened yesterday. Before this experience, he didn't believe in life after death, or in God, but he relied on a scientific explanation of every kind of mystery. Afterwards, he became convinced that it is impossible to die, which in his view was not 'good news'.

(ibid.: 113)

There is no doubt that the life review is a very remarkable experience. Sometimes it has been described as a sort of film seen at a distance, or sets of slides. Some other times, as in the case quoted below, this can be a sort of three-dimensional display of the entire life:

It proceeded to show me every single event of my 22 years of life, in a kind of instant 3-D panoramic review . . . The brightness showed me every second of all those years, in exquisite detail, in what seemed only an instant of time. Watching and re-experiencing all those events of my life changed everything. It was an opportunity to see and feel all the love I had shared, and more importantly, all the pain I had caused. I was able simultaneously to re-experience not only my own feelings and thoughts, but those of all the other people I had ever interacted with. Seeing myself through their eyes was a humbling experience.

(Ring 1980: 44)

For others, it was a reliving of every detail of every moment of their lives, every emotion, and every thought simultaneously as well as the way they dealt with others and how others dealt with them. This can also be a bitter surprise:

Mine was not a review, but a reliving. For me, it was a total reliving of every thought I had ever thought, every word I had ever spoken, and every deed I had ever done; plus, the effect of each thought, word and deed on everyone and anyone who had ever come within my environ-ment or sphere of influence, whether I knew them or not . . . No detail was left out. No slip of the tongue or slur was missed. No mistake or accident went unaccounted for. If there is such a thing as hell, as far as I am concerned, this was hell.

(ibid.: 40)

As Carl Becker has pointed out, probably the most intriguing aspect is the fact that people may report the experience from a third-party perspective, as if they were watching a movie. This seems to indicate that more than a recollection of memory is involved, and perhaps that a 'self' other than the brain is involved in this life review (Becker 1993: 80). There is much uncer-tainty about the nature of the life review, but this remains an interesting phenomenon, which deserve further studies.

What happens after?

The near-death experience has the wonderful power of transforming peo-ple's lives. Most of those who reported the experience claimed to have had significant changes in their lives such as a less materialistic, more spiritual, less competitive view of life and overall a reduced fear of death (Moody 1975; Greyson and Stevenson 1980; Fenwick and Fenwick 1995; Fox 2003). They seem to be convinced that we never die and that the human soul is immortal.

The greatest change is usually found in those who had the most profound experiences, as in the case of those who believed they were going to die and in those who reported a 'life review-type' of experience (Greyson and Stevenson 1980). Positive changes have also been found in those who had an NDE as a consequence of a failed suicide (Roberts and Owen 1988), in children who had an NDE (Sutherland 1995) and in those who came close to death, but did not report or had no memory of an NDE (Kellehear 1996).

The fact that there is a sudden change in the lives of those who had an NDE supports their view that the experience was real and not a hallucination. In this respect, Mark Fox gives a positive suggestion by arguing that:

> Rather, having an experience which may *appear* to the subject to point to the possibility of immortality – such as an OBE whilst resting or sleeping, leading to the conviction that the soul can function independently of the body – may suffice to instil in him or her an often strong and permanent belief that personal death is not the end . . . whether or not such a dualistic view of personhood is correct or even philosophically or psychologically possible is not the issue here. Instead, the conclusions that subjects themselves draw from their experiences are what really matter.
>
> (Fox 2003: 287)

As Paul Badham has pointed out, the after-effects of an NDE are not very different from those reported by spiritual or religious experiences in a broader sense (Badham 2005a). The argument has been explored at length by David Hay, who argued that the after-effects of the spiritual experience can be seen as a 'dynamic force leading to social change, to concern for both others and for the environment and to a far more caring and unselfish style of life' (in Badham 2005a: 202). Melvin Morse, in his book entitled *Transformed by the Light* (Morse and Perry 1992), noted that some of his patients came back to life with 'an increase in the amount of electrical energy, their bodies emitting acceleration of intellect and/or psychic abilities, and even the power to heal themselves'. He gave the example of Kathy, a 45-year-old woman, who suffered from an incurable thyroid cancer and had been given six months to live. It was at that difficult moment of her life that she also developed pneumonia. She was taken urgently to hospital and her heart stopped beating for a while. When she regained consciousness she told others about her wonderful journey on top of a beautiful ridge overlooking a beautiful valley. A being of light came to greet her and touched her 'spiritual body', which was 'filled with light'. Mysteriously her pneumonia had disappeared. A few weeks later, her cancer, too, had inexplicably left her. According to Morse, Kathy's NDE had a direct influence on healing the cancer. He also studied instances in which near-death survivors had returned to life more intelligent than they had been before the experience (Morse 1990; 1994; Morse and Perry 1992).

Atwater in *Beyond the Light* (1995), and it is not a coincidence that most of the NDE books have the term 'Light' in the title, similarly quoted the case of a truck driver who had survived a near-fatal crash and who subsequently began to display advanced mathematical abilities. Literally overnight, he demonstrated a gift for higher mathematics. He was able to write down complicated mathematical equations about which he had no prior knowledge. Gradually, the man began to understand his new abilities and was eventually able to use them in practical applications. In those cases in which near-death survivors claim to have been left with after-effects, Atwater (1995) indicates that 80–90 per cent show a large number of after-effects.

Despite a large number of well-documented positive after-effects, some negative after-effects have also emerged. Among these there is the frustration of not being able to communicate the significance of the experience to others. As has been argued earlier, people who have experienced an NDE may be sure about the authenticity of their experiences. By contrast, especially for those who do not have similar experiences, these are mere hallucinations induced by a dying brain, or by the effect of a certain drug, of no more interest than an especially vivid dream. The fear of being ridiculed or seen as insane by others, has led some people to keep the event private or to share it only with a few family members or friends, even if the experience was very positive (Orne 1995). It has also been observed that how well they were able to integrate the experience into their everyday life can depend on the quality of these relationships (French 2005). Another negative after-effect is the despair at being returned to ordinary life after having experienced such bliss or divine love. Those who knew the person before the event might also experience some problems in accepting and dealing with him or her after the change. It has been claimed that there is evidence of this in a high divorce rate after the NDE (ibid.). Negative long-term after-effects following distressing NDE can include heightened fear of death, flashbacks and other symptoms of traumatic stress disorder (Greyson and Bush 1992).

NDE and *The Tibetan Book of the Dead*

In our Western culture when someone dies, we tend to believe that there is little we can do for the lost loved one. In contrast, Tibetan Buddhists developed a quite different tradition. In Eastern Tibet, especially during the first 49 days after death, the *Bardo Thödel*[11] is read through repeatedly to the deceased along with other practices.[12] Although based on an oral tradition, this text was originally written in the eight century AD and attributed to the Great Guru Padmasambhava, who introduced Buddhism into Tibet. Metaphorically speaking, in Tibetan tradition the 'mental body' that enters a *Bardo* state is conceived like 'a horse, which can be readily controlled by a bridle, or to a huge tree trunk, which may be almost immovable on land, yet once floated in water can be effortlessly directed wherever you wish' (Sogyal Rinpoche 1992: 299). For this reason it needs to be trained.

Various studies have been made in the past 30 years in the attempt to draw some possible parallels between the near-death experience and the *Bardo Thödel*, known in English as *The Tibetan Book of the Dead*.[13] Probably, the most recent analysis has been published by Sogyal Rinpoche in his book *The Tibetan Book of Living and Dying* (1992). In his view, the *Bardo* state, like an NDE, is characterized by extreme clarity, mobility and clairvoyance, which he beautifully relates to a 'body of the golden age' (ibid.: 326). According to him, there are some major commonalities between these two kinds of experiences. These can be summarized as follows:

1   *Vision of a Light.* In the first part of *The Tibetan Book of the Dead* called the *Chikhai, Bardo* is described as the moment of dissolution, which occurs at death. This stage represents the passage from form to formlessness. Here a vision of what is called the primary 'Clear Light of Pure Reality' occurs. If the dying are able to recognize it, they become liberated. Nevertheless, if they don't recognize it, they will have a second chance to see the Secondary Clear Light, which will dawn upon them. The description of the vision of the clear Light in the *Bardo* presents a striking similarity to the 'Light' and the 'Beings of Light' frequently described by NDErs.

2   *Encounters with other beings.* In the second state, the *Chonyid Bardo*, or the 'Bardo of Experiencing Reality', the deceased meet different deities: the Peaceful Deities enveloped in brilliant, colored lights, the Wrathful Deities, the Door-keeping Deities, the Knowledge-Holding Deities, and the *yogins* of the four cardinal points. As Leary has noticed:

> With the powerful vision of these deities, the departed perceive dull light of various colors, indicating the individual *lokas* or realms into which they can be born: the realm of the gods (*devaloka*), the realm of the titans (*asuraloka*), the realm of the humans (*manakaloka*), the realm of the brute subhuman creatures (*tiryakaloka*), the realm of hungry ghosts (*pretaloka*) and the realm of hell (*narakaloka*). Attraction to these lights seems to thwart spiritual liberation and facilitates rebirth.

3   *Negative experiences.* A third, probably less explored parallel between the NDE and the *Bardo Thödel* is the description of 'hellish' experiences. As Sogyal Rinpoche commented: 'Some people report terrifying experiences of fear, loneliness, desolation and gloom, vividly reminiscent of the descriptions of the bardo of becoming' (1992: 328).

Tibetan *delok*

In Tibetan tradition, there is an interesting phenomenon called *delok*, which literally means 'returned from the dead'. The name *deloks* is given to people who seemingly 'die' as a result of an illness, and find themselves traveling in the *Bardo*, before returning to life again. His Holiness the Dalai Lama observed that this argument could offer some interesting parallels with the NDE. In a book called *Sleeping, Dreaming and Dying: An Exploration of Consciousness with the Dalai Lama* (Varela 1998) he mentions the story of a young lady who was instructed by her mother not to touch her body. For a week the mother remained immobile: 'We are not sure whether this person was even breathing, or whether there might have been subtle respiration during this period' (ibid.: 206). When she regained consciousness, she narrates having visited various places.

Another interesting account of this curious phenomenon is featured by Sogyal Rinpoche in his book *The Tibetan Book of the Living and the Dying* (1992), where he narrates the story of a Lingza Chokyi, who lived in Tibet in the sixteenth century. She died and found herself out of the body. She had the vision of a pig's corpse lying on her bed and wearing her clothes. She also saw her relatives and attempted to communicate with her living relatives as they were doing the practices for her death. She felt joy every time the practices were done. Then she heard the voice of someone she thought to be her deceased father, and thus followed him to the *Bardo* realm. Miss Chokyi described this like a place with a bridge leading to hell. There she met the Lord of Death, who was counting the good or evil actions of the dead, as well as people who recounted their stories and a great *yogin* who had come to the hell realms in order to liberate other beings (ibid.: 330). At the end she was sent back because there had been an error of her name and family, and it was not yet her time to die. A similar phenomenon has been encountered in Pasricha and Stevenson's study on NDE in India (Pasricha and Stevenson 1986).

Out-of-Body Experience (OBE)

We currently know that an OBE can be part of a near-death experience but not necessarily (see, for instance, Fenwick and Fenwick 1995). It is sometimes as if the experiencing 'I' has left the body and is sometimes, but certainly not always, as if the experiencing 'I' is floating above the body.

OBEs can occur in a variety of situations such as just relaxing and falling asleep, in waking moments (Green 1968), as a feature of epilepsy and migraine (Blackmore 1982), through electro-stimulation of certain parts of the brain (Persinger 1983; 1987), or in other situations such as dissociative anesthesia induced by ketamine (Jansen 1989; 2001), or profound 'psychedelic dissociation' sometimes resulting from DMT (Strassman 2001).

A collection of experiences describing forms of OBE was published in 1860 by Robert Dale Owen in his book entitled *Footfalls on the Boundary of Another World* (Owen 1980). A well-known example of an out-of-body experience is that of Alfonso de Liguori, who was seen simultaneously by many at the bedside of the dying Pope Clement XIV, while he was starving in a prison in Arezzo (Becker 1993). Carl G. Jung (1875–1961), in *Memories, Dreams, Reflections* (1983) described having had an experience similar to those described above after he had broken his foot and suffered a heart attack in 1944. He wrote:

In a state of unconsciousness I experienced deliriums and visions which must have begun when I hung on the edge of death and was being given oxygen and camphor injections. The image was so tremendous that I concluded that I was close to death . . . It seemed to me that I was high up in space.

(Jung 1983: 322–3)

The psychoanalyst described the reddish-yellow desert of Arabia, the Red Sea, and the Mediterranean:

Far below I saw the globe of the earth, bathed in a gloriously blue light. I saw the deep blue sea and the continents. Far below my feet lay Ceylon, and in the distance ahead of me the subcontinent of India. My field of vision didn't include the whole earth, but its global shape was plainly distinguishable and its outlines shone with a silvery gleam through that wonderful blue light. In many places the globe seemed coloured, or spotted dark green like oxidised silver . . . Later I discovered how high in space one would have to be to have so extensive a view – approximately a thousand miles! The sight of the earth from this height was the most glorious thing I had ever seen . . . I felt violent resistance to my doctor because he had brought me back to life.

(ibid.: 123–5)

Independent of the cause, the most relevant feature of the experience is a sense of realness, which makes it rather different from the sensation of watching a movie, for example. Those who reported an OBE are sometimes sure that their minds have left their physical organism and that they have reached a position where they are able to note their bodies as well as things or events in the physical world from above or from elsewhere.[14] As Peter and Elizabeth Fenwick have pointed out, an intriguing aspect of these experiences is that some people are able to provide accurate accounts of what they believe they have seen while disembodied. In their *The Truth in the Light* (1995), they mentioned the case of a young patient, named Audrey Organ. Little Audrey reported an OBE during a surgical operation (a tonsillectomy) at the age of 5. While unconscious, she was able to see and hear what happened during the operation and reported it to her mother the day after. She said: 'They had funny scissors with long, long handles and they go snip-snip into your throat' (ibid.: 32). Although the return to the body is rarely described,[15] Audrey felt she was being 'pushed like a returning space rocket or maybe how births feels to a baby? – and I came back' (ibid.: 40). Given the age of the child, there is some probability that a dissociative anesthetic, which includes nitrous oxide, was involved.

Although some types of OBE and NDE have been associated with great anxiety and fear, the focus of the anxiety almost never appears to be a specific concern to go back into the body, although a desperate desire to go back to the familiar reality might be present. For example, Ivy Davey had three out-of-body experiences during her second pregnancy. On two of these occasions she felt her 'spirit ("or whatever") floated off to the right-hand corner of the ceiling, and stayed about a foot away for a time, and then came happily back into my body' (Fenwick and Fenwick 1995: 40). The third occasion was different: 'I had the greatest difficulty getting into my body. I can still remember the sensation vividly. I gave three "shudders" before my body "locked" into position.' Mrs Davey adds that although she was up on the ceiling, she didn't see her body (ibid.: 41).

In many ways, the OBE represents a challenge for research on near-death. For instance, Susan Blackmore, known for her skeptical point of view, has argued that

> People really being resuscitated could probably feel some of the manipulations being done on them and hear what was going on. Hearing is the last sense to be lost and, as you will realize if you ever listen to radio plays or news, you can imagine a very clear visual image when you can only hear something. So the dying person could build up a fairly accurate picture this way.
>
> (Blackmore 1991: 39)

Her theories are based on various surveys she made with people who dream as though they were spectators, who are more inclined to have OBEs. She also noticed that people who can more easily switch viewpoints in their imagination are also more likely to report OBEs. Paul Badham has argued in reply that, 'Blackmore's explanatory categories (other than the catch-all category of "lucky guess") suggest that the data cannot be accounted for by such explanations' (2003: 205). Another NDE researcher, the cardiologist Michael Sabom tested Blackmore's hypothesis by asking a group of 25 cardiac arrest patients, who had at least five years history of serious illness, to close their eyes and imagine themselves watching a medical team resuscitate them and to describe what they would have expected to see. The finding was that almost all of them made major errors in describing the resuscitation process (Sabom 1982).

Various studies on out-of-body phenomena have focused on the 'ecsomaticity' (literally, 'out-of-body-ness'). Since the 1960s, a growing number of studies have tried to identify the brain mechanisms responsible for the experience. One of these attempts was carried out by Charles Tart with the use of the EEG. He came to the conclusion that some OBEs were characterized by a flat EEG with a marked predominance of alpha activity in the brain (Tart 1965). A similar result has been shown in similar studies by Mitchell (1973). According to Carl Becker, such theories are inadequate to explain the phenomenon simply because OBEs also occur in many other situations which will be impossible on an alpha or sleep level, such as while engaging in normal everyday activities (Becker 1993: 61).

Another approach is that proposed by the neurosurgeon Olaf Blanke of the University Hospital of Geneva in Switzerland. According to his team, the OBE involves a specific part of the brain, known as the right angular gyrus, which has various involvements with visual information, including the way our body is perceived, as well as touch and balance sensations that all work together to create the mind's representation of the body. Blanke claimed that an out-of-body experience 'may reflect a failure by the angular gyrus to integrate these different channels of information' (Blanke *et al.* 2002). Physical stress, or a lack of oxygen to the brain, as in the case of the NDE, might trigger the experience. So it was for one of his patients, a 43-year-old lady who suffered from epilepsy. The discovery happened accidentally while the team was trying to map the activity of her brain in preparation for surgical treatment. When Blanke and colleagues activated the electrodes placed just above the patient's right ear (the region of the right angular gyrus), the woman began to have strange sensations, which varied according to the amplitude of the stimulation and the position of her body. After the first stimulation, she felt as though she was sinking into her bed and then she felt as though she was 'falling from a height'. After another stimulation she said felt like she was 'floating' about $6^1/2$ feet above her bed, close to the ceiling. When she was asked to watch her legs during the stimulation, the patient said she saw her legs 'becoming shorter' (ibid.). Blanke argued that multiple lobes of the brain play a part in something as complex as a religious experience, but that the temporo-parietal junction, responsible for orienting a person in time and space, is a prime node of that network. Similarly, Michael Persinger, a Canadian psychologist, found that he was able to trigger out-of-body and other paranormal experiences in people by exposing the right sides of their brains to a series of electromagnetic pulses (Persinger 1983; 1999). A part of the brain called the hippocampus is also likely to be very important (Jansen 2001).

One of the most recent investigations of OBE was carried out by Penny Sartori a nurse at the 'Intensive Therapy Unit' (ITU) in Swansea (Sartori 2003; 2005). In order to verify whether or not the experiences of patients, who reported that they 'left their bodies', were hallucinations or some other phenomena, she placed brightly colored cards above the bed spaces of each patient, in order to attract their attention. As soon as the patients regained consciousness and felt better, Sartori asked them if they had obtained any information during unconsciousness. Despite all the effort and preparation made in order to verify the OBE, none of the eight patients who reported an OBE in her group of study had seen the symbols. Does this mean that the OBE is just a mind model constructed by the brain from residual sight, sound and tactile stimulation? One of the most interesting findings of this study was that several patients reported experiences, which appeared to be very accurate. For instance, a female respondent claimed seeing her colon jutting out. As Sartori commented:

> This was correct, the operation did not go to plan and part of her colon had to be exposed at the surface of the skin. The patient would not have expected to see this. However, this could have been seen while she was recovering in ITU, while she was still sedated, or recovering from sedation and could have contaminated her recall of the experience. She reported seeing herself looking as 'white as the paper' I was writing on. This would have been true, as she lost a large amount of blood during this emergency situation. Finally, this lady reported seeing people wearing theatre masks, which is also true. However, she is a retired auxiliary nurse so she would have been aware of the theatre attire prior to her operation.
>
> (2005: 240–2)

As in this case, other OBErs reported accurate descriptions, but these were not verifiable.

The OBEs of Hiroshi Motoyama

For millennia, Eastern cultures have tried to experience OBEs as a result of states of deep meditation (Becker 1983). Interested in the phenomenon, in 2004, while I was a member of the 21st century Centre of Excellence on Death and Life Studies at the University of Tokyo, I was invited to a panel discussion with Hiroshi Motoyama, who is well known in Japan as a visionary and healer.[16] I remember I was amazingly surprised to find out that he regularly practises meditation starting at 3 in the morning until 10 in the morning or noon, or sometimes all day long, without skipping a day. This practice enabled him to learn how 'to exit his body at will'. But this is of course not without an effort. According to him: 'Each session of meditation is comparable to a situation where a samurai warrior stakes his life in a sword duel. It is an extremely difficult task to overcome one's self while withstanding the sensation of pain and discomfort.' This state of pain and discomfort may be well related to the long fasting and other ritual practices, which may have altered his brain function in some way. For instance, there is a growing amount of evidence that people who are sensory-deprived for a long period of time have visual imagery similar to OBEs. However, it was only when this sense of pain and discomfort faded away that his consciousness gradually became clear and transparent, allowing him to experience his first OBE. He said:

> One morning, during an initial training, I began to feel that the pain and the discomfort were gradually fading away and this was accompanied

by my consciousness gradually becoming clear and transparent. It was a peaceful state. Then at the moment when I started feeling peaceful, my soul swiftly went out of my body and I was looking down at my body, which was sitting in meditation, two to three meters above the floor. Even though I, who was sitting in meditation, had my eyes closed, I could clearly see, for example, steps in front of the God-altar, the windows, the ceiling, and the sitting cushion. I felt very strange and mystified, wondering what had happened, but at the same time I also had a feeling that it was nothing extraordinary. In ten minutes or so, I returned to my body. Afterwards, I remember going through a kind of a blissful state for several hours. In less than a month after this experience, I had another experience of the *kundalini* ascending through the central tube of the spinal cord. This experience enabled me to exit my body at will.

(Motoyama 2008)

Hiroshi Motoyama holds the view that thanks to his meditative practices he was able to awaken his soul to a higher dimension of consciousness. I took the opportunity to discuss with him some of the features of the near-death experience, such as the meeting with other beings, or God. He believes that there are many ontological dimensions of beings. Interactions among them can take place on both a vertical and a horizontal level. The latter happens on the plane of the same dimension (e.g. we meet and communicate with other people. Such a communication also happens in the rest of the animal and vegetal worlds. In this sense, a plant communicates with a plant, a rabbit communicates with a rabbit, and so on). According to Motoyama, of a different nature is a 'vertical relationship', which happens between beings that belong to different ontological dimensions. An example of this is the meeting with beings of light, or deceased relatives during a near-death experience (NDE). He suggested that such interaction is possible because there is a field (*basho*) of the same dimension in which multiple beings are simultaneously placed. In one of his numerous publications, he wrote:

In order for beings to exist at all, there must be a *basho* (i.e. field) of the same dimension in which they are placed, wherein each recognizes the other(s) as homogenous with its own being, as well as recognizing its own being as heterogeneous with other being(s).

(Motoyama 2008)

Interestingly, Motoyama coined the terminology, 'World of Places' in order to describe the state of *Samadhi*. He observed[17] that:

When the mind and the object are unified, the subject (the mind) becomes Place, and the new unity is sustained and supported at its base

. . . Unless the mind becomes fundamentally Place (Topos), it cannot be united with the object, for if they are separate, they cannot be one.

(Motoyama 1991: 136)

This could be further supporting evidence that Place is indeed the core aspect of the NDE. Motoyama, who is currently a priest in a Shinto shrine in Tokyo as well as President of the California Institute for Human Science, believes that the human soul survives at the death of the physical body as a soul with a distinct individuality, and it forms a community in the spirit world:

Human beings were created, who in turn can create society, religions, science, and art unique to them. Only the human soul can continue to exist, after death, as a soul with a distinct individuality, and it forms a community in the world of the spirits. The divine self dwells in the created things produced in the natural and human worlds; it is always working (preserving) in order that the beings so produced can continue to exist for a certain period of time under a definite order, organization, and energy. It also works on the souls in the spiritual world; it works, preserves and negates them in ways appropriate to them, so that they can be evolved into higher souls.

(Motoyama 2008)

3

The river of no return[1]

As Edward Hall, the anthropologist, said: 'There is no such a thing as "experience" in the abstract as a mode separate and distinct from culture' (1959: 143). We may wonder, does this claim apply to NDEs? This chapter will address this question by presenting the results of various cross-cultural studies of NDE. It will also introduce for the first time the results of a small-scale study that I carried out in Japan and explore its cultural significance in terms of 'Death and Life Studies'.

Cross-cultural study of the NDE is a relatively new and complex field of investigation. Some researchers hold the view that the NDE is a universal experience, which has basically the same structure around the world, although cultural and religious beliefs influence various details and the way the NDE is interpreted. For example, we currently know that an Indian person is more likely to see Yama, the King of Death, or his messengers called *Yamdoots* (Pasricha and Stevenson 1986), rather than Christ or angels. On the contrary, others, like Cherie Sutherland, have reported cases where the content of the experience was actually different from the cultural or religious background of the person who reported the experience (Sutherland 2007).

Sociologist Allan Kellehear thinks that the idea that the NDE is a universal experience is particularly appealing to those who support a biological explanation of the phenomenon and he considers this kind of conclusion premature on the basis of the limited existing data in non-Western countries (Kellehear 1996). In order to support his view, he offered a systematic comparison of near-death experiences reported in India, China, Western New Britain, Guam, Native America, and New Zealand. He published his results in a book entitled *Experiences Near Death* (1996), in which he came to the conclusion that only two features are universal: (1) the transition into a period of darkness; and (2) the meeting with 'other beings', once arrived in the 'other world'. Other aspects, like a 'life review', are nearly always absent in non-Western accounts. He wrote:

> In every case discussed, deceased or supernatural beings are encountered. There are often met in another realm, which is a social world not

dissimilar to the one the percipient is from. The major differences are that this world is often much more pleasant socially and physically. Clearly, the consistency of these reports suggests that at least two features of the NDE are indeed cross-cultural.

(ibid.: 33)

It is interesting to observe how the concept of 'transition into a period of darkness' is rather different from the vision of a tunnel (also known as 'tunnel effect'). The latter, following Kellehear, is socially constructed:

This darkness is then subject to culture-specific interpretations: a tunnel for Westerners, subterranean caverns for the Melanesians, and so on. NDErs who do not report a period of darkness may not view this aspect of the experience as an important part of their account or narrative.

(ibid.: 35–6)

He gives the example of children's literature in Western societies, which 'is replete with tunnels, extraordinary beings, life reviews, flying experiences, and tales of reunion' (ibid.: 153). Classical tunnel-based stories are those of *The Wizard of Oz*, in which Dorothy is transported inside a 'tunnel' to another place and she meets the 'good witch of the east', or *Alice in Wonderland*, where Alice begins her journey after a long fall down a dark rabbit hole. Moreover, there is Santa Claus who comes every December down the chimney of the house (ibid.).

Kellehear's theory largely contradicts Blackmore's biological explanation that the 'tunnel experience' is caused by a lack of oxygen (*anoxia*) in the brain (Blackmore 2003). Consequently, this causes a random activity throughout the visual system, giving the impression of lots of bright lights flashing in the middle where there are lots of cells, but fading out towards the periphery of the visual system, where there are fewer. As the oxygen level falls even more, the brightness in the middle will increase, leading to the impression of travelling along a tunnel towards the light. Eventually the whole area would seem to be light, giving the feeling of entering the light (Blackmore 1993b).

China

We know relatively little about NDE in China. The most popular work has been carried out by Carl Becker (1981). He made a study of three traditional monks, who were exponents of the foundation of Pure Land Buddhism. Each of the three monks reported a period of illness, during which they all experienced either an NDE or a death-bed vision while still reasonably unconscious. During these accounts neither tunnel experience nor out-of-body experience was reported.

More recently, another study was carried out by Zhi-ying and Jian-xun in 1987. The authors looked at the accounts of 81 survivors of the 1976 Tangshan earthquake in China. Of these, 72 reported an experience similar to a near-death experience (Zhi-ying and Jian-xun 1992). The most distinctive features were: 'sensations of the world being exterminated; a sense of weightlessness; a feeling of being pulled or squeezed', as well as the most common 'feeling estranged from the body, unusually vivid thoughts, loss of emotions, unusual bodily sensations, life seeming like a dream, a feeling of dying, a feeling of peace or euphoria, a life review or "panoramic memory", and thinking unusually fast' (ibid.: 46).

India

More evidence emerged from several studies which were carried out in India. One of these was carried out by Satwant Pasricha and Ian Stevenson (Pasricha and Stevenson 1986). This was based on 16 cases of NDEs in India. The authors observed that experiences were characterized by the meeting with Yamraj, the King of the Dead, or his messengers, called *Yamdoots*, or 'the man with the book', Chitragupta. Curiously, NDErs were often 'sent back' to life because of a mistake in the identity of the person. An example quoted in their study is that of Vasudev Pandey, who was interviewed in 1975. This boy was considered dead and taken to the cremation ground. At this time, some signs of life aroused the attention of those present and Vasudev was removed to the hospital where doctors tried to bring him back to life. He remained unconscious for three days. When he regained consciousness, he told the following story to those who were present:

> Two persons caught me and took me with them. I felt tired after walking some distance; they started to drag me. My feet became useless. Then there was a man sitting up. He looked dreadful and was all black. He was wearing no clothes. He said in a rage [to the attendants who had brought Vasudev] 'I had asked you to bring Vasudev the gardener. Our garden is drying up. You have brought Vasudev the student.'
>
> (Pasricha and Stevenson 1986: 166)

The day after, his gardener, who was also called Vasudev, who was present when Vasudev told his NDE, died.[2]

Once again, the content of an Indian NDE differs from those reported in Western societies where NDErs are not usually able to give a reason for their recovery and if they do so, they are more likely to say that they were 'sent back' because deceased relatives or friends told them that their 'time has not yet come'. A different interpretation of the phenomenon has been given by Susan Blackmore who placed an advertisement in *The Times of India* on 2 November 1991 in order to find potential Indian NDErs. Although she had

19 replies, she was able to interview only nine of them. Her findings differed from Pasricha and Stevenson, who found no tunnel or OBE effects. In contrast, 3 of Blackmore's subjects encountered tunnels or a dark space, and their experiences were in general closer to Western ones. She believes that the cross-cultural similarity supports her contention that NDEs have a biological basis (Blackmore 1993b).

Another study was carried out in India by Osis and Haraldsson (1972–73) in order to determine the extent of cultural variations in death-bed visions in India. A similar investigation was carried out in the USA. They published their results in a book called *At the Hour of Death* (1977), which discusses a large number of cultural variations. One of these regards the vision of beings of light, or religious figure, during the experience:

> The identity of the religious figure [in the vision] was also quite a problem in adult cases. If a patient sees a radiant man clad in white who induces in him an inexplicable experience of harmony and peace, he might *interpret* the apparition in various ways: as an angel, Jesus, or God; or if he is a Hindu, Krishna, Shiva, or Deva.
>
> (ibid.: 37)

Although one might think that the interpretation given varies according to the religious backgrounds, the authors commented that this did not 'significantly affect the purpose' of the figure seen, and the sight of a dead or a religious figure was 'surprisingly similar on both sides of the globe – 78% for the United States and 77% for India' (ibid.: 90–1). An important question about this study is whether these visions were the result of the administration of a particular drug, or if these were real visions. The answer is that the consciousness of over 60 per cent of the people was absolutely clear and no form of sedative had been administered (ibid.: 70). Only in 30 per cent of the cases was it moderately impaired. Although Osis and Haraldsson's research relates primarily to the phenomenology of death-bed visions, which are defined as occurring in the 24 hours before dying, rather than NDEs, the study presents a considerable amount of data able to reinforce later studies into the phenomenology of NDEs.

Melanesia

Dorothy Counts reported three cases of NDEs among the population of Kaliai, in the province of Western New Britain, part of Melanesia (Counts 1983). From these accounts emerged a vision of the afterlife characterized by factories and wage employment. For instance, a person she interviewed found himself walking through a field of flowers to a road that forked in two. In each fork of the road a man was standing persuading the NDEr to come with him. The NDEr picked one of the forks at random:

the man took my hand and we entered a village. There we found a long ladder that led up into a house. We climbed the ladder but when we got to the top I heard a voice saying: 'It isn't time for you to come. Stay there. I'll send a group of people to take you back.' . . . So they took me back down the steps. I wanted to go back to the house, but I couldn't because it turned and I realized that it was not on posts. It was just hanging there in the air, turning around as if it were on an axel (*sic*). If I wanted to go to the door, the house would turn and there would be another part of the house where I was standing. There were all kinds of things inside this house, and I wanted to see them all. There were men working with steel, and some men building ships, and another group of men building cars. I was standing staring when this man said: 'It's not time for you to be here. Your time is yet to come. I'll send some people to take you back . . . you must go back.' I was to go back, but there was no road for me to follow, so the voice said: 'Let him go down.' Then there was a beam of light and I walked along it. I walked down the steps, and then when I turned to look there was nothing but forest . . . So I walked along the beam of light, through the forest and along a narrow path. I came back to my house and re-entered my body and I was alive again.

(Counts 1983: 199–120)

According to Counts, this 'unusual' kind of NDE vision relates to the Kaliai's beliefs that the afterlife is characterized by 'divinely given technologies, including factories, automobiles, highways, airplanes, European houses and buildings in great numbers, and manufactured goods' (ibid.: 130). She also observed how the content of the paradise varies and seems to be culturally defined: 'North Americans and Europeans see beautiful gardens, while Kaliai find an industrialized world of factories, highways, and urban sprawl.' The culturally structured nature of these experiences is consistent with the explanation that out-of-the-body and near-death experience are the result of a psychological state known as hypnagogic sleep. The Kaliai data presented here suggest that this, rather than an objectively experienced 'life after death', is the most reasonable explanation for the phenomenon (ibid.: 132–3).

Other substantial differences between Melanesian NDE and those reported in Western countries arise from her study. There was no claim of viewing the body or possessing a new one, nor were there any reports of floating sensations or feeling exhilarated with the usual feelings of joy and peace. Auditory sensations were absent and most noticeable was the description of a 'journey' along a road or path. No experiencer recalled moving through a tunnel. Only one of them claimed to have met a personage 'dressed in white'. Against these differences, the anthropologist was able to identify a few similarities. She observes: 'Experiencers regretted leaving the place in which they had found themselves, and they also reported encountering others, including some who had died at an earlier time' (ibid.: 131–2).

Visions of the afterlife in Japan

Very little work has been done on NDE in Japan. Two major studies emerged from my investigation. The larger one has been carried out by Takashi Tachibana, an esteemed journalist in the country, who made a popular survey of four hundred individuals who had survived in life-threatening circumstances. In his work entitled *Near-Death Experience* (1994), which is quite popular in Japan, he argues that the most common features of a Japanese NDE are the visions of long, dark rivers and beautiful flowers. Of greater academic relevance are probably the research results of another NDE investigation carried out by Yoshia Hata and his research team at the University of Kyorin (Hata *et al.*, in Hadfield 1991). Researchers interviewed 17 patients, who recovered from a situation where there had been minimal signs of life. Most of them had suffered heart attacks, asthma attacks, or drug poisoning. Eight of them reported memories during unconsciousness (47 per cent). Nine had no memories at all (53 per cent). Of the eight who had an experience, clear visions of rivers or ponds largely prevailed. Such elements have also been emphasized in Takashi Tachibana's popular survey. Probably the most interesting finding of Hata's study is that five of the eight participants (62.5 per cent) reported negative experiences, dominated by fear, pain or suffering. So it was for a 73-year-old lady, who had an NDE as a consequence of a cardiac arrest. She said: 'I saw a cloud filled with dead people. It was a dark, gloomy day. I was chanting sutras. I believed they could be saved if they chanted sutras, so that is what I was telling them to do' (Hadfield 1991: 11).

Negative NDEs seem not to be that common in Western accounts, although as Peter and Elizabeth Fenwick observed, they are probably under-reported because they are less likely to be communicated to others than positive experiences (Fenwick and Fenwick 1995).

A small-scale study

In 2004, I carried out a small-scale study in Japan in collaboration with the 21st Century COE Program on the 'Construction of Death and Life Studies Concerning Culture and Value of Life' at the University of Tokyo. The Chair of the Centre, Susumu Shimazono, has pointed out that the main objective of this program is to explore a variety of issues on 'Life' and 'Death' studies, which in Japanese are called *shiseikan* (or 'perspective on Death and Life') (Shimazono 2004). It is interesting to note here how in Japanese the term 'death' precedes that of 'life'. The interviews for the study were organized by Yoshikazu Honda, Assistant Director of 'The Yoko Civilization Research

Institute' in Tokyo. The three interviewees knew each other, and when I met them in Tokyo, Honda translated.

Case I

Mrs O., a 66-year-old Tai Chi Master, had a very powerful near-death experience which changed her life. Sixteen years before the interview, she was very sick and she vomited dark blood. She lost consciousness and was resuscitated in the emergency care unit of a hospital in Tokyo. The doctor told her later that her heart had stopped beating for a while and that she was considered clinically dead for an unknown period of time (she couldn't remember). She described having a vision of a river which separated her side from that of the Realm of Dead (or 'Yomi'). She said:

> As I got closer, at the very end of the other side of the river, I saw my mother who passed away 18 years ago. I could see only her face because a group of children monks, dressed in white and black, masked the rest of her body. The children were very noisy. I moved closer, to see my mother. She looked very worried and she said: 'Don't come here! Go back!' So I turned back and regained consciousness in the hospital. At that very moment, I heard a nurse calling my name.

A few days after her NDE, another 'strange' event happened to Mrs O. She was still in pain, recovering at home. She said she looked at a picture of a plum tree in full blossom on the wall of her room (this is a rather common image in Japanese houses). Suddenly, she saw the face of her mother staring at her from the centre of a beautiful plum flower. This vision continued for about two weeks. She said: 'When I fully recovered, the face of my mother disappeared from the plum tree.' She felt that her mother had sent her back to our world because she still had several missions to accomplish in this life. The first mission was that she had to become a Tai Chi Master for the good of other people. And so she did. She was still practicing this discipline when I met her.

The second reason was that she had to care for and learn more from her mother-in-law. In fact, four years after her NDE, her husband sadly passed away and her mother-in-law was left all alone because her husband was her only child. Her mother-in-law lived a healthy life and lived until the age of 103.

During the interview, Mrs O. remembered several times when this old woman had been important in her life. She said:

> I was very pleased to take care of her and I learnt so much from her. I never had the opportunity to take care of my own mother while she was alive. When she passed away I was a student in Tokyo, far away from Niigata where my family lived.

Her NDE changed her life in various ways. She became less worried about events in her life. She also understood that we all have a mission in life:

> My mother helped me to see my own path more clearly. I now recognize the power of parents' love for their children. Finally, I had the chance to take care of my mother-in-law and to learn much from her. I feel blessed for what I have experienced. NDE are very rare and precious experiences. Only a few people have had these magnificent experiences.

Case 2

Mrs C. was 66 years old at the time of the interview. She studied Tai Chi and became a Grand Master (the highest level in the discipline). She had an NDE in October 1975 as a result of a long period of sickness. She was considered clinically dead for an unknown period of time. She had a vision of a river which separated her side from that of the 'spirit world'. A rainbow bridge connected the two sides of the river. Once she regained consciousness she gave the following account:

> My father came to greet me. We walked together for a little while and then he left me and crossed over a 'rainbow bridge'. I was about to follow him but he told me not to do so. He said to me: 'Go home, go home!' Then, I woke up.

Case 3

The third person interviewed was Mr C., a 41-year-old musician. He studied classical music and became a professional guitarist. He reported an NDE in December 1981 as a consequence of a terrible car accident.
He said:

> My friend was driving a car and I was sitting in the passenger seat. The car smashed into a bus and I got a hard blow on my head. I was taken to a hospital. In hospital, I was aware of being examined but immediately afterwards I became unconscious and entered a state of 'suspended animation' with dilated pupils for a day (24 hours). Doctors told my parents there was no guarantee of my survival.

Mr C. had a vision of an empty and strange place. He said: 'No one was there. No living things were around me. I remember that I felt serene but lonely. I was amazed at how vast the space was! It was neither too bright nor too dark. It was just there was no living thing there.' He wandered around and reached a wall of bright and magnificent Light in his path. He said:

I saw something glittering in the distance and went to it. Next thing I knew there was a bright huge wall standing in my way. It was made of golden light. There was something I had to go across between the wall and me. I believe there was no river, no bridge or nothing specifically. The wall, which shone gold softly, was made of pure glory and I was sure that there existed whole in it. I moved towards it, being gravitated to it. I have a feeling that I saw many things in this something. Everything happened very quickly. I remember that I saw everything I had experienced. In all the cases the experiences were very unique events, but when they did occur they were the most important experiences in their lives and could be life-transforming. As I have previously argued in Chapter 2, most of those who had a NDE often report a less materialistic, more spiritual, less competitive view of life and overall a reduced fear of death (Moody 1975; Greyson and Stevenson 1980; Fenwick and Fenwick 1995; Fox 2003). They also seem to be convinced that we never die and that the human soul is immortal.

Then I asked him to tell me a little bit more about the sense of gravitation that he felt around the golden wall. He said:

The sense of gravitation toward the light was so strong that I gradually began to lose the sense of distinguishing myself from the light. I was filled with everything. Then I thought something like: 'Would I be dead if the trend continues?', but 'I have achieved nothing in this life!' Then I realized that I had developed a strong feeling of resistance towards this gravitation and the melting into the light. I remember nothing else. The next thing I knew was that I was lying in a hospital bed, and that I was in pain and suffering.

Interestingly, every NDEr we interviewed was absolutely sure that what happened wasn't 'just a dream' but a true experience. This is a common feature of near-death experiences (see, for instance, Greyson and Stevenson 1980). For all the participants it was a pleasant experience. No pain or suffering was reported. Only Mr C. felt 'serene, but lonely'. This differs the research results of Hata and his team at the University of Kyorin (Hata, in Hadfield 1991) in which five out of eight participants had a negative experience.

Vision of beautiful landscapes

In all three cases the individuals reported a sense of emergence into another place (or dimension of reality). Two of them recognized it as the Realm of *Yomi*. They described it as a place of incredible beauty, full of gardens and scented flowers. In both cases, the landscape was described as being particularly bright. According to Mrs O.: 'the ground was filled with beautiful yellow flowers, like a sort of carpet'. She couldn't tell what kind of flowers there were but she noticed the colors were very unusual and very bright. Similarly, Mrs C. said: 'I realized (after a period of unconsciousness) that I was in a place filled with inexplicable gentle light and nice fragrances, as well as beautiful flowers. Then I heard a beautiful voice and music.'

As has been reported in previous studies (Hata, in Hadfield 1991; Tachibana 1994), this kind of vision of a beautiful place seems to be a recurrent feature in Japanese NDEs. One reason could be that nature is strongly connected with spirituality in Japan. For instance, the representations of beautiful and idealistic landscapes are often painted on silk or parchment scrolls, which are commonly used in Japanese houses as an aid to meditation. The Japanese tendency to have near-death visions related to the natural environment could be related to their intimate relationship with nature. This phenomenon has been called 'biophilia' (Wilson 1984). However, there are some exceptions. For instance, Mr. C. did not notice any garden, park or similar, but found himself in a strange place where he had never been before. He said:

> I found myself in a strange place. Soon I realized that something unusual was going on. I had no pain or suffering, either mentally or physically, and I felt serene. But, I didn't have a clue where to turn. I knew I had to decide about something but I had no clue what it should be. I had qualms about it and at the same time I took an interest in it. No one was around me. No living things were around me. I remember that I felt serene but lonely.

The river

Interestingly, two out of three participants described a vision of a river which divided the world of the living from that of the dead. For both of them, to cross the river meant acceptance that they would die. A similar conclusion also emerged from previous studies (Hata, in Hadfield 1991; Tachibana 1994).

A vision of the afterlife is very common in Greek and Roman mythology, where the rivers have been called various names (Chevalier and Gheerbrant 1986: 452). Moreover, it has a strong link with Shinto beliefs where the element of the river (or water in general) has the significance of purification (Kasulis 2004; Bocking 1996). For instance, in the myth of the creation of Japan, Izanagi, the creator god of Japan, travels in the afterlife to meet his deceased wife, Izanami. When he returns from the realm of Yomi (or the 'world of the dead'), he purifies himself in the water of a river. This is because in Japanese tradition the land of the dead is depicted as the land of filth and uncleanliness (Kingsley 1998: 24–5). The latter consideration could be meaningful in the context of the study by Hata and his colleagues at the Kyorin University where five out of eight participants had negative near-death experiences (Hata, in Hadfield 1991).

Meeting with other beings

Two out of three of the participants met other beings. Both Mrs O. and Mrs C. met respectively their dead mother and father, who told them 'do not cross the river' and to go back. Moreover, Mrs O. saw a group of child monks who were with her mother on the other side of the river. She said: 'I saw a large group of children monks running towards me. They were dressed in a white shirt and black skirts. They were aged between 10 and 12, and were all bold.' She immediately associated the group with the terrible noise she was hearing. She said: 'They were terribly noisy and I couldn't understand what they were saying to me.' The third participant, the young musician, was alone: 'serene, but lonely'.

Light in Japan

One participant, Mr. C., had a powerful vision of a wall made of Light and had a form of non-verbal communication with it. He also described a sense of gravitation towards this Light, as if he was melting into it. As we saw in Chapter 2, Ring identified this as the last stage of the NDE (Ring 1980). The other two participants didn't see the Light, but they spoke about bright colours. To illustrate this point, Mrs O. made me look at the flowers in her garden which were incredibly yellow. Mrs C. said that she was in a place filled with inexplicable, gentle, bright light and lovely fragrance.

No one reported a tunnel effect or a transition through a period of darkness, which, following Kellehear (1996), is also one of the two most common elements in NDE from a cross-cultural point of view. Only one participant (Mr C.) referred to a sense of transition, but not in the darkness. He told me he was (1) flying (2) up and (3) at great speed. Both (1) and (2) are quite unusual elements in Western NDE, where people usually are going down along a tunnel, rather than flying up. A common element is the high speed (3).

Life review

No one reported a life review (or a panoramic vision of one's physical life). The only exception might be represented by the musician (Mr C.), who said that he saw everything he had experienced in the wall of Light in front of him. Nevertheless, he couldn't remember what it was. This result confirmed those presented in previous studies (Hata, in Hadfield 1991; Tachibana 1994).

Out-of-Body Experience

No one reported an out-of-body experience. Such a result was also reported in previous studies (Hata, in Hadfield 1991; Tachibana 1994). However, I have recently learnt of the case of an 87-year-old Japanese woman who,

40 years ago, had a very powerful OBE. She was considered clinically dead by the doctors. She described her amazement when she found herself out of her body and looking at her family members crying at her deathbed. Although she tried many ways to attract their attention and to communicate with them (in an attempt to tell them that she was not dead), she did not succeed. She also rang the bell of the ancestors' altar in her house. Her family members heard the sound of the bell and turned towards the altar but they were not able to see her. Finally, after many attempts, she lay down on her corpse and miraculously she came back to life. This was indeed a surprise for everyone!

Border or a point of no return

All three NDErs came to a clear point or border of no return, which was a major component of their experience. Mrs O. described it as a river, which divided her side from the side where she saw the child monks as well as her dead mother who had passed away 18 years previously. Mrs C. described it as a rainbow bridge across a river, and the young musician as a wall of golden Light which blocked his way. For all of them, to cross these points meant that they would die and that they accepted this. Two of them were sent back by their dead relatives (the mother in the case of Mrs O., her father in the case of Ms C.) either (1) because they had a mission to accomplish in life, or (2) because their time had not yet come.

Similar experiences have been widely reported in Western NDE. For instance, we currently know that in India, people tend to be sent back because of a mistake in their identities (Pasricha and Stevenson 1986). A similar phenomenon has been described in case of Lingza Chokyi in the Tibetan *delok* (Sogyal Rinpoche 1992).

On cultural comparison

The cultural comparison between NDEs in different countries is a very difficult topic of investigation, especially in the absence of extensive data. When we think of a cultural comparison of any kind of experience, two different approaches can be taken (Kasulis 1981). One is to look at 'what' is experienced. The other approach is to look at 'how' this is experienced. Let me give an example. If we have two individuals, a Japanese and an Italian, and we asked them 'What is your favourite food?', the Japanese might answer 'sushi', while the Italian might say 'spaghetti'. We all know that sushi and spaghetti have very little in common. Nevertheless, it remains a fact that both the Japanese and the Italian have a favourite food, feel hunger, love food, and so on.

The same thing can be said for the near-death experience. If we look at 'what' has been experienced from a cross-cultural point of view, we may not find many common elements because every experience is unique. Nevertheless, if we start asking how an NDE is experienced, we may come to the conclusion that everywhere in the world many people will report that (1) what happened was 'real' and was not a mere hallucination or a dream; (2) they will emphasize that they travelled to another 'place', as if it is always there but we are not always able to see it; (3) finally, they may say that the experience was one of the more important experiences of their life and that it had a life-changing effect on them, often in a 'spiritual' sense.

Edmund Husserl, the founder of phenomenology, has argued that there are certain cognitive structures (what he called 'eidetic essences') that are common to all people regardless of their cultural context. That is to say that the basis of any near-death experience is found in the same source or power ('energy'), independent of *what* has been experienced. Eastern traditions have grasped this concept in various ways. For example, we find the idea of *Purusa* in Yoga, *Atman* in Vedanta, *Tao* in Taoism, which all refer to the field which is called our 'authentic self' (Nishida 1990).

The afterlife in the Japanese myth of creation

The ancient myth of creation of the Japanese islands is narrated in the first book of the *Kojiki* (or 'Record of Ancient Things'), which was completed in 712 AD.[3] It tells the story of the God Izanagi and the Goddess Izanami who created the numerous islands of Japan alongside many other deities. The myth starts with the description of the gods standing on the 'Floating Bridge of Heaven' (*Ame no uke-hashi*). Izanagi dipped a heavenly jewelled spear into the cosmological brine below and stirred it. Then, when he lifted up the spear, the dripping salt from the tip of the spear coagulated and became the island of Onokoro, the first island of Japan to be created. Izanami and Izanagi decided to go and make their home there. They stuck the spear into the ground to erect the Heavenly Pillar and after dancing around this pillar, they gave birth to more deities, numerous islands and various features of nature such as water-falls, mountains, trees, herbs and the wind.

So, how does this myth relate to the Japanese conception of death and life? Interestingly, there is a part of the myth which is particularly illumin-ating in this regard. This is when the Goddess Izanami dies from a terrible fever while giving birth to the god of fire. Izanagi, bereft, wanted his spouse back and thus decided to travel to the afterlife, or Realm of Yomi, in order to get her back. He calls out to her: 'O, my beloved spouse, the lands which you and I were making have not yet been completed; you must come back!'[4] But it was too late. She had already eaten the fruit in the hearth of Yomi, which meant that she was unable to return to earth without the permission of the *kami* Yomi. She asked her husband to wait for her patiently and not to enter the hall while she was discussing the issue with the *kami*. But being impatient, Izanagi entered the hall. What he saw was dreadful:

Maggots were squirming and roaring in Izanami's corpse. In her heart was Great-Thunder; in her breast was Fire-Thunder; in her belly was Black-Thunder; in her genitals was Crack-Thunder; in her right hand was Earth-Thunder; in her right foot was Reclining-Thunder. Altogether there were eight Thunder-deities.[5]

Izanagi was frightened by this horrible sight and decided to turn and flee. Izanami felt ashamed of his action. Yomi sent his hags to pursue him but he managed to escape them using magic. When Izanagi arrived at the border between the land of the living and underworld, he attacked his pursuers with three peaches he had found nearby.

Finally, Izanami herself came in pursuit of Izanagi. He pulled a huge boulder across the pass to separate Yomi from the land of the living. As Izanagi and Izanami stood facing each other on either side of the boulder, she said: 'O my beloved husband, if you do thus, I will each day strangle to death 1,000 of the populace of your country.' He replied: 'O my beloved spouse, if you do this, I will each day build 1,500 parturition huts, meaning that 1,500 people will be born.'[6] Finally, she told him that he must accept her death. Izanagi promised not to visit her again. Then, they formally declared their marriage over.

Back in the land of the living, Izanagi said: 'I have been to a most unpleasant land, a horrible, unclean land. Therefore I shall purify myself.'[7] Just as the marriage between Izanami and Izanagi brought life to the natural world, their separation signified the beginning of mortality on earth. It is also interesting to notice that once he returned to the world of the living, Izanagi went to purify himself in the water of a river.

The myth is relevant to near-death studies for at least four reasons. The first is the description of the floating bridge of heaven. This is, in fact, a common vision during Japanese NDE. The second reason is that during his visit in the land of Yomi, Izanagi is asked to stop in front of the door of the burial hall. This meant that he was prohibited from going any further. This ban bears some similarities to what is called the border or the point of no return during a near-death experience. Here, the person stops in front of a specific point of no return, for example, a river, a door, a wall, and so on. Only if a person passes over this point will he or she be dead. In a sense the decision whether to die or not is always taken by the living. Ebersole has pointed out that: 'The finality of death is a result of the actions of the living' (1989: 88).

The third interesting aspect of the narration is the description of the dreadful land of Yomi. This can be partially connected to the frightening images of the afterlife in Genshin's *Ojoyoshu*, written in the tenth century.[8] As mentioned previously, Yoshia Hata's research suggests that NDE experiences in Japan generally tend to be negative.

The fourth element is the purification of Izanagi, symbolically using water from a river on his return from the world of the dead. This myth could be associated with the recurrent vision of rivers and water in Japanese NDEs.

The practice of purification is still very popular in Japanese everyday life. For instance, before entering a Shinto Shrine or the house of certain distinguished persons, visitors are asked to purify themselves with water, by washing their hands and their mouths. Moreover, there is another Shinto ritual of purification with water, which takes place during the '*misogi*'. As Kasulis described, although there are no fixed rules, when walking on a mountain path, participants, dressed in white, enter a mountain pool at the base of a sacred waterfall:

> with the water pounding down on his or her head, the devotee stands beneath the waterfall and chants a formulaic incantation. Through the *tama* of the sacred water and the *kotodama* (the *tama* of words) in the chant, the person's impurities are washed away.
>
> (Kasulis 2004: 52)

Another example, which might be familiar to many, is that of a visit to a Japanese restaurant. When you enter such a place, a warm wet cloth is given to you before starting your meal. I have been told that this is not only for hygienic reasons but also for purification.

Death and life in Japan

In Japanese culture there is no clear distinction between life and death. The concept has been well expressed by Kato, who commented that in Japan 'there is a continuum between the living and the dead that makes it difficult to draw clear lines' (Kato, in Martinez 2004: 207). As has been suggested, probably the easiest way to explain this intricate phenomenon is that of the Taoist symbol of yin–yang. The yang (white) never exists purely as yang, but it is always inclusive of some yin (black) and vice versa. Simply stated, for a Japanese person, 'death' is present in a neonate as much as 'life' is present in a sick old man (Kasulis 2004). Such a strict interrelation between life and death appears even clearer by observing Japanese everyday life. A few examples are quoted below.

A notable example is that of the 'cherry blossom festival', which is one of the most important events of the year in Japan. People gather together in parks to celebrate the blossoming of cherry ('sakura') and plum trees. It is also an important moment of reflection on life and death. As Drazen has pointed out in a book called *Anime Explosion!*:[9]

> The blossoms (which someone has linked to the human flesh) appears only for a brief time, then fall to the ground. This is the ultimate reminder that human life is very impermanent, but that, for the short time it is here, it can also be very beautiful.
>
> (2003: 208–19)

Edward O. Wilson has called this sophisticated understanding of the biological, 'biophilia' (Wilson 1984). The term was originally employed to describe the love for nature manifested by field biologists, or naturalists. This occurs as a result of deep-seated emotions, which most of the time are spontaneous and they manifest themselves as a pre-reflective mode of our being. Similarly, other authors have written about a Japanese 'ecocentric' view of human existence (Shaner 1989; Yuasa 1993; Kasulis 2004).

Japanese intimate encounter with the natural world is an integral part of its ancient written history[10] and has been frequently expressed with the dictum *mono no aware*, which literally means to show a 'sensitivity to things'. In Buddhism, for instance, there is a similar expression, which is called to imitate 'the child-like mind', or to show 'one's original face'. As Yasuo Yuasa has observed: 'The child-like mind is originally intimated with his/her world . . . The emotional ties between the child and the environment are powerful and often uncontrolled' (1989: 124). Also Shinto mythology is rich in references to a pantheistic/animistic world-view and in Shinto ritual practices there are many elements which emphasize the encounter with oneself, others and nature in a cultivated harmony.[11] At the core of this phenomenon lies the unifying activity between subject and object, which will be better discussed in the following paragraphs. For instance in 'calligraphy, dramatic theatre, flower arrangement, or the martial arts, one might be instructed to act "naturally" (in Japanese *shizen ni*) in order to become intimate with paper, brush, audience, flowers, or opponent respectively' (Yuasa 1989: 103).

A critique of Japanese love for nature has been put forward by Japanese psychiatrist Takeo Doi, who commented that this could be interpreted as a response to something unsatisfying about the pattern of Japanese social behaviour. In his view, the deep-seated desire for harmony (*wa*) is usually left unfulfilled by a Japanese social consciousness that routinely separates, albeit unconsciously, the outer (*soto*) public face of social obligations (*omote*) from the inner (*uchi*) face reserved for more intimate relationships (*ura*). He concludes that since Japanese are afflicted with this splitting of consciousness they 'seek to become one with nature precisely because of this affliction' (Doi 1986: 155–6). For him:

> Only this would explain why Japanese feel able to breathe again when they confront nature, and why, strangely enough, they recover *kokoro* (heart, mind) that is much more human than the *kokoro* they have when they relate to other human beings.
>
> (ibid.: 151)

The perception of life and death in the country emerges even more clearly from the very peculiar way in which Japanese deal with the problem of abortion with images of *Jizō*, the protector of children. Small statues of the size of little children are placed in cemeteries to apologize to a fetus to be aborted, and as focus of prayers for the soul of the fetus to be reborn into better circumstances. As Patrick Drazen has observed: 'there is a belief (which the West simply does not share) that nothing irretrievable has been lost by an abortion, and that there may be a greater good in the long term (2003: 209). Nevertheless aborted children have a different status from newborn infants (*mizuko*). In dying, they 'go back' to the world previous to life. This can be seen as an anticlockwise process. But where do they go? William LaFleur in his *Liquid Life* (1992) pointed out that in medieval Japan there was a special place for unborn children. This was called the *Sai-no-kawara* (or 'the Riverbank in the land of the Sai').[12] He wrote:

> The sai-no-kawara was envisioned concretely as a riverbank where dead children were gathered. They were thought to be miserable because, on the one hand, they could no longer be with their beloved parents in the land of the living and, on the other hand, they could not cross the river, which is taken to be the boundary between them and a good rebirth.
>
> (ibid.: 58)

Moreover, he observed:

> The sai-no-kaware is not a place found on our eartly maps. It lies in some 'other' world or in something of a borderline location between this world and others . . . Modern people may tell themselves that such locations are 'symbols' of intangible events in some unseen and other world, but it seems fairly clear from the kind of cultic activities that take place in such empirical *Sai-no-kawara* that they have popularly been taken as real nexi with other kinds of space – that is, interstices between the physical and the metaphysical.
>
> (ibid.: 58–9)

All over Japan there are various locations, which are called 'Riverbank of Sai'. One of these is the Nembutsu-ji in Western Kyoyo where curiously there is no river at all. The label is used here to indicate a 'place of power'.

'Place' and the NDE

One of the most fascinating aspects of the Japanese contemporary approach to transcendental states, including the near-death experience, is their understanding in terms of space, or more specifically 'place', in Japanese *basho*.[13] For instance, Hiroshi Motoyama called the state of *Samadhi* 'The World of Places'.

The underlying idea is that our daily reality has an invisible deeper layer, which is different in dimension and is disclosed by the object–subject relation. Nishida called this deeper level of consciousness invisible place, or *basho* (Nishida 1990). He considered the latter to be the sphere of 'authentic self', which he differentiated from 'ego-consciousness', or the consciousness of the temporal self, which he considered an expression of an 'inauthentic self'.[14]

One may wonder, why place? Place is in many ways a mysterious term. In our common language, when we refer to our subjective experience of space we tend to use the term 'place' rather than 'space'. Accordingly, we were born in certain places, we live in certain places, we like to work in certain places, we go to relax in certain places, and so on. Most of these places are not marked on specific maps, but they became special for us because in a way they 'define who we are'. We might keep a photograph of them, a note made in a diary, or we might have spent a word about them with a family member or a friend. Nevertheless, most of these places remain private events of our lives. Following the Japanese tradition, place (or *basho*) represents not only the most intimate aspect of human beings but also of all the existing things (Ichikawa 1979; Watsuji 1988; Nishida 1990; Nagatomo 1992; Yuasa 1993). The concept is implicit in one of the three Japanese terms to indicate a human being (*ningen*), which literally means between a person and a person rather than an individual person (Kasulis 1981; Nagatomo 1992). Japanese philosopher Watsuji described the relationship between body (*ningen*) and space as a 'state of between-ness' (*aidagara*) (Watsuji 1988), while Ichikawa calls this the phenomenon of the 'body–space' (Ichikawa 1979). In other words, the spatial notion of place (*basho*) in Japan is not only a fundamental condition for our life on this planet, but also for our survival. Such an insight serves as a basis for a better understanding of both (1) an individual, and (2) the universal aspect of human beings (Corazza 2005).

The term *basho* was originally used by Nishida in the context of *Logic of Place* (*basho no ronri*), in which according to him the transcendental took place.[15] For Nishida, place (*basho*) indicates that which grounds our being. A recurrent example that he gives is that of a tree in a garden. It is meaningless to say that there is a tree in the garden if we don't assume the existence of a certain *basho*. For the tree to be there, the garden (*basho*) has to support the ground of the tree.

The concept of place can be related to Buddhist notions of 'dependent origination', according to which all phenomena are said to arise and come to be in virtue of dependent origination. We may note, however, that what supports dependent origination is *basho*-being in virtue of which each being is created to *be*, where *basho* means the ontological foundation upon and within which beings are placed (2008). He explained his theory with the following example:

> There was once a newspaper article in which it was reported that a lotus seed was discovered that had been stored in a dry natural environment for three thousand years! When it was planted where someone provided the appropriate conditions such as the appropriate amount of water, and the right soil and temperature, it sprouted new buds and blossomed. In

this case, the seed's discovery by someone and an appropriate natural environment served as relational conditions, with the seed as cause while the blossoming of the flower was the effect.

(Motoyama 2008)

In this example, the lotus flower blossomed despite the fact that it had been stored in a dry natural environment for three thousand years by virtue of being grounded in a spatial *basho*. Thus the same thing may be said about human beings. Watsuji called it a state of 'between-ness' (Watsuji 1996). Similarly, Nishida wrote:

> In order to say that objects are mutually related, constitutive of a single system, and maintain themselves, we must also consider that which establishes such a system within and wherein we can say that such system is implaced. That which *is* must be placed within something; otherwise the distinction between is and not cannot be made. Logically it should be possible to distinguish between the terms of a relation and a relation itself, and also between that which unifies the relation and that wherein the relation is placed. Even if we attempt to think in terms of function, while taking that which is the I as the pure unity of function, insofar as the I can be conceived in confronting the not-I, there must be that which envelops the opposition of I and not-I within and which makes the establishment of the so-called phenomena of consciousness possible within itself. I shall call that which is the receptacle of the ideas in this sense, following the words of Plato's Timaeus, basho [place].

(1970: 273)

According to Nishida, in order to perceive the object of our intention, there must be something like a place, or a field of consciousness, which 'envelops' both subject and object from within. He advanced the hypothesis that:

> If the object is implaced in itself, it cannot become the so-called standard of the content of consciousness. The *basho* wherein the object is implaced must be the same *basho* wherein so-called consciousness is also implaced. When we look at the object itself, we may think of this as intuition. But intuition must also be consciousness.

(ibid.: 9)

This idea of *basho* understood as a field has been explored to some extent in the West. William James, for instance, used the term 'field' in *The Varieties of Religious Experience*, where he observed that human beings have 'fields of consciousness' (James 1902: 189). In more recent years the concept has been recovered by biologist Rupert Sheldrake in his theory of morphic resonance, where he advanced the hypothesis that minds extend beyond brains through fields, which he called 'morphogenetic fields' (Sheldrake 2003; Sheldrake and Fox 1996). The term 'morphogenetic field' was originally employed in biology and literally means 'coming-into-forms'. It designates a structure that is part of the universe and exists everywhere at the same time. According to Sheldrake, it has three major characteristics: (1) it connects together different regions of the brain; (2) it contains attractors; it is about something; it is meaningful; and (3) it links into a unitary system the subject–object relationship (Sheldrake 2003: 44). As a consequence, it is possible for matter to be influenced by these fields at the same time in widely separate areas. This means that a piece of transmitted information modifies a certain field and this field in its turn modifies other similar brains so that they are more likely to reproduce the same kind of behaviour. For instance, when rats in one part of the world were trained to run through mazes, it is alleged that other rats in other places seemed to acquire this ability simultaneously. Another example is when scientists working in different places and not in contact with each other tend to make the same discoveries at more or less the same time. Sheldrake suggests that a more useful term than field (Sheldrake 2003).

Another field theory has been postulated by Jacobo Grinberg-Zylberbaum at the National University of New Mexico, who suggested that the electromagnetic fields which are produced in the brain by the passage of nerve impulses in some way interact with the fabric of space. This interaction between fields and space allows the transmission of an effect from one brain to the next. However, he argues that the transmission is strongest when two people are in similar states, for example, in people who have strong emphatic feeling for each other. His theory supports the view that the activity of the mind can influence activity in the world beyond the brain.

All the field theories which recognize a link between minds can be related to Carl Jung's notion of the 'collective unconscious' (Jung 1936). Jung wrote:

> The collective unconscious is a part of the psyche, which can be negatively distinguished from a personal unconscious by the fact that it does not, like the latter, owe its existence to personal experience and consequently is not a personal acquisition. While the personal unconscious is made up eventually of the contents which have at one time been conscious but which have disappeared from consciousness through having been forgotten or repressed, the contents of the collective unconscious have never been in consciousness, and therefore have never been individually acquired, but owe their existence only to heredity. Whereas the personal unconscious consists for the most part of complexes, the content of the collective unconscious is made up essentially of archetypes.
>
> (Jung 1936: 72)

One of the reasons why Jung adopted this idea was that he found recurrent patterns in dreams and myths, which suggested the existence of unconscious archetypes, which he interpreted as a kind of inherited collective memory beyond the individual brain. He was unable to explain how such inheritance could occur, and his idea is apparently incompatible with the conventional mechanistic assumption that heredity depends on information coded in DNA molecularly. This theory would help to explain why certain images tend to be more recurrent during the NDEs.

Space as consciousness without an object

Zen Master Dōgen observed: 'The ocean is experienced differently by a fish swimming in it, a heavenly being looking at it from heaven, and a person out at sea in a boat' (Kasulis 1981: 85). They are distinct forms of consciousness, which cohabit the same [*basho*] *Space*, the ocean, which is perceived respectively as a 'jewelled palace', a 'necklace' of shining flecks of light, and a 'great circle' (ibid.: 85). In this sense *basho* can be considered as a sort of 'container', or 'envelope'[16] for various kinds of experiences. Now the question of this section is: 'Is there anything in common in the experience of the ocean of the heavenly being, the person at sea and the fish?' The answer is yes. Although they are all different forms of consciousness, they share pre-reflectively the *genjōkōan*: 'the presence of a thing as it is'.[17] Similarly, Husserl (1973) used the famous expression 'back to the things themselves' (*Zurück zu den Sachen selbst*'). To put it simply, to return to the things themselves is

> to return to that world which precedes knowledge, of which knowledge always *speaks* and in relation to which every scientific schematization is an abstract and derivative sign language, as the discipline of geography would be in relation to a forest, a prairie, a river in the countryside we knew beforehand
>
> (Merleau-Ponty 1962: ix)

This refers to a non-conceptual, pre-reflective (or pre-noetic) mode of consciousness that most of the time remains unconscious. In *zazen*[18] it is known as 'consciousness without-an-object (see, for instance, Merrell-Wolff 1973; Kasulis 1981).

Interestingly, in Zen thought, consciousness without-an-object is a state which can be achieved through the practice of 'without thinking'. The latter is a category rather distinct from both thinking and not-thinking. In the opening section of the *Shōbōgenzō*, Dōgen wrote:

> Once, after Master Yakusan Gudō was sitting [in *zazen*], a monk asked him: 'When you are sitting immovably, about what do you think?' The

Master replied, 'I think about not thinking [about anything].' The monk responded, 'How does one think about not-thinking?' The Master replied, 'Without thinking.'[19]

The relationship between thinking, not-thinking and without thinking has been further clarified in phenomenological terms by Thomas Kasulis. In his *Zen Action/Zen Person* (1981), he formalized the relationships among these three categories as follows. Thinking is a noetic attitude of either affirming or negating something. This includes what we typically regard as consciousness – that is 'any mental act whereby we explicitly or implicitly take a stance toward some object, whether that stance be emotional, judgmental, believing, remembering, or assumptive'. Not-thinking is a noetic attitude of negating, denying, or rejecting attitude toward all the mental acts. A classic example is a person who makes the effort to stop thinking about his or her personal problems because he cannot fall asleep. A prevalent misconception of Zen meditation is that this is a form of not-thinking. Dōgen clearly rejected this view by asserting that *zazen* is *not* a conscious effort of blanking one's mind or turning off all conceptual processes. Without-thinking has a completely distinct noetic function from the previous two because it neither affirms nor denies, accepts nor rejects, believes nor disbelieves. In short, it is a pre-noetic (or pre-reflective) mode of consciousness.

Kasulis observes how in ordinary life, pre-reflective experiences are often only fleeting breaks in the continuity of thinking. He gives the following example:

After mowing the lawn, an exhausted man leans his arm on the lawnmower and rests. For a moment or two, his eyes gaze downward and he thinks and feels nothing specific whatsoever. Since for that moment he is not doing anything, we cannot even say that he is making *implicit* thetic assumptions: for that brief period, it is not even an issue whether the grass or even he himself is real. He simply is as he is, with no intentional attitude at all. This does not imply, however, that the experience is devoid of content – even the simplest reflection on that moment would reveal, for example, that he had been gazing on the green of the grass rather than the blue sky. Still, the content was not originally an object of consciousness: the grass was there – it assumed meaning – only through reflection on the original experience. In other words, prereflectively there had been a continuity of consciousness or awareness even with the lack of intentional directionality. Even though the reflection on the act later revealed a content of which one had been conscious at the time of the act, there was, prereflectively, no assumptive, unconscious intentional attitude to constitute that content into a meaning-bearing object.

(ibid.: 75)

In this sense, without-thinking is a prior condition to thinking or not-thinking. As a consequence:

> The more fully one is aware of the prereflective, the more certain one is that the present moment is overbrimming and more than can be circumscribed. Reflective thinking, on the other hand, objectifies the contents of previous experiences, thereby limiting them to a number of significant components. Continuing to reflect, each further bit of analysis uncovers more the experience and makes it richer.
>
> (ibid.: 77)

Nishida conceived the phenomenon of consciousness without an object in terms of 'pure experience' (*junsui keiken*). According to him, this is a primordial and pre-verbal sense of self, which is prior to thought and self-awareness (Nishida 1990). In his early work *A Study into Good* (Japanese: *Zen no Kekyu*), which was published in 1911, he wrote:

> I wanted to explain all things on the basis of the pure experience as the sole reality . . . Over time, I came to realize that it is not that experience exists because there is an individual, but that an individual exists because there is an experience. I thus arrived at the idea that experience is more fundamental than individual differences, and in this way I was able to avoid solipsism.
>
> (ibid.: xiv)

Nishida's notion of 'pure experience' is based on his own experiences in a Zen monastery, but to a lesser extent has been influenced by the philosophy of 'pure positivity', which emerged from the works of Wilhelm Wundt and William James.[20] The uniqueness in Nishida's attempt was to go beyond a common understanding of experience by returning to its root-sources, which are individual, trans-individual and universal.[21] He was certain in this way to connect to transcendental philosophy and metaphysics. Such an attempt was only partially achieved by Husserl's phenomenology, which paid only little attention to altered states of consciousness by limiting its investigation to ordinary states of consciousness. In this sense, Nishida's observation may be beneficial in terms of gaining new philosophical insights about the nature of the near-death experience, which can be considered as a form of pure experience.

Although his language is not always very accessible, Nishida identifies pure experience as

> An animated state with maximum freedom in which there is not the least gap between the will's demand and its fulfilment . . . In a selective will,

freedom has already been lost; yet when we then train the will, it again becomes impulsive. The essence of the will lies not in desire concerning the future but in present activity.

(Nishida 1990: 8)

It has five main characteristics: (1) subject and object occur simultaneously; (2) it is a strict unity of *concrete* consciousness; (3) it is constructed out of past experience; (4) it does not consist of meaning or judgments; and (5) it is passive.

First, during a pure experience, subject and object, and knowing and its object occur simultaneously and they 'are one'. This coincides with the direct experience of something. As Nishida put it: 'When one directly experiences one's own state of consciousness, there is not yet a subject or an object, and knowing and its object are completely unified. This is the most refined type of experience' (ibid.: 3). For example, in our everyday life the moment of seeing a color or hearing a sound is prior not only to the thought that the color or the sound is the activity of an external object, or that one is seeing it, but also to the judgment of what the color or the sound might be. The significance of the first moment of seeing something has been highlighted by Bachelard in his *The Poetics of Space* (1969). He wrote:

One must be receptive to the image at the moment it appears: if there be a philosophy of poetry, it must appear and re-appear through a significant verse, in total adherence to an isolated image; to be exact, in the very ecstasy of the newness of the image.

(ibid.: xv)

He considered this moment as 'a sudden salience on the surface of the psyche' where 'the image comes *before* thought'. He argued that the essence of this very moment reveals the phenomenology of the soul rather than the phenomenology of the mind (ibid.: xx). Pure experience, in these terms is both *Erlebnis* ('immanent lived experience') and *Erfahrung* ('experiential apprehension of the object') as has been previously observed for the near-death experience. This basically means that it incorporates both the noema and the noesis of the experience, which Husserl identified as the moment of consciousness. The *noema* is the meaning (*Sinn*) belonging to the object while the *noesis* corresponds to the constitutive pole, a subjective, lived experience. He largely analysed the relation between these two. As Varela has pointed out:

The concern with the noetico-noematic structure of consciousness makes of the object a subjective meaning for consciousness and relates the immanent and intimate lived experience of consciousness to the external world. Intentionality is this correlation of the lived conscious experience and the object envisaged which dismantles the traps of subjectivism as well as those of objectivism.

(1996: 177)

Second, pure experience is represented by a strict unity of *concrete* consciousness, when the activity of thinking is not yet activated. The primordial state of our consciousness and the immediate state of developing consciousness may at all times be states of pure experience. The consciousness of a newborn infant where the initial sensations are the universe itself is a clear example (Meltzoff and Moore 1999). At this earlier state it is a single system, whose nature is to develop and complete itself.

Third, pure experience is unavoidable because present experience is unavoidable. Whatever the object of an experience may be, whether a physical thing, memory, or concept, that experience occurs in the present. This phenomenon validated the Western phenomenological views on temporality, that both past and future are enfolded in the present (Heidegger 1962; Husserl 1991).

Fourth, pure experience is free of thoughts, judgment and other categories, which arise only when there is a *break* in the unified field of pure experience. This is because it is intuitive. For instance, when we establish a judgment like 'a horse is running' there must be a preceding intuition, 'a running horse', which Nishida indicates as 'pure experience'. As he put it:

As long as consciousness maintains a strict unity it is a pure experience: it is simply a fact. But when the unity is broken and a present consciousness enters into a relation with other consciousness it generates meanings and judgements.

(1990: 9)

For him, thought remains a kind of pure experience only if it is an immediate, unwilled response to what is directly given in experience. This means that thought is not essentially distinguishable from pure experience such as direct perception (although the nature of the object of thought might differ from that of the object of perception).

The notion bears strong similarity to the notion of *immediate apodicticity* in phenomenology, which is prior to the positing of the relation between subject and object. Apparently, Nishida was not well acquainted with the work of Husserl, but they were both influenced by the work of William James (1890; 1902). The main difference between the two is that Husserl proposed a method called *epoché* in order to attain apodicticity, whereas Nishida stressed the valence of *practical* activity. According to Husserl, the everyday self has an innate tendency to think under the command of a natural standpoint (*naturlische Einstellung*) that things in the world outside the self exist as objects and the self exists as a subject opposing to them. He stated that when we suspend such an innate tendency by a disciplined approach (*epochē*), suspending all judgments concerning the relationship between the being of the self and that of thing, a stream of immediate, apodictic perception will be disclosed, a stream operating at the foundation of the world as experienced in the natural standpoint. In contrast, Nishida's experience of immediate apodicticity is by means of *cultivation* and *practice* (Yuasa 1993). Nishida's pure experience can be seen as an ecstatic state, and therein we find an analogy with the experience of *Samatha* meditation (Becker 1992; Austin 1998; Wallace 2003).

Finally, pure experience is passive in the sense that it occurs spontaneously and it is unavoidable.

4

Meeting God in a nightclub?

A popular tale in Japan tells the story of a fisherman who decided one day to visit a dragon palace at the bottom of the sea. His name was Urashima Taro. He was a daydreamer, one of those who are happy just to spend the day gazing at the sky, the shoreline, and the beautiful sea. For him the most wonderful thing was to go out fishing with his boat and spend the entire afternoon admiring the water and imagining what it would be like to be in the middle of the deep blue sea. He did not care about fishing and whenever he caught something, he brought it back home at the end of the day to share it with his old mother. One evening, when he was walking home, he saw a group of boys standing in a circle, shouting and poking at something with a stick. Taro approached them and saw that they were teasing a baby tortoise. With an act of great courage and generosity he saved the baby tortoise and returned it to the sea. A few years after, when he was on his boat, he looked down at the water and saw a large tortoise swimming towards him. It was the tortoise that he had saved from the nasty boys. She had come back as a sign of gratitude to take Taro to the most beautiful place in the world, the Dragon Palace at the bottom of the Sea. Taro didn't hesitate for a second, stepped out from his boat and sat on the tortoise's shell. Down, down, he went, and the deeper he went, the more beautiful the scenery became, until they reached the bottom of the sea. This was as Taro had always imagined it, alive with thousands of brightly colored fish of every shape and size, whose movements filled the water with shining, swirling bubbles, with wonderful flowers that bloomed on rocks and cliffs. Taro was spellbound by everything he saw. There he met the enchanting Oto-hime, the beautiful daughter of the Dragon King, who invited him to live in her palace. From that moment Taro began a new life immersed in pleasure such as no man had ever known: dancing fish, mouth-watering feasts, strolls in the coral garden with the charming, lovely Oto-hime. It was a life beyond his wildest dreams. Wonderful as it was, however, it wasn't long before Taro began to miss his home and his mother. Oto-hime noticed the change and told him that the time had come for him to leave. She gave him a lacquer box as a reminder of the amazing time they had spent together and told him to open it only if he should find himself confused by anything he might see. She also warned him that if he chose to open the box, he could never return to the Dragon Palace. Taro called his tortoise friend and returned to his island. He ran along the beach towards his mother's house. Oddly enough, however, he didn't seem to recognize what he saw. People had changed, the village was no longer the same, and when he came to the place where his house should have been, there was nothing but an empty field of wild flowers! He could not believe it. He was sure that this was his village and his house, but nothing seemed to be the same. And what had happened to his mother? Totally confused he opened the box that Oto-hime had given him. A great cloud of white smoke came out, and it was like all his strength and energy had drained away, as if he weighed nothing at all and was drifting in the wind. Inside the box there was a mirror. He looked at it and was astonished. He saw that his face had changed and that he had a long, white beard! Suddenly everything was clear. While he had been enjoying life in the Dragon Palace, hundreds of years had gone by on land. Urashima Taro looked slowly up to the sky. His life with Oto-hime in her palace in the depths of the sea – had it all been a dream? Or was he dreaming now?

When I first read this tale in a book entitled *Once Upon a Time in Japan* (one of the few available books in English at the Narita Airport in Tokyo!), I was fascinated by it, for it reminded me of the near-death journey in the afterlife. In its simplicity, the story tells us of the possibility that we may leave our everyday reality and enter a different dimension which is much more pleasurable than our present one, but which in a sense does not belong to us. This shift from one reality to another is known in Japan as the 'urashima effect'.

The 'urashima effect' can be a useful metaphor for understanding what happens to those who voluntarily subject themselves to an anesthetic called ketamine with the aim of exploring new frontiers. The effects of ketamine are very significant for our discussion because they present various similarities to the NDE. Although those who were administered this substance did not face the actual threat of death, after an initial impression of dying and leaving the body, they often described entering new realities where they met other beings, such as angels, deceased loved ones, unknown figures and even, more rarely, God, as we saw in NDEs. We might ask: 'Did these people really enter alternative realities, or were they mere hallucinations induced by a drug?', 'Are the experiences similar to the near-death experience?' And if so, 'What are the main differences and similarities?' These, among other questions, will be the basis of the following analysis.

What is ketamine?

Ketamine was originally synthesized in April 1962 by Calvin Stevens, a consultant for a Parke-Davis/Warner Lambert[1] program aimed at finding a safer anesthetic alternative to phencyclidine (PCP). From a clinical point of view, ketamine has been classified as a dissociative anesthetic. The term 'dissociative' suggests that the sensory loss and analgesia as well as amnesia are not accompanied by actual loss of consciousness (Bonta 2004). Sometimes this unique experience incorporates a strong sense of dying. For instance, Barbara Collier, an anesthetist commented: 'Ketamine allows some patients to reason that . . . the strange, unexpected intensity and unfamiliar dimension of their experience means they must have died'[2] (Collier 1972).

This characteristic effect is also produced by a few other dissociative anesthetics, such as nitrous oxide (N_2O), commonly known as 'laughing gas' for its exhilarating effects. Following his explorations with the substance, Humphry Davy published *Researches, Chemical and Philosophical; chiefly concerning Nitrous Oxide (. . .) and its Respiration* (1800), in which he observed that 'nothing exists but thoughts'. He also noticed other interesting effects such as 'an immediate thrilling, a pleasure in every limb, and an intensification of both vision and hearing'. He wrote:

> A sensation analogous to gentle pressure on all the muscles, attended by an highly pleasurable thrilling, particularly in the chest and the extremities. The objects around me became dazzling and my hearing more acute. Towards the last inspirations, the thrilling increased, the sense of muscular power became greater, and at last an irresistible propensity to action was indulged in; I recollect but indistinctly what followed; I know that my motions were various and violent.
>
> (Davy 1800: 458)

William James observed that nitrous oxide can 'stimulate mystical consciousness in an extraordinary degree' and that it reveals 'depth beyond depth of truth' (James 1902: 305). He made these observations in his Gifford Lectures, later published as *The Varieties of Religious Experience* (1902). One of his conclusions was that human beings have additional 'fields of consciousness':

> My impression is . . . that our normal waking consciousness, rational consciousness as we call it, is but one special type of consciousness, whilst all about it, parted from it by the filmiest of screens, there lie potential forms of consciousness entirely different. We may go through life without suspecting their existence.
>
> (ibid.: 305)

Other common dissociative anesthetics are DXM (dextromethorphan), a medicine with anti-tussive (cough suppression) properties, PCP (Phencyclidine), and sometimes high doses of alcohol. It is important to observe that dissociation is a broad term that can include the effects of a very wide range of substances. For instance, Meduna in the 1950s used carbon dioxide to induce NDE-like states as an aid to psychotherapy (Meduna 1950).

Ketamine is currently used in many general hospitals around the world, with a recent increase in use in Emergency Departments and in chronic pain clinics (Parke-Davis 1999–2000; Bell *et al.* 2006; Sehdev *et al.* 2006). It is often used during severe asthmatic crisis, childbirth, and surgical operations, and occasionally in the treatment of migraine and in anesthesia for children (Jansen 2001). It is relatively safe because it does not usually suppress breathing as much as other anesthetics and it has a short duration of action (30–60 minutes). The substance also has good analgesic and amnesic properties. At small doses (0.1–0.5 mg/kg/hr), it appears to stimulate rather than depress the central nervous system (for instance, Jansen 1989), and it has been used for treatment of pain associated with movement and neuropathic pain. However, as I will discuss later in greater detail, at sub-anesthetic doses (10–25 per cent of a surgical dosage), ketamine can produce effects similar to those described during a near-death experience (Moody 1975; Greyson and Stevenson 1980; Fenwick and Fenwick 1995).

In order to prevent dissociative experiences in surgical settings, the drug is often given together with diazepam (Valium®) and other sedatives (Reich and Silvay 1989). Some authors have suggested that the substance can have beneficial effects as an aid in psychotherapy (Grinspoon and Bakalar 1979; Strassman 1995; Krupitsky 1997; Mills *et al.* 1998). However, the use of psychedelics in therapy remains a highly controversial topic in contemporary psychiatry (Jansen 2001; Arnone and Schifano 2006).

Ketamine at rave and squat parties

It is a popular myth that ketamine is a 'horse tranquillizer' used as a recreational drug in clubs, raves and squat parties, among other 'non-clinical' settings. For instance, I remember seeing a front cover of *Mixmag* magazine,[3] showing a raver with a horse's head, with the caption 'Ketamine: only fools and horses?' But these are of course distortions of what the drug is about.

The recreational use of 'K', as it is often called among users, has increased surprisingly during the past ten years and has never been greater than it is today (Morgan *et al.* 2004a; 2004b; 2004c; Hopfer *et al.* 2006). A recent study carried out by an organization called *DrugScope*[4] in 40 drug services operating in 15 UK cities, has shown that ketamine is now one of the 'most sold' drugs in eight of the cities for the first time. In an interview published in *The Guardian* newspaper, Henry Shapiro, head of DrugScope and editor of its newsletter *Druglink*, commented: 'The emergence of ketamine as a key substance of choice is an entirely new phenomenon since we last carried out the survey in 2004 when it didn't figure at all'.[5]

For instance, according to Jamie, a regular weekend user:

The right amount is really enjoyable. It feels like you are floating out of your body, but if you see someone else who has taken ket they are usually staggering around . . . I suppose it's a bit like having all your arms and legs pulled off and put back on the wrong way round.[6]

He commented that ketamine had become in the past few months 'the drug of choice' for a lot of clubbers. 'It has been around on the gay scene for quite a while but now it is everywhere. People often combine it with ecstasy or cocaine or use it at after-club parties.'[7]

The popularity of the non-medical use of ketamine has led to its placement in Schedule III of the United States Controlled Substances Act in August 1999. In some European countries, it became a controlled drug more recently (for example, in February 2001, ketamine became a Class A drug in Italy).[8] In the United Kingdom, it became a Class C drug on 1 January 2006, a development that produced a range of media commentary.

Is ketamine a fun drug?

It may seem difficult to understand why an anesthetic can become such a popular recreational drug. After all, what fun is to be had by lying down on a dance floor? According to Mr B., a recreational user that I interviewed a few year ago, ketamine: 'is an ideal drug because it comes up very quickly and it only lasts for 10–15 minutes or so . . . I used to take it at parties, but also before going to work'.

Several reasons can be identified for the popularity of what I prefer to call the 'non-medical use' of ketamine. First, it has a short duration of action, from 20 minutes to 60 minutes, depending on the amount taken and how it was taken.[9] Second, it is low cost, although new legal controls are likely to raise prices. According to an annual survey in the UK, the price of ketamine starts from £15 for a 'wrap' of a gram (DrugScope 2005). Third, it is considered 'suitable' to be taken in combination with other drugs (Morgan et al. 2004c), since it moderates the 'coming down' effects of stimulants, empathogens and hallucinogens. It is also appealing for its stimulating effects at recreational low doses, because it allows the person to dance, walk or even go to work, as in the case of Mr B. Those who crash on the floor are those who have fallen into a 'K-hole', or have taken high doses of the substance. Finally, it is probably a popular drug because of its intriguing effects. Before exploring these in greater detail, I would like to focus on the numerous risks of taking ketamine in non-controlled clinical settings.

Pondering the risks

Although taking ketamine in a recreational environment seems to be fun for many, it also exposes the user to a large number of risks. The most immediate one is probably the risk of an unwanted experience. For instance, Miss L., a 23-year-old who tried ketamine only once in her life at a disco club, observed:

> I felt a bit paranoid, I was going to die. The first effects started very soon. I felt very confused and normal reality just disappeared. I was dizzy and unable to walk. I started bumping against walls. I wanted to go out from the room where I was, but it was very cold. I had no-one close to help me.

The risk of physical harm from accidents, such as bad falls, is also very high. Evidence has emerged from the National Poisons Information Service in the UK, according to which cases of ketamine intoxication rose from 10 in 1995 to more than 100 in 2001.[10] Ketamine does not lead to physical dependence, but it can generate a strong psychological dependence, similar to cocaine. Tolerance can be developed quickly, hence a larger quantity is required in order to achieve the same effects. This can lead users to take it in intense 'binges'. An immediate risk of taking ketamine in recreational settings is accidents, such as bad falls. The disconnection from the body can be dangerous in almost any situation other than lying down in a safe environment. In addition to this, ketamine is a powerful painkiller, which blocks normal sensations of pain. Other adverse effects can include panic attacks and depression, and when taken in large doses it can exaggerate pre-existing mental health problems. Stimulant-like weight loss and loss of appetite have also been reported after periods of heavy use. The risks of ketamine use are increased if it is used with depressant drugs, such as alcohol. It can suppress breathing and heart function in rare cases, although more commonly it stimulates these functions. It is more likely to suppress breathing (i.e. give rise to a period of apnea) if taken as a fast intravenous injection. When used with stimulant drugs such as ecstasy (MDMA) or amphetamines, it can also cause high blood pressure. A number of reports in the media suggest that ketamine can be used as a 'date rape drug' as high doses can cause amnesia for events that happened while under the influence of the drug. Three days after consumption of ketamine, impairments of working, episodic and semantic memory have been reported (Morgan et al. 2004a; 2004b). One research study has shown that semantic memory impairments associated with recreational ketamine are reversible after people stop or substantially reduce use. However, impairment to episodic and possibly attentional functioning is longer lasting (Krystal et al. 1994; Malhotra et al. 1996; Morgan et al. 2004b). A problem with these studies is that the authors rarely, if ever, provide urine or hair test results to prove that their subjects are not affected by other drugs at the time of testing. Cannabis and alcohol are particularly likely culprits as many ketamine users smoke cannabis and drink alcohol daily (Jansen 2001). Some users also experience mild forms of schizophrenic-like symptoms and perceptual distortions associated with the use of ketamine for a short period after they have stopped taking the drug (Morgan *et al.* 2004c). Initially, from its anesthetic use, clinicians reported confusional states, vivid dreams and hallucinations as well as flashbacks (Siegal 1978). The risk of death in general is not high. According to a report by the European Monitoring Centre for Drugs and Drug Addiction, only 12 persons have died as a result of ketamine use (seven in the US, and five in Europe) in the previous 10 years. Only three of these deaths were for ketamine alone (EMCDDA 2003).

Experiments in voluntary death? Ketamine research study

The following sections will be based on results that emerged from a research study that I carried out among a group of 36 ketamine recreational users, who tried the substance in order to experience its intriguing effects. Timothy Leary called these 'experiments in voluntary death' (Leary 1997: 375). In order to fully grasp the meaning of these experiences, I suggest that you suspend any possible judgment or habitual thought about drug-related experiences, and try to assume an open and unprejudiced attitude towards the accounts that you are about to read. The discussion will continue in the next chapter where I will present a comparison between ketamine experiences and those reported by a group of 36 individuals who had NDEs as a result of either (1) a cardiac arrest or (2) other life-threatening circumstances, but always while awake.

Methodological issues

For recruitment purposes, a general request was made via popular announcements and through a network of informants for persons who would be willing to provide an 'account' of their ketamine experience(s). The study was also advertised on the Internet. A web-site was created and kept updated for the first two years of the project.[11] This facilitated easier and faster access to information. If respondents had both a previous recreational ketamine experience and recollected what they believed to be an NDE, they were invited to fill in a validated and standardized 16-item questionnaire, known among researchers as the 'Greyson NDE Scale' (Greyson 1983). This has been successfully validated in previous NDE studies (Parnia *et al.* 2001). A score of 7 or over is accepted as compatible with an NDE.

Those 36 respondents who described an experience suggestive of an NDE and also reported a minimum score of 7 on the NDE scale were invited to a face-to-face interview. Answers to the questionnaire were used as a basis for the discussion, which was carried out as an open-ended interview. Subjects' interviews were recorded and notes were taken as well. Overall, 65 subjects made at least an initial electronic contact and sent me online their ketamine experience(s). After an initial analysis, 40 subjects were invited to fill in the Greyson scale, and four of them did not reach the cut-off score of 7. In those four cases, most of the psychoactive experiences reported involved either vivid dreams or auditory/visual hallucinations, but did not include any experiences suggestive of an NDE. All participants gave informed consent to participate in the study and stated that they had fully recovered and that they did not develop a problematic use of the substance. The SOAS, University of London, Ethics Committee granted the study approval. Interviews were held in the UK, Europe, Tokyo and the USA.

Socio-demographic profile

All the participants had a well-defined socio-demographic profile. A male component slightly prevailed (56 per cent), although the female group was also significant (44 per cent); 94 per cent were single. The youngest person I interviewed was 21 years old and the oldest 45 years old.

Fifteen participants were in full-time occupation (42 per cent), thirteen were students (36 per cent), five (14 per cent) were unemployed and three (8 per cent) were involved in other activities. In this category I have included two individuals who were engaged in military service, and one young mother who was taking care of her newborn infant.

Sixteen participants (44 per cent) were educated to BA level. Three (8 per cent) had a lower degree. Fifteen (42 per cent) had a Masters degree and three (8 per cent) had reached a PhD level.

Regarding nationality, 9 individuals (25 per cent) were from the UK, 23 (64 per cent) from continental Europe, 2 (6 per cent) from the USA and 1 (3 per cent) from Japan. Participants of one nationality often advised me to interview friends of the same nationality.

Use of ketamine

All 36 participants had tried ketamine at least once. Twelve had consumed the substance less than 5 times, five between 5 and 10 times, while the majority of the group were more experienced ketamine users, having taken it on up to 2,000 occasions. These figures did not necessarily indicate the current use of the drug. In 25 per cent of the cases, the last occasion of ketamine use had occurred within the last month, but none of them had taken it within the previous week. In the remaining cases, last occasion of use occurred in the previous 1–60 months. Typically, ketamine was taken intranasally (29 per cent), but 9 per cent of the participants had injected it intramuscularly, 19 per cent intravenously, and 5 per cent had smoked it. No ketamine ingestion was reported. Ketamine typical dosage ranged between 20 and 150 mg, although most participants were guessing the dose and had no objective evidence of the purity.

Interestingly, all those I interviewed claimed that the first consumption of ketamine had resulted in the most intense experiences. As a consequence, some participants stopped taking it because 'it didn't work any longer'. Some others carried on taking it for its 'stimulant' effects. This phenomenon has been observed in previous studies (Jansen 2001: 28). Participants asserted that after a while its effects turned out to be similar to those induced by cocaine, but nevertheless they preferred ketamine because it was cheaper on the street market.

A relatively high number of people (12) claimed to have used ketamine in order to stimulate their 'creative insights'. Most of these were musicians, street artists, singers, writers or art students. As Susan Blackmore has pointed out in an article published in the *Daily Telegraph*, this phenomenon has been little emphasized in academic studies.[12] She explains how a wide range of substances, including ketamine, inspired her work and career. Francis Crick claimed that he was under the influence of small doses of LSD when he first deduced the double-helix structure of DNA nearly 50 years ago,[13] and Kary Mullis, who won a Nobel Prize in 1993, said that the idea for the Polymerase Chain Reaction, which revolutionized the role that DNA samples play in crime detection (among much else) came to him while he was affected by LSD. He discussed this in a BBC *Horizon* documentary called 'Psychedelic Science'.

Use of other substances

All 36 participants had smoked cannabis at least once in their lives or had taken MDMA (also known as 'ecstasy'). Thirty-four (94 per cent) had tried an amphetamine of some sort (especially 'speed' powder), 91 per cent cocaine, 97 per cent LSD, and 86 per cent 'magic mushrooms' (psilocybin). They were less likely to have taken anabolic steroids (6 per cent), solvents (5.5 per cent) or opiates (16 per cent).

Perception of time

To the question 'Did time seem to be speeded up?', 47.7 per cent of the participants (17) answered that everything seemed to be happening at once, or that time stopped, or lost all its meaning. This was followed by 16 participants who perceived a temporal acceleration, especially during the initial part of the experience, while three (8 per cent), perceived a complete absence of time during the experience. In most of the cases, the initial 'rush' ended in timelessness and only at this stage did time lose all its meaning. Miss C., a 21-year-old girl, who was also the youngest person I interviewed, commented: 'Initially, it goes very quickly. You hear a buzzing sound[14] and images pass very fast in front of you one after the other. You go down a dark spiral with a light at the end. Once you are there, the real time doesn't exist any more.'

In a few other cases the buzzing sound was generated by the acceleration of 'travelling down' a dark tunnel. It was also described as a strange noise. Participants often tried to reproduce it during the interviews.

Frequency of visions

'Were your thoughts speeded up?' Several participants observed that the word 'thoughts' was unsuitable to describe their experiences, because they were devoid of rational thinking. Mr T., a 23-year-old, observed: 'On ketamine you don't think like you do in the everyday life. Ketamine does everything for you. You cannot control it. It goes very fast!' Participants seem to prefer the term 'vision'. Mr. W, another interviewee, said: 'Having a ketamine trip is like watching a movie. You see one scene after another, but you never know what is coming after.'

Other participants came to similar conclusions. Miss C., a 22-year-old, said: 'Ketamine visions go from 3D to 2D. They run very quickly. Do you know when you take a picture? Ketamine has the same click, click, click . . . effect and everything becomes flat, like in a photograph.'

The majority of the group reported that their 'visions' were very fast (38.8 per cent), 30.5 per cent faster than usual, and 30.6 per cent did not notice any change.

Life review

The third question on the Greyson NDE Scale concerns the vision or sense of reliving life events, which Moody (1975) called the 'life review'. Some (11 per cent) of those interviewed answered that they were able to remember past events, while (17 per cent) said that their past flashed out of control in front of them.

Such visions were described as extremely vivid and always as visual records. Miss B., a 21-year-old student, commented: 'It was like I was watching the movie of my life. I never thought it possible.' She described her life review as happening in reverse order (from the present back to her birth). The case of Miss E., a 32-year-old, was rather different. She visualized only a very specific moment of her life:

> I was surprised, and a bit scared, when I saw myself in my family house at the age of 16. My father was staring at me. Suddenly the vision stopped on the face of my father and I have heard a voice saying: 'Have you seen the eyes of your father?' So I looked deeply into his eyes and I saw lots of sorrow and disappointment about my behaviour. It surprised me a lot because I had completely forgotten about the event. I wasn't a good daughter at that time and this has left me with many regrets.

Miss E. told me that after this experience she made many attempts to stay in touch with her father. Sadly, he passed away two years after the experience. She said: 'I always will be thankful to that experience, because it helped me to understand my past mistakes and to regain a good relationship with my father shortly before he passed away.'

Understanding of the universe

The majority of those interviewed (53 per cent) felt a sense of total understanding of the universe. So it was for Mr B., a 32-year-old, a regular ketamine user who said:

> My ketamine experiences helped me to understand that all things in the universe, material and spiritual, originate from the same source and are related to each other as if they were one family. Past, present, future are all contained in the same life force from which we originate. Only few times I have reached this dimension on ketamine. I have been doing it for several years now, but nothing happens any more.

Six of them (16.6 per cent) answered that they 'understood everything about themselves or others'. Miss S., who took some ketamine powder at home with her boyfriend, said:

> For the first time I was seeing myself so clearly in another [her partner] and then as divided into many other people and the entire cosmos. I felt a strong sense of unity. It will never happen again.

Other participants came out with statements such as: 'I thought I was dead'. 'I didn't exist any more as "me", but I actually was a small part of a cosmic system', or 'I spoke a universal language, which regulates the entire earth and the planets', or 'I enjoyed a state of absolute freedom while melting down with the universe in its totality'. Some said that the experience made them understand the meaning of the Tao, where the yin (feminine, dark and passive) alternates with the yang (masculine, light and active).

Eleven (30 per cent) did not report these kinds of experiences.

Sense of peace and joy

Twenty-six participants (72 per cent) reported a strong sense of peace or pleasantness; 17 per cent reported a feeling of relief or calmness. The experience was rather different for the 19 per cent who had frightening or unpleasant experiences.

Most of the accounts that I have collected were given by people who took the substance in what could be perceived as relatively positive circumstances in terms of their emotional state, such as the visit of a friend, or at an open-air party, which may have contributed to their positive outcome. Clearly, ketamine is only sometimes a 'bad trip' anesthetic (Strassman 1997). It has been claimed that these bad experiences cannot have been NDEs, for some have assumed that the NDE is always peaceful (Moody 1975; Ring 1980). However, Peter and Elizabeth Fenwick in *The Truth in the Light* (1995) have hypothesized that negative experience among NDErs may be underreported because the persons who had them may be less inclined to communicate them. Karl Jansen also addresses the point in detail, stressing that many NDEs reported throughout history, especially in medieval times, were highly negative, hell-based reports (Jansen 2001: 93).

Some 47 per cent of the participants claimed that their ketamine experience was very 'joyful' and 30 per cent felt 'happy'.

Unity with the universe

The majority of those interviewed (59 per cent) felt united with the entire cosmos. 19 per cent felt no longer in conflict with nature or outside of it. Some individuals claimed they took part in the 'fabrication of the universe', or felt a 'cosmic union with earth', as if they were able to understand its constitutive principle by means of the principle within the self. For example, Mr P. was listening to a piece of music when he injected 100 mg of ketamine (IM). He said:

> I gradually lost my senses. The music was very distorted. I tested myself by asking basic questions about mathematics, the names of those I love, etc., then suddenly I wasn't interested in this any more. So I tried to concentrate on 'who I am' and I lost the interest again. Visions become blurred. It wasn't meaningful who I was any more, because I existed anyway. Then I tried the experience of death. I was going down a tunnel. I saw the planet Earth. I could feel the relationship between the human soul, Earth and the planets. I thought I was a doll, you know the *matryoshka*[15]? I was the *matryoshka* of the entire system. I understood that earth is inside something else. I felt its gravity. All this is embraced within a system. I was nothing, but I knew that my place was on Earth.

Another participant said:

> Two years ago I was with my friends in Valencia. We went to the beach that day and we had some ketamine. We sat on the sand. The effects started very soon. I felt dizzy and I had to lie down. I closed my eyes. The first thing that I remember is that I felt somehow I was going very fast and that I left my body. It was not frightening. Subsequently I saw a tunnel and a tiny little light which grew bigger and bigger. I was

approaching this light when I heard a voice telling me to go back. So I asked 'Why? I don't want to go back.' I had no reply. A being of light appeared. He wanted to show me something. A big screen also appeared. I saw earth and the planets. I have heard them breathing. I touched the stars and talked to the Sun (God). I cannot remember what he said but it was amazing. I kept thinking that it was wonderful and amazing. And then, suddenly, I was lying back on the beach!

Meeting with God

Eight per cent of participants saw an unusual bright light, while 72 per cent had no special light experience at all. A relatively small number of participants (19 per cent) felt themselves surrounded by a brilliant light of mystical and otherworldly origin, which was described as at the end of a spiral or a tunnel. Four of them communicated with the Light, which they thought to be God/Goddess. I have been told that this was in the form of non-verbal communication. Three of them were not able to report the contents of the communication, because they 'forgot all about it'. So it was for Mr D., a 33-year-old, who commented:

> The light was very bright and emanating warmth. I could easily stand the heat. It was like facing God. We spoke. I cannot remember what he said, but I remember that I couldn't lie. It is hard to describe, I never experienced such an intensity of feeling.

In contrast, one of the interviewees gave a detailed account of his experience. Here is an abstract:

> I heard a buzzing sound and I found myself going very fast along a dark tunnel, which ended in a bright Light. It was God. I talked to God and I asked him to take me. And he [God] said 'Yes'. Then I got very scared and I replied that I had to take care of my daughter. So he told me to go back. My auntie came to take me. I asked: 'Where are we going?' She replied: 'Don't worry!' She took me to a very shining and beautiful place with lots of mountains. I saw many dead people there in white clothes. Then I saw a group of children playing. I asked my auntie: 'Who are they?' She replied that they died many years ago in a school bus accident. Then I thought of my daughter and I felt the need to come back. My auntie understood this without the need to speak and she told me to go back.

While describing the travel back into his body, he said: 'It was very violent. Do you know the feeling when someone hits you on your body? And I came back.'

The Light was described as being 'bright', 'brilliant', 'radiant', 'like the sun' and not necessarily big. It was also 'warm' and 'welcoming', 'scented', 'full of energy', 'pure love and compassion', 'vibrating sounds' (like mantras or 'heavenly music'). As noted earlier, it was usually located at the end of a tunnel, and it was never described as a known religious figure, like the Buddha or Jesus. This aspect of the non-ketamine NDE has been clearly highlighted by Peter and Elizabeth Fenwick in their book *The Truth in the Light* (1995). The authors noticed how the Light is rarely seen as Christ, even if the person who reported the experience was a Christian:

> Most of us, whether Christians or not, have an 'identikit' image of Christ. . . . No one has any notion of what actually Christ looked like. There is no description of him in the New Testament. We have no idea whether he was fair or dark, short or tall, even whether he had a beard. It is highly unlikely that his hair was auburn, a colour quite atypical of Mediterranean races. In fact the first Christian images bore much more resemblance to the sun god Apollo – blond and beardless – than to the consensus we have finally arrived at after more than a thousand years of artists' impressions. I think we have to make a distinction between the feeling of the presence of Christ in the experience, and the image which the perceiving brain creates to fit it, which is simply drawn from the picture-bank of memory.
>
> (ibid.: 62–3)

In summary, a different image of God emerged from the interviews. Rather than an external entity, God appeared to be part of each individual. This feature has been characterized as 'entheogenic' (from the Greek *entheos*, or 'divine within'). Explanations of what is happening in these experiences can become very controversial and will be discussed in the final chapter of this book.

About the senses

To the question, 'Were your senses more vivid than usual?', 73 per cent answered that they were very vivid. 17 per cent said that they were more vivid than usual, and 22 per cent noticed no difference.

Among those who experienced a change, some interesting sensorial effects were described. For instance, a 22-year-old girl I interviewed in Berlin referred to what she called 'the paper effect'. She said:

> You feel like you are made of paper. There is no consistency. You are pure soul. I named this the 'paper effect' . . . The experience happens very quickly. Visions are like glued on your eyes. You are a part of them. There is no right or left. Everything looks very much the same.

It has also often been observed that the last thing noticed before becoming 'dissociated' was also the first element of the experience. The same girl gave the following example:

> I lay down on the carpet of my room ready for the ketamine trip. This was the first thing that I saw when the effects started. I was travelling into it at great speed. The carpet turned up to be a labyrinth with no way out. It was all yellow, red, blue, and green. It was a very long trip. It took me an hour and a half to come out.

One participant had what he considered to be a birth-related experience. She said:

> I took some K powder with a few very good friends of mine. It was summer and we were sitting on top of a roof garden. The weather was really amazing, very bright, very sunny. The first effects came up very quickly, a few minutes after the last line. I bent my head on my friend Bua's shoulders, who was sitting close to me, ready to go for the trip. I remember I was looking at his long dreadlocks hair before closing my eyes and this was also the first image of my ketamine trip . . . suddenly I found myself travelling inside his hair at high speed towards the roots. The hair became a tunnel, which was getting darker and darker. Patterns then appeared one after the other, very quickly. Once I came to the end of tunnel I saw an open sepulchre. This was the most interesting and fascinating part of the experience. I looked inside but I couldn't see anything because it was very dark. I heard a child crying. The cry was coming from the inside. I had the absolute conviction of having travelled into the depth of my unconscious. I was that child inside the uterus of my mother.

Psychiatrist Stanislav Grof called these 'near-birth experiences' (NBEs) (Grof 1979; 1985).

Extra-sensory perceptions (ESP)

A small minority of the group, 5.5 per cent of the participants, had what they thought were extra-sensory perceptions and felt that 'the facts had been checked out'. These included reports of telepathy and other psychic abilities, like precognition of facts. Some 19 per cent reported extra-sensory perceptions but 'the facts had not been checked out'. Females were more likely to answer 'yes' to this question.[16] A young woman described being able to listen to other people's thoughts while affected by ketamine: 'I knew what people were about to say before they actually spoke. This happened several times. I was also more aware of the large amount of energy inside my body.'

Another felt her legs were growing taller than Centre Point in central London:

> I remember one day I was dancing on K in a club in Soho. I felt very light. Suddenly, I felt my legs growing bigger and bigger. I had the impression of having reached the ceiling. So I left the venue and went out to get some fresh air. It was very difficult to walk. I stopped in front of the Centre Point. I felt I was higher than the building. Amazingly, I was able to look down on Trafalgar Square and the Thames. It was a very unique experience.

Another girl, Miss A., told me: 'I was thinking about someone, and that someone turned up at my door.' Another person had a similar experience with e-mails. She was thinking of someone and this someone was at that moment sending her an e-mail (even if they didn't communicate for long).

Mr. Z., a 32-year-old who took ketamine for several years but gave it up 'because it was time to move on with my life', said that he developed an interesting connection with his girlfriend, especially while they were both taking ketamine on a regular basis. Once they had the same dream. They were cruising around the San Francisco Bay on a boat full of golden coins.

Another participant, Miss L., told me that she once went to play bingo on a small dose of ketamine. She predicted the lucky numbers and won some money!

Some 17 per cent of the participants claimed to have had visions of the 'world future', whereas 8 per cent had visions of their 'personal future'. One of these was Mrs C., a 38-year-old, who gave me the following account:

> I saw my two children on a boat ten years before I gave birth to both of them. They were smiling and they looked very happy together. My daughter wore the same shirt my mother bought her on the occasion of the Holy Communion.

Mr W., who used ketamine extensively in meditational practices and described himself as someone 'who died various times within the ketamine context', had the following vision about the future of Saddam Hussein during the First Gulf War:

> I was in Australia during the lead-up to the first Gulf War. I had decided to use the substance to get a better look at Saddam Hussein. I did a substantial dose for my body weight and set the intention prior to going under. There was the familiar high-pitched frequency followed by a soft plopping sound and I was in one of Saddam's palaces facing a furious, heavily built man with a thick mustache. He was pacing up and down on the marble floor when he must have noticed me. He came at

me with a sword and we battled briefly before he backed away. It was then I could see with the eyes of my Spirit that he was one of the Atlantean black magicians who have had to reincarnate. With that, I knew he was going to fall hard.

Mr W.'s experience is also interesting for a quite different reason. It shows how sometimes there is a connection between the last thing in one's mind, or seen in the room (or surrounding environment) before the drug took hold and the first element of the experience. In contrast, according to the literature, an NDE does not usually seem to be overly influenced by the final sights and sounds experienced before the NDE commences. This may be due either to the phenomenon not occurring or to it being underreported. The phenomenon has also been observed in previous ketamine studies (Lilly 1978; Moore and Alltounian 1978; Jansen 2001). For instance, Karl Jansen has observed that people in his study were more inclined to see a 'syringe, rather than Pearly Gates, as syringes are sometimes amongst the last things people see on "the way out"' (Jansen 2001: 77).

Out-of-Body Experience (OBE)

Some 33 per cent of participants were absolutely sure that they had left their bodies and that they existed outside them. For instance, Mr P., a 33-year-old, observed:

> On ketamine you are like a disembodied eye, which has a depth and wanders around. You move by the power of your thoughts. You look left, you move left, you look right, you move right. On my way I met people I didn't know before. I saw many villages with streets like normal streets in this world. I was like a camera wandering around. I saw many different landscapes and empty factories. I could hear melodies and I have tried later to reproduce them in my music.

One of the things that is striking about these accounts is that some of the subjects could see their bodies. Mr A., for example, clearly saw his body and his friends around him, while looking down from the ceiling. He said:

> I was with my friends at home watching TV. We decided to try some 'Special K'. I had never heard about it before. I had a line. Everything was very fast. After a few seconds I was outside my body, up to the ceiling of the living room watching down. I was very scared. I thought I was dead. I saw my body and my friends close to me lying on the couch. I wanted to talk with them but I couldn't. I was sure I was dead. Then when the effects started fading away, I floated back into my body very slowly, from the belly button upwards to the head. My senses returned,

everything was normal again and I understood I wasn't dead. I don't think ketamine is fun!

Another participant had a similar experience while he was dancing at a squat party:

> I felt immediately very dizzy on standing up. I came out and I felt I couldn't walk, so I crashed on the floor next to the nearest corner. I started getting higher and higher until I was convinced that I was dead. I got very scared when I saw myself from above. I couldn't remember doing ketamine. I looked very dreadful there on the floor. I floated in and out the room for about 20 minutes. I was fully aware of the music. I visited other rooms and I could see other people dancing and other things like the furniture of the place, but I couldn't speak. I felt like I belonged to another life. After being out of body/dead?, I came back into my body. I felt very shocked and I went home. Taking ketamine was a big mistake! It was too strong and I got sick too!

Encounter with other beings

The sense of transition into another reality was the commonest feature among the 36 accounts that were collected; 44 per cent had the feeling of entering a clearly mystical or unearthly world, 25 per cent a strange or unusual place, while 30 per cent did not report this kind of experience. In this different dimension of reality, 30 per cent of participants met other beings, such as angels or unknown creatures, or heard a voice of a mystical or unearthly nature.

Sometimes, as in the case of Mr F., they did not see these entities, but they were able to sense their presence. Mr F. observed:

> I travelled down into a tunnel at great speed. I entered a landscape of breathtaking beauty. I had a sensation of 'knowing' the place, but I also knew that it was in 'another' space. I wasn't worried at all. I moved around and I felt I was accompanied by millions of beings, I didn't hear them or see them. I just knew they were there with me. I felt joy and love of knowing we were all one. I was communicating with them by telepathic thoughts. I find it hard to explain. The only way I can describe it, is that we are all parts of a whole system. While there, I have connected with the information of the entire universe and I knew everything and then some more.

Other participants met religious figures, or 'Beings of Light'. I recorded the story of Miss G., a 32-year-old, who had the following experience after her first use of ketamine:

I was with two good friends of mine in a caravan in Southern Spain. Only my boyfriend took ketamine with me. The first thing I remember after the hit is that I was in India, inside a cave. The burner, which was inside the caravan, turned into a statue. It wasn't the Buddha but a similar image. I spoke with this statue but I cannot remember what we said. Everything was very calm. I wasn't worried about anything. I never felt so safe and well, like when you wake up and your partner is holding you in his arms. It was the most amazing thing that you can experience.

Some 14 per cent heard a voice they could not identify. Miss S. reported:

I saw myself in a small room with no furniture apart from a bed. It looked like the cell of a prison. I was sitting on the bed facing down, while holding my head with my hands. I looked very sad and uncomfortable in that empty environment. Then I heard a voice asking me a very weird question: 'Do you think you are God?' This happened few years ago, but I still think about it.

As reported in NDE literature, the messages conveyed by the voice usually had a strong existential meaning (Fenwick and Fenwick 1995). In the accounts that have been collected, the voice was often thought to be God.

Another interesting feature of the NDE is the encounter with relatives or friends, who apparently come to greet the persons or send them back to the 'world of the living'. Only 17 per cent of those I interviewed had a similar experience on ketamine.

Point or border of no return

Some participants (16.6 per cent) came to a sort of 'barrier' or a 'point of no return', which was described as the limit between earthly life and the next life. It could be a bridge, an edge, a gate, or remain undefined. Participants often felt a certain resistance 'to go back' because the sense of peace and pleasantness they felt in this 'other realm' was very high; 22 per cent came to a conscious decision to return to life. According to Mr W., who was mentioned above, the point of no return is just an illusion. He said: 'the death point, as it is generally understood, is merely the body's fear at being left. Once you know that, you can move freely between the levels.'

After-effects

Although the after-effects of ketamine have been extensively studied by anesthesiologists in clinical terms, very little attention has been paid to the changes reported by those who had an experience similar to the NDE.

Reduced fear of death

The majority of those I interviewed reported a reduced fear of death (46 per cent). This is an interesting result if we consider that respondents did not find themselves in life-threatening circumstances. One conclusion that might be drawn from this is that it is unnecessary to face death to report a reduced fear of death afterwards. On the contrary, an experience that gives a person an intuition of dying might be enough to stimulate the conviction that death does not exist and that the human soul is immortal.

Some participants manifested a deeper appreciation for the natural world in terms of both animistic and pantheistic beliefs. Most of these insights originated while under the effects of ketamine.

Synchronicity and psychic abilities

Another after-effect of ketamine experiences was the tendency of some participants to become more interested in interpreting their life events in terms of 'meaningful coincidences'. Miss A., for instance, noted that she experienced many 'strange' coincidences while taking ketamine (this does not necessarily indicate that she was under the effects of ketamine when these events happened). She also reported having powerful precognitive experiences. One of these was about the death of her grandmother. She received the actual news only a few days after the experience. Some other participants were sure that the use of ketamine had developed a 'new potential' or a telepathic sensitivity.

Interests and activities

Some participants claimed that their experiences with ketamine had a significant impact on their interests and activities. Some became more interested in practices such as yoga and meditation. A participant commented: 'After my ketamine experiences I became attracted by the idea of karma and reincarnation. I am sure that death doesn't exist, and that the human soul is immortal.'

Summary

In terms of the 'Greyson NDE Scale', all the main features of the near-death experience were reported by the ketamine group under study here. All 36 participants were sure that what happened was real and not a mere 'hallucination' induced by ketamine. The accounts include visions of beautiful landscapes or peaceful environments where they met luminous divinities (30 per cent) as well as frightening *sumi* (with non-human faces), strange animals, and unknown or unseen presences (16.6 per cent). Some 16.6 per cent met dead relatives or friends. An interesting result in this sense was that all 36 visited a certain place, 'good' or 'bad'; 44.4 per cent described it as clearly mystical or unearthly. Events that happened 'there' were described with extreme clarity and accuracy even several years after the experiences.

Some 19.4 per cent felt surrounded by an unusual light of mystical or otherworldly origin. This has been described as 'bright', 'radiant', 'rather small', 'full of energy' and/or 'pure love and compassion', and 'vibrating sounds like mantras'. Two participants reported out-of-body experiences, which in both cases were unpleasant; 33.3 per cent were absolutely sure they left their bodies and that they temporarily existed outside them; 11.1 per cent were able to remember past events, while 16.6 per cent claimed that their past flashed out of control in front of them (the 'life review') and 52.7 per cent felt a total understanding of the universe, expressed in such statements as 'we originate from the source and relate to each other as if we were one big family'. Some respondents said that they had participated in the 'fabrication of the universe' or felt a 'cosmic union with earth', as if they were able to understand its constitutive principle by means of a principle within the self. One participant had birth-related memories, also known as near-birth experiences (NBEs). A small minority of the group reported extra-sensory perceptions. These included an enhanced level of telepathy and other apparent psychic abilities, such as precognition (including vision of the world's future reported by 16 per cent). A point or a border of no return was reached by 16 per cent.

In the following chapter, these results will be systematically compared with those obtained in a study carried out by Peter Fenwick on 36 subjects who reported NDEs as a result of either cardiac arrest or some other life-threatening circumstance. However, before proceeding to this comparison, a few remarks are necessary about the limitations of my study. This may be useful for those interested in conducting further investigations.

It is important to observe that not all ketamine users have experiences similar to near-death experiences. Currently it is impossible to predict who will have an NDE-like one. Those who took part in the study contacted me because they were willing to share their ketamine experiences. This may have over-estimated the real occurrence of the near-death type of experience among ketamine users. Jansen, for instance, suggested that NDEs happen only to 12 per cent of ketamine users (Jansen 2001). This means that 88 per cent do not have one, and might not be aware of these effects. Another relevant observation is that according to those I interviewed, the NDE-like experiences were more likely to happen on first exposure to ketamine. Although further studies are required, this preliminary result suggests that it is not a recurrent effect. On the contrary, those who continued with consumption noticed that its NDE-like effects gradually faded away. Moreover, all the accounts that I collected inevitably dealt with *memories* of an experience and not with a direct experience. In this sense what has been called 'false memory' could play a role, especially when the memories were reported a long time after the event. For instance, this possibility is supported by results in experimental research, which have shown that eyewitness testimony is unreliable, including testimony of anomalous experiences (French 2005). An exemption to this observation is represented by those who reported an NDE as a result of a cardiac arrest and were interviewed immediately after the experience (e.g. Parnia *et al.* 2001; Sartori 2005). Furthermore, since most of the interviewees used other recreational drugs, one could ask if the NDE-like states they described were associated with the ketamine use or are more appropriately to be considered a result of ketamine/polydrug intake instead. One could also wonder if findings similar to those described here might have been observed for other psychoactive compounds (e.g., dimethyltryptamine; Strassman 2001). The present data would have been less difficult to interpret if they were the result of a prospective, double-blind vs placebo, study with volunteers who had no history of ketamine use. Although sometimes carried out (Krystal *et al.* 1994), prospective studies with psychotomimetic drugs can raise ethical concerns.

There were further potential sources of uncertainty in this study. The interviews were not carried out close to the time of the ketamine experiences, and so there was no possibility of employing toxicological tests to confirm the interviewees' statements about the drugs they had taken. It therefore cannot be ruled out that other drugs (e.g., cannabis) had recently been self-administered (Jansen 2001). Finally, participants often had great difficulties in articulating their experiences. Although some details can be described, the essence of these experiences is inexpressible and beyond thought: in one word, it is 'ineffable'.

5

Gaining new insights

The aim of this chapter is to shed new light on the hidden potential of human nature by comparing the ketamine and near-death experiences. Are they identical? If not, what are the main similarities and differences? What can we learn from this? To help make the comparison, experiences that took place under three different circumstances were considered: (1) ketamine use; (2) cardiac arrest; and (3) various life-threatening circumstances in which subjects were awake (e.g. car accident, childbirth).

Comparison of ketamine and NDEs

Methodological issues

The ketamine research results presented in the previous chapter were compared with those obtained from a similar study carried out by Peter Fenwick on 36 cases of NDE that followed either (1) cardiac arrest or (2) some other life-threatening circumstance during which the subject was awake. The data from both these NDE groups ('a' and 'b') are available at the Religious Experience Research Centre (RERC)[1] Archive at the University of Wales, Lampeter.

For clarity, groups 'a' and 'b' will sometimes be combined together under the name 'NDE group' in the following discussion, but a distinction between the two will be made when appropriate.

Interviews with the ketamine and NDE group subjects were held following completion of a semi-structured questionnaire known as the 'Greyson NDE Scale' (Greyson 1983: 369–75).

Demographic profile

The NDE group was older than the ketamine group. As noted before, the latter was mainly composed of subjects aged between 20 and 35 years old. In contrast, Fenwick's group members had an age of 35 or more. In both cases, the male component was slightly larger (53 per cent in the NDE group;

56 per cent in the ketamine group). In the ketamine group, the majority were either students (36 per cent) or in full-time employment (42 per cent). In the NDE group, many of the participants were retired (47.5 per cent).

Sense of dying

In all groups, the experience often began with a strong sense of dying and of leaving the body, which was reported by 33 per cent of the ketamine group, 53 per cent of the NDE cardiac-arrest group 'a', and 87 per cent of the NDE other-circumstances group 'b'. This was followed by a strong sense of peace and well-being, which was higher in the NDE groups: 93 per cent in cardiac-arrest group 'a' and 90 per cent in the other-circumstances group 'b', but only 72 per cent in the ketamine group. Conversely, a feeling of joy was highest in the ketamine group at 47 per cent, compared with 45 per cent in the other-circumstances group 'b' and only 27 per cent in the cardiac-arrest group 'a'.

Timelessness

The perception of time was reported to alter for the majority of the two groups (69 per cent in the ketamine group; 67 per cent in the NDE group). After an initial rush or acceleration in the perception of time, there was a sense of timelessness, described in terms that suggested 'time' had lost its meaning. Some of the participants explicitly used expressions such as 'I was not aware of time' or 'time had no meaning'. The exception here might be the life review, an experience during which time acquires a particular relevance, through the disclosure of life events.

In both groups, 'thoughts' and visions were sometimes described as speeded up (70 per cent in the NDE group; 69 per cent in the ketamine group), although there were also states in which there appeared to be little logical thought but more of an experiential mental state focused on visions.

Life review

An infrequently encountered feature was the life review. Findings seem to be very similar among the three groups. Some 16 per cent of the participants in the ketamine study reported such an experience. In the NDE study, it was reported by 14 per cent in cardiac-arrest group 'a' and by 16 per cent in the other-circumstances group 'b'.

Visions of other 'places'

While time had no meaning, space – or more specifically the sense of 'being-in-a-place'[2] – was always present. This was the commonest feature among all the accounts that I considered in this study. In near-death and ketamine cases, these 'other places' were depicted in various ways. Although they could vary from heavenly gardens to open sepulchres, from rural villages to forests, experiences were never 'placeless'. All the respondents in the three groups claimed that there was no other way of knowing or sensing those places except by being there, and they found it difficult to articulate the experience in words. For instance, a respondent in the near-death group observed:

> The Lord took me to a garden where surely beauty had found its name. This was an old-fashioned, typically English garden with lush green velvet lawn, bounded by deep curving borders brimming with flowers, each flower nestling within its family group, each group proclaiming its presence with a riot of colour and fragrance as if blessed by a morning dew. The entrance to the garden was marked by a trellis of honeysuckle so laden that you had to crouch down to pass beneath while at the other end a rustic garden gate led to the outside. It was here that my walk through was to end as I was gently led through to the other side. It was at this moment that the realization that I was going to live came to me and I would have to face the consequences of living. There followed two weeks as I lay in a coma in between worlds.

It could be argued that the intuition of one's death here and now, which may have been present to all group participants, renders the temporal dimension of existence less relevant than the spatial domain, which therefore largely prevails. As we saw in Chapter 3, this suggestion is supported by a Japanese theory of place (*basho*). For instance, Hiroshi Motoyama, after many years of meditative practice, called the state of *Samadhi* the 'World of Places' (Motoyama 1991). The concept is also implicit in some Eastern philosophies, including Buddhism, according to which temporal consciousness applies to the field of our ordinary experience and relates to the self-consciousness of individuals ('ego-consciousness'). This is viewed as 'inauthentic' and 'insufficient'. Space-consciousness is different in nature, for it makes a connection to a deeper level of consciousness, unlike the surface time-consciousness within the field of ordinary experience (see, for instance, Yuasa 1987; 1993).

Hence, it could be suggested that transcendental consciousness is place-bound (Corazza 2007b). I will discuss this idea in greater depth in the next few sections and then move on to the comparative discussion by highlighting differences between the ketamine and near-death experiences.

What is it like to be in a transcendental place?

There is a lack of relevant literature on the spatial dominance of place during the near-death experience. Researchers have focused on other elements of the experience, such as the tunnel, or the transition into a period of darkness, the light, and the meeting with others (see, for instance, Kellehear 1996). It will therefore be valuable if I pay special attention to the spatial element of being-in-a-transcendental-place, which as noted above, was the most common element that I found in both the NDE and ketamine groups. The descriptions furnished by participants suggest that the experience of 'being-in-a-place' is characterized by four main constitutive elements, which can be summarized as follows: (1) the experience of things-events; (2) non-homogeneity of space; (3) multi-sensoriality, including synesthesia; and (4) a higher level of activity, or a faster information exchange.

The experience of things-events

The recurrent feature of 'being-in-a-place' during a near-death experience first suggests that the experience cannot be isolated from what I call 'things-events'. By things-events I mean that which the experience is *about*. As pointed out in the previous chapters, no two near-death accounts are the same, although there are similarities between the dynamics of the happenings. Many things-events happen 'there', and nearly always the protagonists are able to produce interesting narratives of these things-events, which are remembered vividly for years. All the accounts I have collected, far from describing quiet, uneventful experiences, were rich with actions (e.g. involving motion, decision-making, use of various senses). At any stage, things-events were never rigidly imposed on those who reported the experiences, who instead were always able to modify the events-things to various degrees, as in the case below:

> I saw something glittering in the distance and went to it. Next thing I knew there was a bright huge wall standing in my way. It was made of golden light. There was something I had to go across between the wall and me. I believe there was no river, no bridge or nothing specifically. The wall, which shone gold softly, was made of pure glory and I was sure that there existed whole in it. I moved towards it, being gravitated to it. I have a feeling that I saw many things in this something. Everything happened very quickly. I remember that I saw everything I had experienced. The sense of gravitation toward the light was so strong that I gradually began to lose the sense of distinguishing myself from the light. I was filled with everything. Then I thought something like: 'Would I be dead if the trend continues?' but 'I have done nothing in this life!'. Then I realized that I had developed a strong feeling of resistance towards this gravitation and the melting into the light. I remember nothing else. The next thing I knew was that I was lying in a hospital bed, and pain and that I was in pain and suffering.

For many of those interviewed in both groups, the experience generally involved a movement, or a motion within a definite place (often explicitly emotional).

Even if the 'travelling self' remained in one place (e.g., a garden, a village, a temple), the situation was never entirely stationary because it always involved a focus or an action within a place. So it was for a Japanese lady who found herself in a beautiful garden covered by bright yellow flowers. The next thing she saw was a river in front of her:

> As I got closer, at the very end of the other side of the river, I saw my mother who passed away 18 years ago. I could see only her face because a group of children monks, dressed in white and black, masked the rest of her body. The children were very noisy. I moved closer, to see my mother. She looked very worried and she said: 'Don't come here! Go back!' So I turned back and regained consciousness in the hospital. At that very moment, I heard a nurse calling my name.

As illustrated by this case, things-events sometimes have a cultural undertone. For instance, as previously observed, the vision of beautiful gardens with many flowers was quite common among the Japanese group, as well as the vision of a river which divides the world of the living from the world of those who have passed away (the 'realm of Yomi').

Less reported is the 'travelling self' moving from place to place. So it was for another participant, who visited several villages in another realm and finally ended up in the countryside, where he was surrounded by empty factories:

> On my way I met people I didn't know before. I saw many villages with streets like normal streets in this world. I saw many different landscapes and empty factories.

One of the remarkable things about these accounts is that the transition from one place to another is always reported as happening by mere 'power of thought', rather than by transportation. For instance, the participant above described streets as being 'like normal streets in this world', but he mentioned no cars, buses, trains, planes, and so on. He visited the countryside, but why did he not drive or take a train there? This is yet another feature of the NDE that we shall have to explain.

A possible answer is that the 'travelling self' is already a means of transportation and that there may be a fundamental equation between personhood and embodiment. The idea that the soul has a mobile post-mortem body is an ancient belief reflected in such terms as the Egyptian *ka*, the Greek *ochema*, and the Sanskrit *kosha*, *deha* and *sarira*, which indicate 'vehicles of consciousness', some of which pass into post-mortem realms. The subject has been explored at great length by Dutch philosopher Johannes Jacobus Poortman (1896–1970) in his book *Vehicles of Consciousness* (1978), in which he formulated the concept of a hylic pluralism. According to his research, the notion of a body-vehicle is supported by evidence found, for example, in the Rig Veda, the Upanishads, the Old Testament, the pre-Socratic philosophers, Plato, Aristotle, certain Epicureans and Stoics, Plotinus, Porphyry, Iamblichus, Proclus, Origen, Saint Paul, many Gnostics, Augustine, Thomas Aquinas, Descartes, Paracelsus, Swedenborg, and several modern philosophers, novelists, and scientists.

Non-homogeneity of space

Afterlife places in both groups were often described as having particular qualities, which made them different from the places we inhabit in everyday life. In the ketamine group, 44 per cent had the feeling of entering a clearly mystical or unearthly world. Affirmations like 'It was Heaven!' were quite common.[3] Experiences of Hell were also reported; 25 per cent described a strange or unusual place, while 30 per cent did not report this kind of experience.

Did these people really go to heaven or hell? It is, of course, very hard to answer the question. According to Le Goff (1981), heaven, hell and purgatory are all forms of what he called 'spatialization of thoughts', which he considered a product of our imaginations.

More flexible in this regard is the Doctrine Commission of the Church of England who recently revised their views:

> No one can be compulsorily installed in heaven, whose characteristic is the communion of love. God whose being is love preserves our human freedom, for freedom is the condition of love. Although God's love goes, and has gone, to the uttermost, plumbing the depths of hell, the possibility remains for each human being of final rejection of God, and so of eternal life.
>
> (Church of England 1995)

According to the Commission:

> In the past the imagery of hell-fire and eternal torment and punishment, often sadistically expressed, has been used to frighten men and women into believing. Christians have professed appalling theologies which made God into a sadistic monster and left searing psychological scars on many. Over the last two centuries the decline in the churches of the western world in the teaching of everlasting punishment has been one of the most notable transformations of Christian belief. There are many reasons for this change, but amongst them has been the moral protest from both within and without the Christian faith against a religion of fear, and a growing sense that the picture of a God who consigned millions to eternal torment was far removed from the revelation of

God's love in Christ. Nevertheless it is our conviction that the reality of hell (and indeed of heaven) is the ultimate affirmation of the reality of human freedom. Hell is not eternal torment, but it is the final and irrevocable choosing of that which is opposed to God so completely and so absolutely that the only end is total non-being. Dante placed at the bottom of hell three figures frozen in ice – Judas, Brutus and Cassius. They were the betrayers of their friends, and through that they had ceased to have the capacity for love and so for heaven. Annihilation might be a truer picture of damnation than any of the traditional images of the hell of the eternal moment. If God has created us with the freedom to choose, then those who make such a final choice choose against the only source of life, and they have their reward. Whether there be any who do so choose, only God knows.

(Church of England 1995: 198–9)

The concept of the non-homogeneity of space is an intriguing topic of study which has been overlooked in contemporary literature. An exception is found in the work of Mircea Eliade (1907–1986), who explicitly stated that the non-homogeneity of space is an assumption that 'precedes all reflections on the world and allows the world to be constructed, because it reveals its fixed points (the sacred places)' (Eliade 1959: 21). In his book *The Sacred and the Profane* (1959), he observed that space for a religious person is always non-homogenous. He wrote: 'For religious man, space is not homogeneous; he experiences interruptions, breaks in it; some part of space is qualitatively different from others' (ibid.: 20). In phenomenological terms, this suggests that the perception of the sacred is active on a pre-noetic (or 'pre-reflective') level of consciousness, which becomes fully available only during peculiar circumstances, as for instance in a near-death experience.

The case for the non-homogeneity of space has ancient roots. It is common knowledge that cathedrals, churches, temples and other places of ritual importance were built in certain places chosen in relation to the lie of the land, the flow of the water, the direction of the wind, the vegetation, and so on. This kind of awareness is also known as *geomancy*. In China, ancient practices based on a system of understanding the balance of energies, or the flow of the 'chi' in places, such as the *feng-shui*,[4] are still present and regularly practised today. Despite these ancient beliefs in the power of places, and a current revival in their practice, most of us today tend to consider one location very much like another.

A multi-sensory experience

Auditory experiences were also common in both groups. For instance, at the beginning of the experience, a noise or a buzzing or a ringing sound was often heard: 'I heard a loud buzzing sound in my ears, followed by a travel into a narrow tunnel. I left the physical world as well as my body. I thought I was dead, but I wasn't scared at all', said Jo, a young physician who took ketamine in his lab. Other sounds were also reported. Another respondent heard a 'sweet sound of bells' coming from the Light. Chants (like the reading of sutras) were mentioned in the Japanese accounts. A Japanese participant described these sounds as being quite disturbing: 'I saw a large group of children monks running towards me. They were dressed in a white dress with black skirts (a typical costume for Japanese monks). They were aged between 10 and 12, and they were all bold. They were terribly noisy, and I couldn't understand what they were saying.' Some other times, harmonious music was heard: 'I remember I could hear melodies, I never heard before. I have tried to reproduce them with my music', said Mr S., a young composer who lives in London.

As I highlighted in a previous study (Corazza and Terreni 2005), the idea of representing the 'sound' of the NDE in music was carried out in an original composition by Arnold Schoenberg (1874–1951), namely his *String Trio* (Op 45), a work commissioned by the Department of Music of Harvard University. The story behind this composition is quite singular. In August 1946, Schoenberg had a heart attack, which was nearly fatal. His heart stopped beating for a while and he 'returned' to life only after an injection in the cardiac muscles. As he revealed in a letter dated 9 May 1946, his *String Trio* is an attempt to reproduce all the phases of his travel in the after-life (ibid.: 47).

'Thermal space' was also described. For example, the vision of the Light was associated with warmth. So it was for Mr D. who said: 'The light was very bright and emanating warmth. I could easily stand the heat. I was also more aware of the large amount of energy around me.' Similarly, Mr F. said: 'I saw a distant light, which was growing bigger and bigger. There was a strong feeling of love and warmth. I was attracted toward it, but I knew that it wasn't my time to go there.'

Olfactory sensations were sometimes described. For instance, the pleasant fragrances of flowers or the wild scents of the forests were reported by one participant in the ketamine study and by all the participants in the Japanese study. I did not record any touch or taste sensations.

In conclusion, sensorial experiences in both the ketamine experience and the NDE can be important. In the ketamine study, 73 per cent felt that the senses were 'incredibly more vivid', whereas 17 per cent asserted that they were 'more vivid than usual'. A recurrent observation was that colors were brighter than usual. A Japanese lady claimed that 'the ground was filled with beautiful yellow flowers, like a sort of carpet'. Although she couldn't tell what kind they were, she noticed that the color was very unusual, for they were 'particularly bright'. Another participant observed that once he had travelled down along a dark tunnel 'there was much light. Everything was exceptionally bright, although my experience was dreadful.'

Synesthesia

Synesthesia is defined as the interchange of sensory images from one sensory organ to another (Marks 1978, as cited in Domino 1989), such as 'seeing' a sound, or 'tasting' a color. Sensory categories are also referred to as modalities, and so synesthesia is also known as a sensory cross-modality, or crossing of the senses (Cytowic 1995). The phenomenon appears to be more prevalent in individuals with artistic or musical backgrounds (Domino 1989), a group well represented among those interviewed as part of this work. Many were able to see sounds or hear colors during the experiences. Calvin, a young man in his twenties, gave the following account:

> On 'K' I was not only able to see the colors but to smell them. Even now, after two years from my last ketamine experience, I am able to recognize the difference between the smell of green or red. It is such an incredible experience!

Extraordinary communication abilities

Another feature commonly reported by the ketamine and the near-death groups was communication with other entities, such as the spirits of deceased loved ones, the Light (or God), Beings of Light, strangers or other entities. It has often been reported that the communication happened without speech, by the power of thought alone. How is it possible? A similar phenomenon is telepathy, which has been studied scientifically for more than 100 years. The most cited experiments are probably those known as 'Ganzfeld' (or 'total field') experiments, which use audio and visual sensory deprivation in order to test telepathy. Participants sit in a relaxed state in dim red light, with half a ping-pong ball covering each eye. In another room, a 'sender' concentrates on a picture or video clip, selected at random from a pool of possible targets. After the session is over, the participant is shown four pictures or video clips and asked to pick one that most closely corresponds to impressions he or she may have received during the test session. By chance, participants would select the correct target picture roughly one time in four, with a hit rate of 25 per cent. A meta-analysis published in 1985 covering 28 studies showed an overall hit rate of 37 per cent (Honorton 1985). A published meta-analysis of the same data (Hyman 1985) again showed that the odds against chance were very high. Unfortunately, the Ganzfeld procedure bears little resemblance to apparent telepathy in everyday life. Also, in most Ganzfeld and other tests on telepathy in parapsychology laboratories, the 'senders' and 'receivers' are strangers, whereas apparent telepathy in real life is said to take place more readily between people who know each other well, such as intimate friends and family members. Psychiatrist Berthold Schwarz described 505 episodes that appeared to involve telepathic exchange between himself, his wife Ardis, their son Eric and

daughter Lisa. Like Freud, Jung and other psychoanalysts who had an interest in the subject, Schwarz observed several ways in which apparent telepathic
communication is influenced by unconscious psychological processes.

Rupert Sheldrake has recently attempted to explain telepathy in relation
to his theory of the 'sense of being stared at' (Sheldrake 2003). Sheldrake
believes that the experiments which he and other collaborators have carried
out over the past few years have produced some evidence for telepathy, but
so far the scientific world is generally not convinced. The debate gave rise
to a special edition of the *Journal of Consciousness Studies* entitled 'The Sense
of Being Glared At: What Is It Like to Be a Heretic?' (2005). One of
Sheldrake's studies involved the investigation of possible telepathic communication in connection with e-mails. On each planned session, there were
four potential e-mailers, one of whom was selected at random by the experi-
menter. One minute before a prearranged time at which the e-mail was
to be sent, the participant guessed who would send it. Fifty participants
(29 women and 21 men) were recruited through an employment web-site. Of
552 trials, 235 (43 per cent) guesses were hits, significantly above the chance
expectation of 25 per cent. Further tests with five participants (four women,
one man, aged 16–29) were videotaped continuously. On the filmed trials,
the 64 hits of 137 (47 per cent) were significantly above chance (Sheldrake
and Smart 2005). The problems associated with studies of this nature have
been addressed by a range of authors, such as Michael Shermer, author of
Why People Believe Weird Things (2002) and David F. Marks and Richard
Kammann, authors of *The Psychology of the Psychic* (1980).

Differences between ketamine and near-death experiences

What seemed to be initially a largely anecdotal observation that ketamine
and near-death experiences are sometimes the same has in fact turned out
to be a valid line of enquiry for providing further suggestions about the nature
of both these states. Many of the participants in all three groups shared the
feeling of dying, of travelling at high speed along a tunnel, of entering another
'place'. Rare in both groups was the life review. However, I would now like
to focus on the major differences between the two states, which emerged for
the first time from this study.

Encounters with other beings

Particularly significant was the finding that encounters with deceased or
religious beings were mentioned by 57 per cent in the NDE cardiac arrest
group, by 47 per cent in the NDE other-circumstances group, but by only
17 per cent in the ketamine group. Of the encounters that included religious
figures in the two near-death groups, the majority included encounters with
Jesus. Such visions were not reported in the ketamine group: here 'beings of

light' were not attributed any definite or recognizable personality. A possible reason for such a significant difference is that ketamine users had induced the experiences themselves and so during the journey were less likely to have a psychological need for support from a recognizable and comforting presence. Far more helpless are those who have experienced a car accident or other emergency, like a cardiac arrest. In this case, there is a serious threat to life. Nevertheless, the argument becomes more complex if we consider that the majority of those who had a ketamine experience had the absolute conviction of dying or being dead during the experience, and they had completely forgotten about the fact that they were under the effect of the substance. It is also possible that the NDE groups, being from an older generation, had more of a Christian upbringing or were more Christian-oriented, and therefore were more likely to experience or interpret spiritual presences as Jesus.

Vision of the Light

The vision of the Light was much higher in the two NDE groups (73 per cent for cardiac arrest; 72.5 per cent for other circumstances). A similar result emerged from a study carried out by Sam Parnia and Peter Fenwick at the Southampton Hospital on cardiac arrest survivors (Parnia *et al.* 2001), in which 75 per cent of the participants experienced the Light. Conversely, light was reported by only 19 per cent of ketamine users. In both studies the Light was described as having particular qualities, such as a luminous color (silver, gold, or white) and with no shadows. It was 'brilliant like the sun', emanating pure love and compassion, and warm and welcoming. It was often identified as God or the Absolute. Non-verbal communications with the Light (God) were often reported. Curiously, regardless of the cause of the experience, the persons were not usually able to remember the content of the message. When this was remembered, in both NDE and ketamine cases, the Light (God) had sometimes apparently sent the person back to life because s/he had to take care of a family member or other dear persons.

Interestingly, those who claimed to have met the Light in the ketamine group gave very detailed accounts of their experiences, but they could not report the final message given by the Light. This phenomenon, although underreported, has also emerged in previous near-death studies. But how can it be that such an inspiring aspect of the experience is so easily forgotten, especially when the experience as a whole is characterized by full clarity? Several possible explanations for this phenomenon can be suggested. First, the person's ordinary mind was unable to process and store the information adequately because the information was communicated too quickly (although it may be difficult to explain while only the communication with the Light was too fast) or for some other reason, such as a change in normal mental functioning in the ketamine and NDE states.[5] A second, connected possibility is that messages were received at a pre-noetic or pre-reflective level of consciousness, which most of the time remains unconscious and non-verbal: hence the message is not accessible and cannot be described to others at later interviews. Yuasa (1993) referred to this as the region of 'dark consciousness'. If this is the case, then these may contribute to the life-changes that may happen to those who 'spoke with the Light'. Third, it is possible that those interviewed did not want to disclose the information, perhaps because it was too personal. Fourth, it is possible that the forgetting serves to protect consciousness from the knowledge of 'the Light' and the 'inner workings' of the universe, knowledge that would make life difficult and distressing. In other words, the amnesia acts as a psychological/spiritual protective mechanism against 'too much truth', a kind of replacing of the samite over the Holy Grail to deliberately shield its light. The most 'scientific' hypothesis within the contemporary paradigm is that the data are not remembered for the same reason that large parts of dreams are not remembered and fade as the sleeper wakes. There are several theories of this kind, which make no reference to spiritual or paranormal realities. NMDA receptors are closely involved in memory formation, and those in certain parts of the brain may play a central role in the recollection of conversation. If NDE, ketamine experience, and dreaming involve blockade of these sites, as Jansen suggests, then we can expect incomplete memories to form and subsequent gaps in the recollection of the experiences.

Many participants in both studies referred to visions of 'lights'. I have recorded some of these statements: 'I saw a light silver, white and red'; 'The light was orange'; 'I saw a red triangle rising up from the very dark ground'; 'I saw the light as my physical form would have'. The experience sometimes seemed to be characterized by brighter colors, which were described as more vivid than usual. This aspect has also been pointed out in previous NDE studies (Moody 1975; Greyson and Stevenson 1980; Ring 1980). The light was usually located at the end of a dark tunnel or tunnel-like alternatives, such as a cave, spiral, valley, or just a general period of darkness.

Being one with the cosmos

It is interesting that although the ketamine group subjects were less likely to meet the Light, they were more likely to report a sense of harmony and unity with the universe (52 per cent). This kind of experience was reported by only 20 per cent of subjects in the cardiac arrest group and 30 per cent of those in the other-circumstances NDE group. As noted in Chapter 4, some individuals felt they were taking part in the 'fabrication of the universe' itself or were able to understand the constitutive principle of the universe by means of the principle within the self. The idea that we are all interconnected with the entire cosmos is an ancient belief. For instance, the Delphic exhortation to 'Know Thyself', inscribed at the Temple of Apollo, could be interpreted as more than a call for moral self-knowledge: it could also be understood as a call to look 'inwards' to find the intelligible order and the God within (Marshall 1992: 81). In modern times, mystical intimations of the order, life, unity and interconnectedness of the universe have sometimes been called 'cosmic consciousness' or 'cosmic mystical experience'. It constitutes a particularly expansive kind of 'extrovertive mystical experience', a type of mystical experience in which the world or some its contents become a focus of special insight or unity (Marshall 2005).

Marcia Moore, in her book *Journeys into the Bright World* (Moore and Alltounian 1978), has offered several personal accounts of 'cosmic union' that took place while she was under the influence of ketamine. As Karl Jansen has commented, her book is 'of particular interest in that it was written by a woman, as writing about psychedelic drugs is an area still largely dominated by men, with rare exceptions' (Jansen 2001: 55). Her cosmological intuitions were sometimes followed by considerations about the universe as an organized intelligence.

On a less mystical, more theological level, the recognition of an 'order' within the cosmos has been expressed by Richard Swinburne: he notes that 'the universe might so naturally have been chaotic, but it is not – it is very orderly' (Swinburne 1979: 136). He argues that after some exploration, the universe becomes organized to the explorer's eyes. Once we accept the order, we can either explain it in scientific terms, or we can seek an alternative explanation in terms of a free and conscious intelligence ('God'), which lies behind it. He argues for the completeness of the second choice.

Point or border of no return

Another interesting peculiarity of the ketamine experience is that only a marginal number of participants have approached 'a point of no return'. This can be identified as an edge, a wall, a river, among other patterns. This is in significant contrast to Fenwick's study, in which 77 per cent had the 'point-of-no-return' experience. There are at least a couple of possible explanations for this. First, ketamine users knew from the beginning of their trip that they would 'come back', for the substance has a short duration of action. Second, it is possible that the ketamine experience does not always lead to the deeper stages. Its effects could easily depend upon the quantity of the substance taken and the personal characteristics of the experiencer.

When there is no light at the end of the tunnel

According to Mr W.:

> One of the most disturbing aspects of ketamine is how it can pitch even the most experienced psychonaut straight into hell. There's really no other word for it and even if you are not a believer, you know it's hell. It's

the most dreadful feeling you can imagine. It's like being frozen in time (perhaps Dante was right). There's no way out and the overwhelming sense is that this awful state is eternal. You just know it's going to go on and on for ever.

It has been claimed that ketamine experiences tend to be more hellish than 'natural' near-death experience (Moody 1975; Strassman 1997; Fox 2003) and also to feel 'unreal' in comparison (Fenwick 1997). However, it is unlikely that there is a 'natural' NDE as such. As we have seen, most near-death experiences have an obvious trigger circumstance, such as cardiac arrest, sensory deprivation, meditation and even stimulation of certain parts of the brain.

A systematic analysis of the 36 ketamine accounts shows that these 'more hellish' and 'unreality' claims can easily be contradicted. One of the most striking conclusions is that the majority of those interviewed (72 per cent) felt a strong sense of peace and pleasantness, and in 40 per cent of the cases, 'joy' was described.

In Fenwick's NDE study, a sense of peace and pleasantness was higher at 93 per cent, but only 26 per cent felt joy, less than with ketamine. This result indicates that the NDE-like ketamine experiences are not more 'hellish' than standard NDEs. Such a conclusion has recently been reinforced by Mark Fox's observation: the fact that most reported cases are overwhelmingly positive in nature 'does not necessarily indicate that negative experiences are in the overwhelming minority, and may simply be indicative of the fact that respondents are more likely to report positive experiences than negative ones' (Fox 2003: 260–1).

It has also been pointed out that the assumption that transcendental experiences are very positive and pleasant experiences is false, driven by baseless 'New Age' optimism. For instance, *The Tibetan Book of the Dead* is full of references to hellish moments. Why should the NDE always be a blissful and positive experience? As noted in Chapter 4, further evidence of negative NDEs emerged from the research work of Yoshia Hata and his research team at the University of Kyorin in Japan (Hata *et al.*, in Hadfield 1991). The team interviewed 17 patients, who had recovered from comas with 'minimal signs of life' after heart attacks, asthma attacks, and drug poisoning. Eight reported memories during their apparent unconsciousness. Five were of negative experiences, dominated by fear, pain or suffering.

One finding of particular interest was the case of Mr P., mentioned in Chapter 4, who had a negative NDE as a result of a suicide attempt and a positive experience after taking ketamine. This is a rare case of someone who had both experiences. The first was the result of an attempted suicide at the age of 18:

I suddenly felt that I was travelling down a tunnel and at the end there was much light. Everything was exceptionally bright, although my experience was dreadful. I was sure I was in hell. I saw three *sumi*. They tried to torture me. They didn't look very human.

Several years after this episode, he tried ketamine for the first time while he was at home listening to some music:

I thought I was dying and the feeling was very similar to my suicide. I went to the toilet and I had the feeling of passing through the door. Then I went back to the room and I lay down on my bed. I gradually lost my senses. The music was very distorted. I tested myself by asking basic questions about mathematics, the names of those I love, etc., then suddenly I wasn't interested in this any more. So I tried to concentrate on 'who I am' and I lost interest again. Visions become blurred. It wasn't meaningful who I was anymore, because I existed anyway. Then I tried the experience of death. I was going down a tunnel. I saw the planet Earth. I could feel the relationship between the human soul, Earth and the planets. I thought I was a doll, you know the *matryoshka*? I was the *matryoshka* of the entire system. I understood that Earth is inside something else. I felt its gravity. All this is embraced within a system. I was nothing, but I knew that my place was on Earth.

Another example is quoted in Jansen's *Ketamine: Dreams and Realities* (2001: 99–107). In this case, it was clear that the near-death experience and the ketamine experience were identical. The person interviewed was a man who had lost his partner in a fire. He had an NDE while trying to rescue her, and then had the same experience while taking ketamine for the first time a week later.

Ketamine and the brain

The effects of ketamine on the brain have been studied by Karl Jansen, who proposed a ketamine model of the near-death experience (1989; 2001). He suggests that both ketamine and the NDE involve events at glutamate receptors called N-methyl-D-aspartate (NMDA) receptors, which are fundamental for vital functions such as memory and learning.

It has been discovered that a sudden deprivation of oxygen in the brain, as occurs in a heart attack or brain damage, triggers an abnormal release of a neurotransmitter called glutamate,[6] which kills neurons by over-stimulating them. The phenomenon is known as 'excito-toxicity' (Jansen 1989; Fenwick 1997). These nerve cells quickly die, and there is a loss of further neurons from related chemical reactions. Glutamate works by attachment to NMDA receptors, proteins on the cell surface. Ketamine is one of the drugs that block these proteins, and it can therefore prevent glutamate from harming neurons. When the brain suffers an injury such as a stroke, neurons release glutamate onto nearby neurons, which become excited, overloaded with calcium, and die. Normal neurotransmission is altered during injury, causing excess calcium to activate enzymes, which eventually leads to destruction of the cell. Since this occurs through glutamate receptors, including NMDA receptors, scientists believe that damage can be stopped through the use of agents that block the receptors. One of these is ketamine.

Several objections can be made to Jansen's ketamine model of the NDE. As David Fontana has pointed out, ketamine does not 'reproduce NDEs or any other mental state' (2005: 398), but it may eventually facilitate the conditions under which these states can occur. However, this is not the same as 'reproducing them'. Thus even if glutamate inhibition (or any other abnormal, chemically induced brain process) is present during the NDE, it is too strong to say that it has *caused* or *created* it. It may merely be a facilitating condition. Another observation emerges from the fact that out-of-body experiences, which sometimes occur as part of an NDE, do not involve an excessive release of glutamate, and they can occur when the individual is perfectly well both physically and mentally (ibid.: 399). The same is true of some mystical experiences that are phenomenologically very similar to NDEs, but which again can occur when there is no sign of any physical or psychological trauma (Marshall 2005: 95–6).

However, rather than entirely reducing this phenomenon to a neurobiological event, Jansen has been prepared to consider a wide range of hypotheses in his book *Ketamine: Dreams and Realities* (2001). For example, he does not dismiss suggestions that 'the brain can act as a transceiver, converting fields beyond the brain into features of the mind, in a manner similar to the way a television converts waves in the air into sounds and vision' (ibid.: 92). From this particular perspective, only one of several that he explores, the effect of 'ketamine on the brain can be seen as a metaphorical "mental modem", which can potentially "connect" the mind to "everything else", allowing a peek behind the curtain at the inner workings of this and other realities' (ibid.: 44). But he also warns that ideas such as these 'must be approached with care, as there can be a risk of collusion with maladaptive beliefs of persons suffering from a serious mental illness requiring medical treatment' (ibid.: 44), and unlike Stanislav Grof, a psychiatrist who clearly favors such hypotheses (Grof and Grof 1986), Jansen does not commit himself to any particular view. His warning was aimed at ideas expressed in works such as Stanislav and Christina Grof's article 'Spiritual emergency: understanding and treatment of transpersonal crises' (1986), which he considered to be a potentially hazardous path for psychiatry to pursue.[7]

6

Explaining the mystery

There are currently various scientific explanations for the near-death experience. These can be classified into three main approaches, which, however, are not mutually exclusive: (1) the mind/brain identity (or neuro-reductionist) theory; (2) psychological explanations; and (3) the transcendental (or 'survivalist') approach.

Mind and brain identity theories

Also called as 'neuro-reductionism or eliminativism' (Varela *et al.* 2001), this approach tends to confine human existence in terms of brain functions and sees consciousness as a mere product of the brain. Those who follow this approach assume that there is no physical understanding of the self or mind. A notable example is Francis Crick, who discovered the structure of DNA with James Watson and received a Nobel Prize for this work. Towards the end of his brilliant career, which embraced the study of both human genes and brains, he came to the conclusion that we 'are nothing but a pack of neurons'. In his book *The Astonishing Hypothesis* (1994), he wrote:

> The Astonishing Hypothesis is that 'You', your joys and your sorrows, your memories and your ambitions, your sense of personal identity and free will, are in fact no more than the behaviour of a vast assembly of nerve cells and their associated molecules.
>
> (ibid.: 3)

In other words, according to Crick, the ultimate task of scientific endeavour is to explain consciousness in terms of brain mechanisms. I find this indeed a very 'astonishing hypothesis'. In recent years this approach has been revolutionized by computational processing as well as by the arrival of brain imaging technologies, such as functional Magnetic Resonance Imaging (fMRI), positron emission tomography (PET) and recently magnetic encephalography (MEG). Thanks to these new tools of science, various physiological explanations have been proposed to account for the near-death experience. These include oxygen depletion in the brain (also known as 'cerebral hypoxia'), which is common in a dying brain (Blackmore and Troscianko 1988), but, as we have seen, the NDE can also be experienced in other situations. Whinnery and Whinnery (1990) conducted a study of more than a thousand fighter pilots and examined the relations between NDE and the so-called G-LOC syndrome (i.e. acceleration-induced loss of consciousness). This state could be observed in pilots during extreme acceleration, which can result in low blood levels in the brain. The researchers noticed a large number of features which are common to the NDE:

> Tunnel visions and bright lights, floating sensations, automatic movement, autoscopy, OBEs, not wanting to be disturbed, paralysis, vivid dreamlets of beautiful places, pleasurable sensations, euphoria and dissociation, inclusion of friends or family, inclusion of previous memories or thoughts, the experience being very memorable (when it can be remembered), confabulation, and strong urge to explain the experience.
> (Whinnery 1997: 245)

An objection to anoxia is that it generates confusional thinking, while NDEs are characterized by extreme clarity of thought (French 2005b). Blackmore (1996a; 1996b), for instance, has argued that this varies a great deal according to the type of anoxia, its speed of onset, and the time until oxygen is restored.

Other theories have recognized the centrality of neurotransmitters. These can include endorphins (Carr 1982; Sotelo et al. 1995), which are naturally released in the brain during particularly stressful moments and can cause pain reduction and pleasant sensations, and other features similar to those manifested during an NDE. Jansen (1989; 2001) has argued that endorphins are not hallucinogenic, but he observed that a sudden increase of the neurotransmitter glutamate both during an NDE and a ketamine experience might be indirectly responsible for aspects of the phenomenon. As we saw in Chapter 5, he proposed a ketamine model of the NDE. Others have addressed serotonin pathways (Morse et al. 1986), activation of the limbic system (Lempert et al. 1994) and temporal lobe anoxic seizures, but none has yet been shown to be responsible for the phenomenon.

The methodological presuppositions of the neuro-reductionist approach have been considered a violation of our human experience by an increasing number of scholars (see, for instance, Varela 1996; Damasio 2003). The main problem with this approach is that the 'objective' measurements of the brain do not allow investigation of the 'subjective' aspects of the human experience. As Leder has put it: 'By not including the "subjective" side of the experience in the reflection, we assume only a partial reflection and our question becomes disembodied' (1990: 7). The argument has been well explored by Thomas Nagel in his article entitled 'What is it like to be a bat?' (1974), where he deals with the 'what it is like' ('subjective') character of human experience. He argues that an organism endowed with a sonar system like a bat does not perceive what an organism equipped with a visual apparatus (like a human being) can perceive. In other words, the fact that an organism has a 'conscious' experience means basically that there is something 'to be' that organism. As Nagel described it, when we say that another organism is conscious, we mean that 'there is something it is like to be that organism . . . something it is like to be *for* the organism' (Nagel 1974: 436); 'the essence of the belief that bats have experience is that there is something that it is like to be a bat' (ibid.: 438).

The subjective aspect of the human experience was central, for instance, to Western phenomenology, which started from the irreducible nature of conscious experience as distinct from the mental content as represented in the 'philosophy of mind'. In this respect, Merleau-Ponty (1962) discusses the distinction between an 'objective' body, which can be identified with its anatomical description and a *lived* body, which contrarily lives through and sustains the act of perception. Along the same lines, in Japan, Yasuo Yuasa indicated this as a new research direction that he called 'subjective science', which 'attempts to restore the wholeness of mind while keeping a certain cooperative relationship with objective science' (Yuasa 1989: xv). This is a science that focuses on the inner cosmos of human subjects. In his work, Yuasa compared and opposed his concept of 'subjective science' with that of 'objective science' and argued that we cannot appreciate the meaning of truth *in toto*, unless we delve into the inner cosmos buried in ourselves (Yuasa 1993).

According to Francisco Varela, the reductionist approach considers the 'subjective' side of human experience as unreliable and unsafe, and regards it as a second order of expression to an objective knowledge, which is considered valid and scientific (Varela *et al.* 2001). This attitude has its own risks. Probably the most insidious one is derived from the argument that the NDE is a mere product of the brain. None of us can deny that the experience and the brain activities are interconnected. A large number of clinical studies provide evidence of such a relation. Let us take an appealing example such as that of the smell of lavender (*Lavandula angustifolia*).[1] Masatoshi and his colleagues at the Tohoku University in Japan have shown from a PET measurement that the lavender aroma produces 'a metabolic reduction in the right superior temporal gyrus and the right postcentral gyrus and activations in the left posterior part of the cingulate gyrus' (Itoh *et al.* 2004: 109). These results mean that smelling lavender aroma induces not only a state of relaxation but also increases an arousal level in the subject taking part in their experiment. Other examples are a brain contusion or a lack of oxygen supply, which can result in the loss of consciousness, and a tumor, or a trauma of the temporal lobe, which involve certain distortions of consciousness processes that are distinct and different from those associated with pre-frontal lesions. Infections of the brain or administration of certain drugs with psychoactive properties, such as hypnotics, stimulants, or psychedelics, are conducive to quite characteristic alterations of consciousness. Recent successful results in neurosurgery have shown how there can be a clinical improvement after the intervention. All these situations demonstrate that there is a close connection between consciousness and the brain; however, they do not necessarily prove that the brain actually produces consciousness. In other words, the fact that the mind and the brain are related to each other does not prove they are the same.

Psychological explanations

There are various psychological explanations of the NDE. One of these was formulated by Noyes and Kletti (1976), who state the NDE should be seen as a form of depersonalization, which occurs as a defense mechanism against the perceived threat of dying. Another psychological theory considers the near-death experience to be analogous to birth, while the 'tunnel effect' and the emergence into a bright light have been interpreted as a symbolic re-living of the birth process. The tunnel is the birth canal and the white light is the world into which we were born. This theory was promoted by the late astronomer Carl Sagan. In his words:

> The only alternative, so far as I can see, is that every human being, without exception, has already shared an experience like that of those travellers who return from the land of death: the sensation of flight; the emergence from darkness into light; an experience in which, at least sometimes, a heroic figure can be dimly perceived, bathed in radiance and glory. There is only one common experience that matches this description. It is called birth.
>
> (Sagan 1979: 303–4)

Sagan's theory was influenced by the work on death and dying carried out by Stanislav Grof and Joan Halifax (1977), who also advanced various parallels between mystical experiences, NDE and drug-induced experiences (especially LSD and ketamine). At a conference in London at Rudolf Steiner House,[2] Stanislav Grof argued that the NDE, far from being proof of an afterlife, recalls universal symbols of life and death, which are surprisingly common among different cultures. He went on to relate scientific theories about the universe to birth experiences. His idea seemed to present some similarities with C.G. Jung's 'archetypes' of the collective unconscious (Jung 1936).

Various scholars have found these theories inadequate to explain the NDE for several reasons. For instance, according to Susan Blackmore, a newborn infant would not see anything like a tunnel as it is being born. This is because the birth canal is stretched and compressed and the baby is usually forced through it with the top of the head and not with the eyes (which are closed anyway) (Blackmore 1982). In order to test her theory, Blackmore carried out a study where she interviewed some people born normally and others delivered by Caesarean section. Almost exactly equal percentages of both groups had a tunnel experience (36 per cent) during an NDE (ibid.). Other objections have been proposed by Carl Becker. He observed:

> The newborn's eyes are generally blurred by tears. They are often closed, either from relaxation, napping, or blinking . . . Even if their eyes are open and free of tears, they are often completely devoid of attention, like adults who may be momentarily oblivious to their physical surroundings even when their eyes are open.
>
> (1993: 113)[3]

And even if the newborn infants were able to perceive their surroundings with any kind of completeness or uniformity at birth, the birth experience and the death experiences with which we are concerned are not sufficiently analogous to reduce NDEs to memories of birth (ibid.: 115).

Transcendental hypothesis

This approach, also known as the 'survivalist hypothesis', strongly supports the view that a detachable soul leaves the body at the moment of the near-death experience and that this provides evidence of our survival after the death of the body (see, for, instance, Badham and Badham 1982; Rogo, 1982; Sabom 1982). This approach is mainly based on the experience as it appears to those who have had an NDE. As Paul Badham put it:

> The hypothesis appears to be supported by the claims made by many resuscitated persons that at the moment their hearts stopped beating they found themselves outside their bodies looking down with interest on the attempts made by the medical teams to revive them. What makes these claims evidential is that their observations seem to be extraordinarily accurate, and to accord with what would have been seen if they genuinely were looking down from above.
>
> (2003: 192)

Implicit in the survivalist hypothesis is a dichotomic way of thinking according to which soul and matter are two separate and incompatible entities. Before we move on with our discussion, it is relevant to observe how the term 'soul', or *anima*, has intentionally been avoided in contemporary debates and replaced by 'consciousness' or 'mind'. I find it rather a dismissive attitude because the concept of the human soul is not only fundamental in various religious traditions, but it also contains all the elements we need 'to define human uniqueness: mind, spirit, essence, immortal being, personhood, identity, selfhood' (McPhate, in Deane-Drummond and Scott 2006: 100).

Even this approach has its own limitations. The most remarkable one is that by losing sight of mind–body wholeness, the mind (or soul) is considered a disembodied entity, which is totally unrelated to the rest of the body. In order to overcome such a limitation, the Church of England Doctrine Commission has recently redefined the concept of the soul as follows:

> It would not be possible to speak of salvation in terms of destiny of souls after death, if the soul were thought of as the detachable spiritual part of ourselves. If the essential human being is an embodied whole, our ultimate destiny must be resurrection and transformation of our entire being . . . to speak thus is not to abandon talk of the soul, but to seek its redefinition.
>
> (Church of England 1995)

Interestingly, this redefinition of the soul provides a more inclusive concept of what it means to be a human being as an 'embodied whole' and refers to the resurrection of a new form of embodiment, rather than a disembodied soul. Similarly, Keith Ward has observed that 'the idea of resurrection is the idea of a new embodiment which is so closely related to this one that it can be best spoken of as the "same body transformed", rather than as quite a new body' (Ward, in Lorimer 2004: 169). In his view, the doctrine of resurrection is popularly misunderstood because of three Catholic doctrines, namely, (1) that the soul is created by God at a specific point (which makes one think it is a thing); (2) that the soul is naturally immortal (which makes one think that it could just go on for ever without a body); and (3) that the body is resurrected (which makes one think that the very same body climbs out of the grave). He suggested that 'to get the orthodox view, one has to have some grasp of the idea that the soul is the Form of the body, and yet that it is a substantial Form, capable of (un-naturally) existing with just conscious contents' (ibid.: 169–70).

The value and the necessity of recovering a concept of the soul in the contemporary debate on consciousness has been emphasized by Paul Badham, who argued that:

> The concept of the soul is a necessary ingredient of any faith, which wishes to affirm that we are more than physically determined creatures, and that we have the potentiality for moral and rational growth and for developing a spirituality, which can ultimately transcend our bodily death.
>
> (Badham 2005b: 219)

Although, for Badham, the soul is clearly difficult to define, he also encourages a rational explanation of it, which he thinks possible (ibid.: 220). Although I fully support this view, I would like to suggest that the near-death experience is proof of something more immediate than our survival after death, something that is much more concerned with our here and now. My assumption here is mainly based on the fact that the survivalist hypothesis seems to be inadequate to explain the cases of those who did not experience a situation of temporary death as we have seen, for instance, in the ketamine study.[4] Nevertheless, it can be argued that the fact the persons did not die on these occasions contradicts their accounts of dying and of leaving their bodies. How is it possible? The argument has been extensively treated in the work of Yasuo Yuasa (1925–2005), which will be discussed in length in the next chapter. As he confirmed during a personal discussion,[5] as well as in some of his publications (Yuasa 1993), the idea that during an NDE an immaterial soul leaves the body and enters the Divine or Ultimate reality, represents a new contemporary form of dualism, which does not reject *in toto* the previously accepted reductionism that the mind is the brain (ibid.: 41). In order to overcome such a limitation, he attempts to inspire reconciliation between body and mind by offering a new reflection based on the unexplored spiritual potential within the body. Particularly interesting in this respect is his body scheme, which will be discussed in Chapter 7.

Others, such as Susan Blackmore, have criticized the survivalist hypothesis, assuming that the observations made during an NDE could be explained as a combination of 'information available at that time, prior knowledge, fantasy or dreams, and lucky guesses, and information from the remaining senses' (Blackmore 1996b: 480). Chris French (2005) has stated that these arguments have to be approached with care because they deal with memories of an event and not with a direct experience. In this sense, 'false' memories could play a central role, especially when these were reported in long-term retrospective studies. His argument is supported by results in experimental research, which have shown that eyewitness testimony is unreliable, including the testimony of anomalous experiences. An exception to his observation is represented by those interviewed immediately after the experience, such as after recovery from cardiac arrest (e.g. Parnia *et al.* 2001; Sartori 2005).

7

Rethinking embodiment

In the concluding chapter of *Religion, Spirituality and the Near-Death Experience* (2003), Mark Fox observes that 'twenty-five years after the coining of the actual phrase "near-death experience", it remains to be established beyond doubt that during such an experience anything leaves the body' (ibid.: 340). One of the reasons for the continuing uncertainty could be that the research directions taken so far have been epistemologically insufficient to handle the complex nature of the experience. We may wonder: 'Has something important been left out of the discussion?' As a contribution to this field of enquiry, I would now like to put forward a set of observations to support a theory of embodiment. I shall attempt to open the door to a new perspective on the NDE, one designed to bring out the non-dualistic, non-reductionist nature of the experience. For you to fully appreciate this new view, I invite you to suspend for a moment any knowledge or beliefs you may have about the near-death experience. The discussion will be strongly influenced by an Asian, more specifically, a Japanese, theory of mind–body, which rejects any kind of dualism. As we have seen, essential to this approach is the view that bodily activities are primarily considered in terms of space (*basho*) rather than time. In some ways, this viewpoint contradicts a common Western notion of embodiment in which 'time' (mind) is primary and 'space' (body) is secondary (Yuasa 1993). Watsuji (1978) called the characteristic of spatial or environmental relatedness a state of 'between-ness' (*aidagara*), which he considered to be the foundation of our being. The relevance of this approach is validated by recent developments, especially in neuroscience, in which consciousness, far from being considered a neural correlate (NCC), has been recognized as dependent on the dynamic interrelations between self, others and the surrounding environment (Varela *et al.* 1991; Panksepp 1998; Damasio 1999; Zahavi 1999; Thompson 2001). This realization is a fundamental prerequisite for removing those barriers that separate mental from physical phenomena.

The body as a higher form of knowledge

We humans have a terrible habit. We tend to identify ourselves with our rational minds. This puts a great limitation on us, a trap that condemns us to think that we 'have', rather than we 'are' our bodies. According to an Asian, especially Japanese view, the rational self, or the one that answers to our name, is only a superficial part of ourselves, which we tend to assume is the entirety, when in fact it is only a small part of an immense manifestation of activities, both physical and mental, of which we are normally unaware. If we look at this phenomenon from a transcendental point of view, it would probably be correct to say that the superficial self has mistakenly usurped the place of a timeless universal entity that Yuasa called 'Bright Consciousness' (Yuasa 1993). Metaphorically speaking, we are icebergs floating in the deep sea, with one-fifth above the surface and four-fifths below. However, we usually assume that the totality of ourselves is just the one-fifth above. The NDEs are a manifestation of the remaining four-fifths. It may sound a paradox when put in words, but as we have seen in the previous chapters, it is an insight to be taken from the accounts of those who reported these kinds of experiences (or at least some of them), and it can be a meaningful insight for everyone. These people felt a strong sense of unity with the universe, and some of them took part in the fabrication of the universe itself, as if they were able to understand its constitutive principle by means of the principle within the self. But how do we relate to this totality? And, overall, how is it possible to explain such a relationship in terms of embodiment? To start with, I would like to assume the point of view of the body as experienced 'from within'. When considered in this way, the body becomes an indefinite entity, which is always changing and has no physical boundaries or delimitation such as the skin. I have called this the 'extended body' (Corazza 2007c).

Within such a wider and more comprehensive, or 'holistic', notion of the body, the near-death experience no longer challenges one's understanding of what it means to be human.

Extended bodies

This more 'holistic' perspective on the body has been extensively studied by Hiroshi Ichikawa (1931–2002). His primary objective was to reveal 'the nakedness of Being' by looking at the phenomenon that he called the 'body-space', namely the body that is extended in space. As Nagatomo remarks, his aim was to 'elevate the human body, long degraded within the Western philosophical tradition, to the dignity of the spirit' (Nagatomo 1992: 3). In his book *The Body as the Spirit*, published in 1979, Ichikawa argued in favor of the unity of spirit and body by supporting the view that the body is the spirit, a counter-thesis to the well-known Cartesian dualism where mind and body are conceived as kinds of extremes. According to Ichikawa: 'our concrete life in its great part is spent within a structure which cannot be reduced either to the spirit or to the body' (ibid.: 5). This being the case, 'we should consider this unique structure itself as fundamental, and regard the spirit and the body as aspects abstracted from it' (ibid.: 5). The idea that the 'body *is* the spirit' must then be understood in terms of some 'fundamental structure' that allows us to understand the sense of unity, which according to Ichikawa, embraces both the spirit and the body. His starting point was the understanding of the body as 'lived from within', which far from being a disembodied being focusing on intellect or rationality, 'carries the sense of the subject being incarnate or embodied, while, nevertheless, simultaneously being an epistemological center of consciousness' (ibid.: 5). Ichikawa characterizes it as follows:

> Although it is not quite an appropriate expression, we live it from within, grasping it immediately. This body is a basis (*kitai*) for our action, penetrating through a bright horizon of consciousness to an obscure, hazy horizon. It is always present in front of, or rather *with* us. In spite of this, or because of this, it in itself remains without being brought to awareness. In this sense, we should say that we do not *have* the body, but we *are* the body.
>
> (ibid.: 6)

Ichikawa proposed a threefold classification of what it means 'to be a body'. The first category is called the 'innate body-space' (*seitoku-teki shintai kūkan*). This can be defined as the body delimited by the skin that we see reflected when we look at ourselves in a mirror. The second category that Ichikawa identifies is the 'semi-definite body-space' (*junkōsei-teki shintai kūkan*). This is the body that expands through the use of tools. A classic example is the stick in the hand of a blind person. In this case, the stick becomes an extension of the blind person's arm. At the same time, a computer can be seen as an extension of the brain, a telephone as an extension of the voice, a pen as an extension of the finger. When you drive your car, you may perceive the car as an extension of your legs, or when you wear your clothes, you may perceive them as an extension of your skin, as so on. According to this approach, we humans work via extensions.

The third category is what Ichikawa defines as the 'indefinitely varying body-space' (*fukaku-teki na kahen-teki shintai kūkan*). Going far beyond the previous two body-spaces, it has three main characteristics: (1) it is always changing; (2) it is temporary; and (3) it is non-habitual.

One of the most outstanding aspects of Ichikawa's theory is that it conceives of the human body in terms of 'corporeal extensions', which articulate themselves on these three different levels. This view has several implications for consciousness studies, particularly in the field of visual perception (O'Regan and Noë 2001). For instance, we currently know that the perception of visual space does not arise from a unified model of space in the brain, but from numerous spatial maps, many of which are located in the cortical areas involved in the control of bodily movements (for instance, of the eyes, arms, and so on) (Rizzolatti *et al.* 1994). This basically means that experiential space is not a uniform container, but rather a medium molded by our sensory and moving bodies: our movements 'progressively carve out a working space from undifferentiated visual information' and this 'movement-based space ... becomes then our experiential peripersonal visual space' (Rizzolatti *et al.* 1997: 191). In more general terms, some current studies on visual perception have hypothesized that seeing is a way of acting: it is visually guided exploration of the world (Thompson 2001). As Kevin O'Regan and Alva Noë put it in a recent article: 'activity in internal representations does not generate the experience of seeing ... the experience of seeing occurs when the organism masters what we call the governing laws of sensorimotor contingency' (O'Regan and Noë 2001). In this respect, Ichikawa has suggested that when we touch an object, for instance, a pen, the perception of it does not happen passively on the *surface* of our body, but it is rather the manifestation of a bodily 'extension' towards it (in Nagatomo 1992: 13–15). In other words, we are able to detect the pen's shape and/or hardness not by mere contact with the surface of our hand but rather by means of a corporeal extension toward it, or what he called a 'bodily dialogue' (*shintai teki taiwa*) (Ichikawa, in Nagatomo 1992: 13). This hypothesis has been supported by James Gibson's finding that we will score high (about 95 per cent) in the recognition of objects when we touch them (active touching), but we will score low (about 45 per cent) when we are touched by the objects (passive touching) (Gibson 1966). From Ichikawa's point of view, in the absence of a 'dialogue' with the object of our intention, we will not be able to determine a depth (or an 'inner horizon') to things around us. In recognition of this characteristic, we do not make contact with the world by means of the *surface* of the perceptual organs, nor do we passively receive a given stimulus from the external world. As Nagatomo observed: 'the latter is implied by the phrase body dialogue, since a dialogue is by definition a dialogue only when two or more participants are actively engaged' (Ichikawa, in Nagatomo 1992: 13).

In our everyday life, we are largely unaware of this bodily 'dialogue', which acts on a pre-noetic (or 'pre-reflective') level of consciousness. Following Ichikawa, this is characterized by an intentional structure, which is constitutive of consciousness (ibid.: 46).

The notion that a human organism can extend beyond its physical boundaries is radically different from a conventional viewpoint, according to which our perceptions of external objects are supposed to be located inside our heads, rather than outside it, and experienced there by an inner subject.

This idea has been called the 'Cartesian Theater', a metaphorical movie screen on which the drama of conscious experience unfolds before its viewing Cartesian subject (Dennett 1991: 39). In contrast, Ichikawa has a more dynamic understanding in which perception is held to reach out and actively engage with the world:

> The retina does not directly touch the objects that make up the land-scape, for example, but the act of visual perception extends as far as these objects seen, enabling the individual to feel depth in the scenery. Therefore, as visual perception is lived, it extends to the objects seen.
>
> (Ichikawa, in Nagatomo 1992: 13)

Additional evidence for this position emerges from the fact that babies are born with interpersonal body schemas for facial imitation. A growing number of studies have shown that newborns (less than an hour old in some cases) can imitate the facial gestures of another person (see, for instance, Meltzoff and Moore 1999). This phenomenon, also known as 'invisible imitation', supports the view that infants use parts of their bodies (invisible to themselves) to imitate the movements of others. For this kind of imitation to be possible, the infants must be able to match a visual display outside them (in this case, the facial movements of others). Therefore, there must be an underlying 'bodily scheme' which organizes experiences of their own bodily positions and movements, to which the newborn can relate the gestures of the other person. If imitation requires a scheme, then this scheme should be present from birth, rather than being an infant's acquisition as Piaget has postulated (1962). As I will note in the next section, Yasuo Yuasa identified this as the level of kinesthesis in his body scheme.

Yasuo Yuasa's body-scheme

This more holistic perspective on what it means to be a human being will now be discussed in terms of 'body-scheme'. In phenomenology, the concept was first introduced by Merleau-Ponty, who recognized the centrality of the *lived* body, or the 'habit body' (*le corps habituel*) as a built-in-body-scheme (*le schéma corporeal*). Its primary function is to integrate all the somatic sensations, which form the basis of kinesthesis (see below), and to direct them toward the thing-event of the external world. An elaboration of Merleau-Ponty's scheme has been presented in more recent years by Yasuo Yuasa, who incorporates an Asian mind–body theory. According to Professor Yuasa, the body is endowed with multi-layered information circuits, which have been largely ignored in the Western tradition, and for this reason his approach remains relatively exceptional. This model, known as Yuasa's body-scheme, can bring new insights to the field of near-death studies because it gives particular importance to bodily unconscious activities. In contrast, these were left implicit in Merleau-Ponty's body-scheme.

Yuasa's body-scheme regards the *living* body as a system of information, which constantly renews itself and is analysable in terms of energy phenomena, 'because if information passes through a circuit, there must be a carrier of this information, and this carrier must be understood as energy-phenomena' (Nagatomo 1992: 60). This concept of energy is too complex to be defined clearly and will probably be one of the major areas to be developed in the future. In Yuasa's view, the body-scheme is constituted of four main information sub-systems, which will now be discussed. These are: (1) the sensory-motor level; (2) the kinaesthetic body; (3) the autonomic nervous system; and (4) the unconscious quasi-body.

The functioning of these four circuits is particularly useful when we try to understand the sense of oneness, which is achieved in some Asian traditions of self-cultivation. As Nagatomo commented:

> Yuasa offers a comprehensive and deeper analysis of the body than most philosophers, East and West, have thus far provided. His concept of body-scheme purports to explicate the inseparability and the oneness of the lived body-mind as it is *achieved* through the Eastern *praxis* of personal self-cultivation.
>
> (1992: 59)

In our everyday life we are constantly engaged in an infinite number of outside perceptions. We meet people, we talk, we eat, we listen to music, we enjoy ourselves in many other ways. Following Yuasa, these perceptions are the setting of our first information system, which connects the body with the external world. He calls it the 'external sensory-motor circuit' (*gaikai kankaku undō kairo*) (Yuasa 1993: 43).

On a 'sensory' level, our sensory organs constantly receive information from the external world through the nervous system. This is a *passive* function. For instance, when we hear a song we love, our ears send it to the brain by converting it into a series of impulses (an information input) traveling through the sensory nerves. On a 'motor' level, our motor organs (our hands and our feet) act in the world. This is an *active* function. Once the brain receives a stimulus transmitted from the sensory organs, various centres respond to it by sending an information output to the motor nerves, which control the muscles in the limbs. In response to the song, we may start to move or dance. This is called a 'circuit' because it incorporates a process of information that leads inwards and then returns outwards:

> When the sensory organs such as the eyes or ears receive a stimulus entering from the outside, they send it to the brain by converting it into an

impulse (an information input) travelling through the sensory nerves (for example, an optical nerve) . . . When the brain receives a sensory stimulus from the distal organs, various sensory centres in the cortex respond to it, and synthesizing the information in the frontal lobe, the brain forms a judgment. When a situation in the external world is recognized by means of this process, the frontal lobe sends out a centrifugal impulse (an information output) by way of the motor nerves, which control the muscle of the limbs.

(ibid.: 43)

Henri Bergson (1859–1941) examined this circuit in detail and called it 'the sensory-motor apparatus' (*les appareils sensori-moteurs*). He thought it was designed for the 'utility of life', such as everyday activities. Eating, walking, dancing are all actions that relate to the external world and therefore involve a 'sensory-motor circuit' (*un circuit sensori-moteur*). Similarly, Maurice Merleau-Ponty (1908–1961) calls this the 'sensory motor circuit' (1962: 102). In the opening section of his most important work, *The Phenomenology of Perception* (1962), he wrote: 'Our own body is in the world as the heart in the organism; it keeps the spectacle constantly alive, it breathes life into it and sustains it inwardly, and with it forms a system' (ibid.: 203). The body represents for Merleau-Ponty the first instrument through which we 'act' upon the world that is already given (material world) and the world that is coming to birth (mental representation of it). In this sense, for him as well as for Bergson, the functioning of the 'sensory-motor circuit' constitutes the most fundamental aspect of the human being.

The second system of information is linked to the relationship between perceptual cognition and action. Yuasa calls it the 'circuit of coenesthesis' (*zenshin naibu kankaku kairo*) (Yuasa 1993: 45). It deals with internal sensations of the body, and mainly consists of two circuits: (1) the circuit of *kinesthesis*; and (2) the circuit of *somesthesis*. The former is connected to the motor nerves through which the cerebral cortex sends commands to the four limbs (hands and legs). The muscles and the tendons in the motor organs are equipped with sensory-motor nerves, which inform the brain of their condition. Called the 'circuit of *kinesthesis*', this is the information system that supports 'from below' the working of the 'external sensory-motor circuit'. In other words, it lies on the *periphery* of the so-called ego-consciousness, and it is linked to functions such as thinking, willing, feeling and imagining. Nevertheless it would be a mistake to consider it as limited to these functions since the kinesthesis is directed towards the world. The founder of phenomenology, Edmund Husserl (1859–1938) spent much of his time on the problem of the 'kinaesthetic body', which occupies an important place in his published and unpublished work. As he wrote: 'The kinesthesis of the body is existing latently at the base of the intentional functioning of consciousness' (Husserl 1973: 84–5). Its important role within the functioning of the human body has also been analysed in terms of 'passive synthesis', 'intentionality', or 'pre-reflective' (or 'pre-noetic') experience, which is a mode of consciousness prior to that of self-awareness. Inheriting the idea from Husserl, Merleau-Ponty proposed the concept of *body-scheme*, which took him to new mind–body theories. At the heart of this concept lies the relationship between the body and the world, perception and action, or sensation and movement.

A second circuit concerning the inner condition of the body is the *circuit of somesthesis*, in which the nerves send the information to the brain on the condition of the organs. This system comes to our attention, for instance, when we are sick. Then at this time we are able to distinguish various parts of our body, such as the heart, lungs and stomach, which otherwise remain generally unnoticed. In a broader sense, it can be conceived of as a feedback apparatus. In short, we can say that coenesthesis is the awareness of one's body condition.

The combination of somesthesis and kinesthesis gives rise to what is called *coenesthesis*, which, following Yuasa, is our second circuit (Yuasa 1993: 47). What is most important about this circuit is that it maintains a constant link with an automatic memory. For instance, when we learn to perform a dance thorough repeated practice, we reach a stage in which our body *knows* immediately what the next move will be, that is, unconsciously and without requiring any thought. As Yuasa has put it:

> There is *an automatic memory system* at the base of consciousness for judgment, which stores past data, and checking a failed datum, it directs the datum in order for it to be a successful (execution) next time. The repetition of this process is training. In other words, training is to *habituate* the body in a definite direction. For this purpose, the capacity of the memory system must be enhanced.
>
> (Yuasa, in Nagatomo 1992: 62)

This means that the connection between coenesthesis and the automatic memory system, both of which belong to consciousness, does not require any conscious effort of recall: the body *learns and knows* by itself.

In many ways, this idea reflects the concept that Merleau-Ponty called 'habit-body' (*le corps habituel*) and Bergson called 'learned memory' (*le souvenir appris*), both of which designate an internalization of bodily movement for the utility of life (Nagatomo 1992: 63). Such ideas may enrich the contemporary debates on consciousness, in which the psychophysiological functions of the human body are largely left out.

The third information system in Yuasa's body-scheme is the circuit of the 'autonomic' nervous system, which is called the 'emotion-instinct circuit' (*jōdō honnō kairo*). Yuasa wrote: 'This circuit has a very close relationship with human instincts such as sexual desire and appetite. For this reason, I call it the emotion-instinct circuit' (1993: 49). It has the function of maintaining life. When the first circuit (external sensory-motor) is not active, as in the case of anesthesia, the emotion-instinct circuit is still functioning. In the absence of the latter, we have no life. Compared to the others, this circuit remains largely unexplored (along with the somesthesis of the second circuit). Investigations remain focused on the first two levels. Its 'autonomic' function is an unconscious function, which, seen from a psychophysiological point of view, cannot be specifically located in any section of the brain or body. Because of the difficulty in studying this circuit, many contemporary researchers have abandoned reductionism and moved to correlative dualism, taking the mind to exist independently of the brain (body).

There are still many unresolved issues concerning the problem of the third level, the emotion-instinct circuit. Most attention has been paid to the first circuit and to the kinesthesis of the second circuit.

A major difference between the function of the external sensory-motor circuit and the autonomic nervous system is that the former is voluntary, while the latter is usually not. For instance, anyone can decide to shut off, to a certain extent, the stimuli received through the sensory organs, but we cannot control the activity of other internal organs, such as the pulsation of the heart or the digestive function of the stomach, which are performed independent of the will, and most of the time we are unaware of these. For instance, on an airplane we can use ear-plugs to reduce the noise, or we can wear an eye mask to block out the light. But usually we cannot stop the rhythm of our breathing in order to avoid the peculiar smell of the passenger sitting next to us. Most of the activity of the 'autonomic nervous system' is thus unconscious. The term 'autonomic' itself suggests that the activity is self-regulated, independent of the will. In this regard, Ivan Pavlov (1849–1936) first discovered the above mechanism from a psychological point of view. If a bell is rung whenever a dog is given food, and if this is repeated, the dog starts salivating upon just hearing the bell (a sensory stimulus). A secretion of saliva occurs due to the activity of the parasympathetic nerves in the centre of the medulla oblongata. This is usually an autonomic function, occurring reflexively with food in the mouth as a stimulus. Here there is no direct relationship between hearing the bell (a sensory stimulus to the cortex) and the secretion of saliva (an activity of the autonomic nerves). However, in the case of the dog's Pavlovian conditioned reflex, which occurs only upon repeated reception of a stimulus (food), secretion can now occur at just the sound of the bell. This is a reflex conditioned through habituation. In this case, the stimulus to the sensory organ and the activity of the autonomic nerves are connected by the function of emotion rooted in instinct.

To explain this example in term of the three body-information systems, we can say that the information entering the first circuit (external sensory-motor) reaches the third circuit (emotion-instinct). An emotional response to the information rebounds back to the second circuit (coenesthesis), which habituates the body, thereby establishing a connection between these three circuits. The important point in this example is that the function of emotion creates a new temporary circuit, which connects the cerebral cortex (and its sensory-nerve input) with the cortex beneath it (autonomic nerves).

In other words, Yuasa's schematization suggests that the control that one can exercise on these circuits decreases as one progresses from the first level to the third level. As Nagatomo observed: 'The difference in control correlates with an awareness of the body which decreases in transparency, or increases in opacity as one moves from the first to the third circuit' (1992: 65–6).

Being more aware of our autonomic system can be very beneficial. This is also the goal of Asian self-cultivation methods, the goal of which, as Yuasa stresses, is to change the patterns of emotional response (i.e., complexes in personality) by controlling emotions and integrating the power of the unconscious (see, for instance, Yuasa 1993).

This goal depends mainly on the body, not the mind, as there can be no conscious will to suppress emotions. For instance, Yuasa emphasizes the importance of breathing exercises, which are fundamental in all forms of Japanese training and self-cultivation methods. In this case, a person can consciously control the rhythm and pattern of their breathing, which consequently will affect the autonomic nervous system which is closely connected to emotion:

> The function of the autonomic nerves is deeply linked to emotions (both positive and negative emotions such as anger, sorrow, hatred, joy, love and peace, that is, pleasure and pain). If the negative emotion is always stressed, a pathological state will result, but on the other hand, if the positive emotion is always strengthened, it will nurture more mature psychological traits (that is, the pattern of emotion as a habit of the mind/heart).
>
> (Yuasa in Nagatomo 1992: 68)

Andrew Weil (1997) points out that a focus on breathing disengages us from our outer thought processes, enlivens us and restores harmony to the whole nervous system. Renee Welfeld (1997) reminds us that each part of the breathing process can also have a symbolic meaning. Each time you inhale, you begin life anew as you re-establish the cycle that initiated life outside the womb. With the space that follows inhalation, the promise of a new beginning can be deeply felt. Exhalation represents the emptying out, a moment of surrender and trust that the next breath will be made available to you again. The moment after the exhalation is a time to pause, reflect and feel a profound sense of well-being, a time to be at the centre of your universe. Celebrate the flow of vitality throughout your system and into your organs.

Again, for a better understanding of this concept we need to examine the relationship between the body and the environment. In our daily life, we receive physical and psychological stimuli from the surrounding environment, and the manner in which we respond to these depends very much upon the individual. In other words, the response will be connected with the emotional response (or habit of the heart-mind) unique to that person. When this emotional response is distorted, a complex is formed, resulting, for instance, in a neurosis. In this case, stimuli from outside enter the body through the external sensory-motor circuit and proceed to influence the functioning of the autonomic nerves.

In summary, there are three main information circuits in this paradigm. The first is the sensory-motor system, which deals with the external world. The second is the circuit of coenesthesis, which is the system of self-apprehending sensation in one's body. The third is the emotion-instinct circuit of the autonomic nervous system, which is connected with the unconscious. Following Yuasa (1993), we can add to these a fourth circuit called the 'unconscious quasi-body', which incorporates a vast region of the mind and body that was only implicit in Merleau-Ponty's body-scheme.[3]

The term 'unconscious' here indicates that this is an *invisible* circuit, which cannot be detected in the ordinary field of consciousness in everyday life, but only in particular altered states of consciousness, such as near-death experiences or meditative states. As Nagatomo has pointed out: 'Awareness of this order remains *dark* and *invisible* to most people under normal circumstances' (2006: 7).

The term 'quasi-body' indicates that the body at this level does not conform to the idea of the body-subject or the body-object, which have been discussed previously. In Yuasa's words:

> This fourth circuit is an *invisible circuit*, insofar as we examine it anatomically, and so it cannot be perceived by means of external perception. And when it is viewed psychologically, it is a *potential circuit below consciousness*, which consciousness in an ordinary circumstance cannot detect.
>
> (Yuasa, in Nagatomo 1992: 69)

Nagatomo suggests that in order to gain access to this deep region of the self, 'we must allow the body to speak to the mind, and a conscious mind must learn to listen to the unconscious. In practical terms, an entry into this order will open up through breathing exercises and meditation' (Nagatomo 2006: 8).

Yuasa has observed that the unconscious quasi-body 'designates a pathway of emotional energy flowing in the unconscious, and is a quasi-body system which activates physiological functions together with the objective body' (Yuasa 1993: 119). However, it may be rather difficult to understand from a Western point of view, when Yuasa talked about 'a pathway of emotional energy' he was referring to the life-force *ki* – or, the Chinese equivalent Qi or *ch'i* – which is said to circulate though an invisible system of channels present in the body, known as ki-meridians, or 'acu-points'.[4] These are essential in treatments such as acupuncture, which aim to support the life-activity of living organisms, and which regard the living body as a comprehensive whole of vital energy or life-energy. This outlook differs from conventional medical practice and biological science, which have tended to have a reductionist and materialist approach to the body. The medicine of *ki*-energy is accepted by many people who are engaged in the practice of alternative medicine (see for instance, Becker 2002).

Ki-energy

In ordinary usage 'ki' means 'air' or 'state of mind'. In ancient Chinese philosophy, 'qi' (or 'ki') referred to the vital energy that fills each human body as well as the whole universe (Shimazono 2004: 287). It is by means of the *ki* that we are 'animate corpses' and through which we interconnect with other human beings and the surrounding world.

Ki-energy is not present in a corpse. It is applicable to various factors such as climatic conditions, an arising social condition, as well as psychological and pathological conditions. For instance, a Japanese person might say that 'heaven's *ki* is bad' when there is bad weather. Or when two persons are getting on well together, they use the expression '*ki ga au*', which literally means that 'ki accords with each other'. In contrast, when a person faces an unstable situation, which generates fears or suspicion, an expression such as '*ki mi ga warui*' may be used, which means 'the taste of ki is bad'.

According to Yuasa, '*Ki* energy has a psychophysiological character that cannot be properly accommodated within the dualistic paradigm of thinking' (Nagatomo 1992: xii). Similarly, Suzuki has pointed out: 'This is a difficult term to translate into English. It is something imperceptible, impalpable that pervades the entire universe' (Suzuki 1959b: 149).

Professor Hiroshi Motoyama has been conducting research in the field of *ki*-energy employing a measuring device that he invented called AMI (Apparatus for Meridian Identification), an apparatus for measuring the function of meridians and their corresponding internal organs.[5]

An example of how *ki*-energy is used in meditation to achieve a *kundalini* experience is given in the following account by Motoyama. After practising meditation for six months, sometimes all day long, he observed:

When I was gathering my consciousness into the lower abdomen in order to balance ki-energy in my body, so that the energy of the upper part of my body would become evenly distributed, while the lower part would be packed with the energy, I suddenly experienced, after engaging in this practice for less than twenty minutes, a pillar of hot and voluminous fire shooting up from the base of my spine through the central tube of my spinal cord. My entire body was scorching hot, and no sooner had I realized it than my body swiftly became afloat twenty to thirty centimetres in mid-air, even though I was still assuming a meditation posture. Although my body was terribly hot and my consciousness was almost hazy, I could clearly grasp the event that was taking place. After ten to twenty seconds, my body descended to the floor with a thump. For about a week after this experience occurred, I felt my entire body to be extremely hot. This was an experience of awakening the *kundalini*.

Prior to this practice I had been engaging in 'winter practices' outside in which I poured buckets of ice-cold water over my body. I did this regularly from toward the end of January through to the beginning of February. I recall myself shivering in the dead of the winter because it was cold. After pouring many buckets of water, I would stand naked in the cold wintry wind for about an hour while praying to God. My body felt like it was frozen; when I pinched the skin of my body, it was like pinching thick plastic. However, after awakening the *kundalini*, I no longer felt cold at all during such 'winter practice', and in fact when I poured buckets of water over my body, I could see white vapors rising from all over the body. I felt good, because my entire body was hot.

After having repeatedly gone through the ecstatic state and the awakening of the *kundalini* for several months, I became able to receive the flow of God without having to enter into any ecstatic state. Consequently, I came to realize that I could exist out of the body while being elevated to the world of God. Accordingly, I gradually became awakened to the world of the divine self [*purusa*] through the power of God. This was the awakening of a super-consciousness of the divine self.

(Motoyama, 2008)

The notion of *ki*-energy, or simply *ki*, without specification that this is a kind of energy, is useful for understanding how mind and body relate. Yuasa wrote:

The substance of the unknown energy *ki* is not within our [present] understanding. It is a flow of a certain kind of energy unique to the living organism which circulates in the body, although it is uncertain yet what generates such a function. To be more specific, when the flow of *ki* is examined psychologically, it can be perceived as an extraordinary sensation, as a lived body's self-grasping sensation in a unique situation on the surface of the circuit of the coenesthesis (e.g. a case of a *ki*-sensitive person).

(Yuasa, in Nagatomo 1992: 70)

The *ki*-meridians operate at the level of the skin, which is also the boundary wall between the internal and the external body.[6]

Yuasa claimed that the function of the quasi-body has an immediate effect on both body and mind and for this reason can be viewed as a 'breakthrough' point capable of transforming the existing scientific paradigm in so far as it is still influenced by Cartesian mind–body dualism:

> The *ki*-meridian system is related closely to both mind and body, both spirit and matter, and is a middle system that influences them. For this reason, it is a third term which cannot be explained by Descartes' mind-body dichotomy, but it forms a mediating system that links the mind and the body. Herein lies, it seems, a *break-through* point that reforms the paradigm of empirical science [established] since Descartes.

(Yuasa, in Nagatomo 1992: 71)

This observation has implications for near-death experiences. During an interview I carried out with Yasuo Yuasa,[7] he suggested that the near-death experience could easily represent a way of access to the unconscious quasi-body. The NDE allows the person to step directly into the unconscious quasi-body. The first three circuits are shut down and the individual's body will die. In the case of the NDE, there is no longer a clear awareness of the external world. Both sensory and motor organs are no longer functioning, or their activity is drastically reduced. In Yuasa's view, this could be the reason for the sense of dying, during which ego-consciousness gradually disappears. After an initial phase of transition, often described as a tunnel experience, the mind arises out of the unconscious quasi-body into what has been described as a different realm or dimension of reality. This emergence allows the person to understand him/herself as a disembodied 'soul' or 'mind'. According to Yuasa, this is because the 'quasi-body' has no anatomical counterpart and our sensory perceptions cannot detect it. Yuasa encouraged further study of this circuit, which he considers to be the most fundamental for maintaining life rather than the body. He often emphasized the connection between the unconscious quasi-body and *ki*-energy, which could possibly explain the strong sense of unity with the cosmos that emerges from both the NDEs and ketamine experiences.

Concluding thoughts

The idea that we are extended in space beyond our conventional boundaries has been little explored in Western thought, and it will probably be one line of enquiry to develop in future research. In many ways, it allows us to glimpse a new world-view by offering us a better understanding not only of what we are, but also of what we can be. As Michael Murphy has pointed out in *The Future of the Body* (1992), the body is endowed with extraordinary capacities, the manifestation of which makes us aware of our general ignorance about the reaches of human nature. Scientific discoveries have contributed to a deeper knowledge of the self and the universe around us, bestowing upon us knowledge and understanding that was unavailable in earlier times. The challenge of the future will be to gather together evidence of our extraordinary ability to connect with the universe, so that it can be seen and known as a whole. Fundamental to this new perspective is an Asian view of embodiment according to which the body cannot be considered apart from place (*basho*), which represents the 'ground of our being'. Evidence for this has emerged in the present research from the accounts of those who had profound transcendental experiences as a result of close encounters with death or through the effects of dissociative drugs such as ketamine. Some reported a powerful sense of harmony and unity with the universe, and even a sense of taking part in the 'fabrication' of the universe. Some had the impression of dying and entering other realms of reality where they met God or other beings.

In many ways, the value of these experiences goes far beyond the question of scientific proof of an afterlife and brings us directly to our immediate experience of the here-and-now and the sense of meaning and purpose that we may experience in this life. It also goes beyond reductionism and the attempt to locate the soul or consciousness in some part of the brain. Even more profoundly, the experiences can suggest to us that what we label 'I' is only a small part of a deeper intelligence that is immanent within all creation. They invite us to recognize and seek out this intelligence or power that seems to reach within and extend beyond the physical body, which, as William Blake reminds us, is a portion of Soul discerned by the five Senses, the chief inlets of Soul in this age.

Notes

I The mind–body connection

1 Some of the arguments presented in this chapter were published as a lecture series in O. Corazza (2008) *The Japanese Philosophy of the Body*, University of Wales, Lampeter, and discussed at the international workshop 'Rethinking Embodiment', which she organized for the Centre for the Study of Japanese Religion (CSJR) at the School of Oriental and African Studies (SOAS), University of London, in June 2006.

2 This dictum first appeared in the fourth section of the *Discourse on the Method* (1637) and later in the first part of the *Principles of Philosophy* (1644).

3 *Discourse*, 1637, in R. Descartes (1979), *The Philosophical Works of Descartes*, vol. 1, trans. Elizabeth S. Haldane and G.R.T. Ross, Cambridge: Cambridge University Press, p. 101.

4 Even today, very little is known about the functions of the pineal gland. As Rick Strassman has pointed out:

> The pineal gland of evolutionarily older animals, such as lizards and amphibians, is also called the 'third eye'. Just like the two seeing eyes, the third eye possesses a lens, corneas, and a retina. It is light sensitive and helps to regulate body temperature and skin coloration. Melatonin, the primary pineal hormone, is present in primitive pineal glands. As animals climbed the evolutionary ladder, the pineal moved inward, deeper into the brain, more hidden from outside influences. While the bird pineal no longer sits on top of the skull, it remains sensitive to outside light because of the paper-thin surrounding bones. The mammalian, including human, pineal is buried even deeper in the brain's recesses and it is not directly sensitive to light, at least in adults.
>
> (2001: 60)

Interestingly, the human pineal gland becomes visible in the developing fetus at seven weeks, or 49 days, after conception. As Strassman observed: 'This is nearly exactly the moment in which one can clearly see the first indication of male or female gender. Before this time the sex of the fetus is indeterminate' (ibid.: 61).

5 *Kami* in Japanese Shinto religion is a divine force of nature. These are anthropomorphic with human forms and actions (rather than being referred to a location, a rock, a mountain). According to some calculations, there are more than eight million gods in the Japanese tradition. As gods, they often appear – to borrow Nietzsche's phrase – 'human, all too human'. In fact, Japanese *kami* were thought to be once humans. Divinized ancestors have, in a sense, the prerogative of being

'all too human' simply because they still are. Sometimes they resemble the gods of the ancient Greeks – not only are they many but also because they can be vain, angry, passionate, resentful, and so on (LaFleur 1992: 55).

6 In a way, Watsuji's interest in space is a response to Martin Heidegger's emphasis on temporality, which he well expressed in his *Being and Time*. As Watsuji commented: 'His attempt to grasp the structure of man's existence as temporality was extremely interesting, but my concern was this: while temporality is presented as the subject's (*shutaiteki*) structure of being, why is not spatiality equally well presented as a fundamental structure of human being?'

7 This refers to the phenomenon in which a limb is lost but feels as if it is still there. The limb is a phantom, but it feels real.

8 Francisco Varela, from a videotape recorded on January 7, 2001, from *RAI Educational*, Italy.

2 Journeys in the afterlife

1 From personal correspondence with Yoshi Honda, Assistant Director of the Yoko Civilization Research Institute in Japan.

2 The *Kojiki* was completed in 712 AD. Until then, the ancient Shinto beliefs were not recorded in writing, but rather transmitted by an oral tradition. The idea of writing down the religious beliefs, the property of the ancient Chinese system, was probably introduced to Japan by Buddhist missionaries sent by the King of Korea from 522 AD.

3 *Kojiki*, trans. Philippi (1968: 61).

4 Ibid., p. 62.

5 Ibid., p. 68.

6 Ibid., p. 68.

7 Albert Heim, in a paper given at the Swiss Alpine Club in 1892, 'Remarks on fatal falls', trans. R. Noyes and R. Kletti, *Omega* 3.

8 The *Myth of Er*, narrated in Plato's *Republic*, Book 10.

9 Karl Jansen, personal communication, April 2006.

10 The Church of England Doctrine Commission (1995) has recently rejected the idea of hell as a place of fire, pitchforks and screams of unending agony, describing it as essentially a point of complete isolation (i.e. as a non-place, devoid of coordinates) for those who reject the love of God.

11 According to Varela:

> [The term] *bardo* (Sanskrit *antarābhava*) refers generally to the intermediate state between death and rebirth, where the mindstream wanders in the form of a 'mental body' while seeking a new embodiment. The *bardo* is considered to be an important opportunity for tantric practice, for it is at the point of transition from death into the *bardo* that the clear light nature of consciousness becomes manifest. Likewise, during the *bardo*, the mind experiences numerous appearances, said to be in the form of peaceful and wrathful deities. If the practitioner can realize these appearances as the nature of the mind itself, he or she can attain liberation.
>
> (1998: 228)

12 This is the period of time of the *Bardo* of becoming. A particular emphasis on spiritual practice is given to the first 21 days.

13 See W.Y. Evans-Wentz (ed.), *The Tibetan Book of the Dead, or the After-Death Experiences on the Bardo Plane, according to Lama Kazi Dawa-Samdup's English Rendering* (1927, 3rd edn, London: Oxford University Press, 1957).

14 Interestingly, this is never from below.
15 An exception is found in the work of Johann Christophe Hampe, who in his *To Die Is Gain* (1979), argues that the return to the body takes place via a reversal of the process by which they left. For instance, if subjects journeyed along a tunnel, they return though a tunnel. As he wrote about a case in his study: 'once more he experiences night, the black tunnel, and then what we call waking up' (Hampe 1979: 90).
16 The occasion was a panel discussion entitled 'Spirituality, Life and the Body' at Professor Motoyama's Institute in Tokyo in October 2004.
17 In this regard, Motoyama observed:

> Although it is not the customary practice in academic scholarship to cite personal experience in order to illustrate a point which an author wishes to make, I will cite my own experiences because I believe they are unique and valuable for learning about the nature of mystical experience and what it means for the academic investigation on this topic.
>
> (Motoyama 2008)

3 The river of no return

1 Part of this chapter has been published as 'The Spirit of Place: Visions of the Afterlife in Japan', in F. Cariglia (ed.) (2007) *Sopravvivere: Il velato destino della personalità*. Proceedings of the 11th International Congress on Borderland Experiences, San Marino, pp. 23–8.
2 The full form of this account was published in their article, 'Near-Death Experiences in India: a preliminary report', *Journal of Nervous and Mental Diseases*, 174 (1986): 165–70.
3 See Chapter 2, note 2.
4 *Kojiki*, trans. Philippi (1968: 61).
5 Ibid., p. 62.
6 Ibid., p. 68.
7 Ibid., p. 68.
8 Interestingly, Professor Shigetoshi Osano made a parallel with the Hell in *The Divine Comedy* of Dante Alighieri (Osano 2003: 19).
9 *Anime* is a word commonly used to describe Japanese animation.
10 For instance, the deep emotional affinity between persons and nature is well expressed in the classic texts of ancient Japan such as *Man'yōshū, Kojiki* and *Tale of Genji*.
11 An example is given by divination, which involves offerings of natural goods such as fruits and eggs.
12 Etymologically, there are several doubts about the origin of the world *Sai*. The most likely hypothesis is that it may originally have been written with a Chinese ideograph meaning 'boundary' (LaFleur 1992: 230).
13 *Basho* literally means 'place' (*Platz* in German).
14 At the center of temporal consciousness lies the self-consciousness of the individual. This consciousness of self-identity remains present during the passage of time and it exists from birth to death of the self. The idea of self-consciousness is viewed as inauthentic in Eastern philosophies as well as in Buddhism. More specifically, Eastern mind and body theories say that we should rather note the relationship between the body and space which underlies and substantially restricts the time-consciousness appearing on the surface of consciousness within the field of ordinary experience.

15 As Nishida wrote:

> The logic of place, which is Absolute Nothingness, neither confronts object-ive logic nor excludes it. Place reflects all individuals and their mutually determining way of being within itself and realizes them as its own self-determination . . . The logic of place is not the form of thinking of the subjective self. Rather, it is the form of the self-expression of Reality.
>
> (ibid.: 371)

For him, only a logic of place allows transcendence because it connects us with what is prior to, and source of, both seeing and knowing and that which is seen and known. At the basis of Nishida's notion of place is that the individual is the self-determination of the universal (place or Absolute Nothingness) and as such transcends generic concepts. Such a view is in radical contrast to Western 'object-ive logic', which, strictly speaking, never fully transcends the individual structure.

16 The terms 'container' and 'envelope' were often used by Edward Casey in order to describe place (Casey 1982; 1988).

17 This is a common argument in Zen in order to emphasize the pre-reflective experi-ence, rather than being a statement about the nature of the universe (Kasulis 1981: 86).

18 *Zazen* literally means 'seated meditation'. In Zen, this practice aims to calm the body and the mind in order to achieve a state of 'without-thinking'.

19 Dōgen Kigen, *Dōgen zenji zenshū* [Complete Works of Zen Master Dōgen], vol. 1, p. 90.

20 At that time, there was a trend in philosophy based on 'pure positivity' starting with the emergence of a new philosophy represented by Wilhelm Wundt (1832–1920) and William James (1842–1910) in the United States, as well as Gustav Theodor Fechner (1801–1887) and Ernst Mach (1838–1916). They all advocated a new form of empiricism, which Wilhelm Wundt called 'pure experience', James 'radical empiricism', and Mach 'empirico-criticism'. Their attempts were to reduce experience to its pure and direct form. In this context, Nishida wrote his first book called *An Inquiry into the Good* (1990).

21 In order to grasp the essence of the subjective existence, and to drop into the core of pure experience, Nishida looked at Greek philosophy, and took up Aristotle's *hypokeimenon*, where reality is perceived not in the direction of consciousness, but in the direction of objects. Aristotle's notion of the individual is a *seen* indi-vidual, not an active one and thus based on the logic of objective thinking. Nishida went beyond this view, which for him was insufficient. An individual is not only a single individual, but has to be understood in the dynamic interaction between two or a myriad of acting individuals. He argued that the individual is charac-terized by the *place* where it lies, and this place must be sought in the field con-sciousness of 'transcendental predicates'.

4 Meeting God in a nightclub?

1 The pharmaceutical company, which was previously a subsidiary of Warner-Lambert, was absorbed into Pfizer in 2000 and other licensed companies such as Fort Dodge.

2 As mentioned in Jansen (2001) *Ketamine: Dreams and Realities*, p. 98.

3 *Mixmag*, February 2006.

4 *DrugScope* is the UK's leading centre of expertise on drugs. The aim of the organization is to inform policy and reduce drug-related risk. It mainly provides

quality information, promotes responses to drug taking and undertakes research at local, national and international level.

5 Interview, 'Special K, the horse pill taking over from ecstasy among clubbers', *The Guardian*, Tuesday, 6 September 2005.

6 Interview, 'Government moves to control ketamine', *The Guardian*, Monday, 30 May 2005.

7 Ibid.

8 For additional information, see *Decreto Ministeriale* 8/2/2001, http://gazzette.comune.jesi.an.it/2001/194/2.htm

9 For instance, when injected intramuscularly (IM) (50–100 mg), the first effects start quickly in less than two minutes and they will last for about an hour. When taken intranasally (the most common route of consumption among recreational users, in 'lines' of 20–50mg each), the effects commence within 5–10 minutes and last for about 30 minutes. They last much longer when taken orally, but the first awareness of the effects begins in 15–20 minutes. Intravenous injection is relatively uncommon (recreationally). It is essentially identical in effect to IM injection, but leads to a much quicker onset – usually within 10–15 seconds of dosing.

10 *The Guardian*, Tuesday, 6 September 2005.

11 The web-site was www.ornellacorazza.com

12 Susan Blackmore, 'I take illegal drugs for inspiration', *Daily Telegraph*, 21 May 2005, pp. 17–18.

13 'Nobel Prize genius Crick was high on LSD when he discovered the secret of life', *Mail on Sunday*, 8 August 2004.

14 She made a buzzing sound to help her description.

15 *Matryoshka doll*, or a Russian nested doll, is a set of dolls of decreasing sizes placed one inside another. Its name is a diminutive form of a Russian female name 'Matryona'. A set of *Matryoshka* dolls consists of a wooden figure which can be pulled apart to reveal another figure of the same sort inside. It has in turn another figure inside, and so on. The number of nested figures is usually six or more. The shape is mostly cylindrical, rounded at the top for the head and tapered towards the bottom, but little else; the dolls have no hands (except those that are painted). The artistry is in the painting of each doll, which can be extremely elaborate. *Matryoshka* dolls are often designed to follow a particular theme, for instance, peasant girls in traditional dress, but the theme can be almost anything, ranging from fairy tale characters to Soviet leaders (from 'Matryoshka Doll', Wikipedia).

16 There is some evidence that women are more likely to have a more significant experience than men when given ketamine (reviewed by Jansen 2001: 55).

5 Gaining new insights

1 RERC (formerly RERU, the Religious Experience Research Unit) was founded in 1966 by Sir Alister Hardy. Its aim was to contribute to the understanding of transcendental, spiritual or religious experiences, their role in the evolution of consciousness and religious reflection, and their impact upon individual lives and on society. He initially collected and classified around 4,000 accounts of contemporary religious experiences (Franklin 2006). Today the RERC Archive contains over 6,000 accounts.

2 A few preliminary remarks about this terminology are in order here. Although the idea may seem strange at first glance, the concept of 'being-in-a-place' can be framed within the context of the Western phenomenological tradition. Thus, Martin Heidegger (1962) proposed 'being-in-the-world' (*In-der-Welt-sein*) as a fundamental mode of our existence. A major difference between the state of 'being-in-the-world'

and the state of 'being-in-a-place' concerns directionality. While 'being-in-the-world' refers to an outer space, 'being-in-a-place' refers to an inner space: the ability to function in the outer world by those who report the experiences under study here is drastically reduced (e.g. by a heart attack or anesthetic). In phenomenological terms, the *Dasein's* activity of *Verstehen* (the German word for 'understanding' – in rational terms) is no longer functioning. In a sense, the 'being-in-a-place' forms a lower stratum on which the 'being-in-the world' takes place. Similarly, Japanese phenomenologist Hiroshi Ichikawa spoke about the phenomenon of 'being-in-an-ambience' (Ichikawa 1979).

3 A 1982 Gallup poll found that the belief in an afterlife is synonymous with belief in heaven. It was also found that in the United States 77 per cent of those who believe in the afterlife believe in heaven and 64 per cent thought they had a good possibility of going there; 34 per cent of doctors and 8 per cent of scientists were found to believe in the existence of heaven (Gallup 1982).

4 The term *feng-shui* literally means 'wind and water' and symbolizes the subtle energies that flow through the environment.

5 Anthropologist Edward Hall made a distinction between fast and slow forms of communication (Hall 1959). He classified as 'fast messages' those received from a cartoon, a headline, a TV commercial, propaganda, and so on, while 'slow messages' are those received from a book, poetry, art, TV documentary, and so on. He also observed that 'a fast message sent to people who are geared to slow format will usually miss the target' (ibid.: 5).

6 Glutamate is responsible for nerve signalling, passing messages in a chain from one neuron to another. As a signal reaches the end of one neuron, a neurotransmitter is released. The neurotransmitter then attaches to the receptors, the proteins located on the surface of the next neuron, in the same way that a key fits a lock. Glutamate promotes the firing of neurons.

7 Personal correspondence with Dr Karl Jansen.

6 Where have you been?

1 The term 'lavender' comes from the Latin root *lavare*, which means to 'to wash'.

2 Thursday, 10 July 2003, 'The Roots of Human Violence and Greed', Stanislav Grof, Rudolf Steiner House, 35 Park Road, London NW1.

3 See Fantz and Miranda (1975).

4 Some of the other situations that can result in reports of NDE are: in people who were extremely tired; during rapid acceleration during training of fighter pilots (Whinnery and Whinnery 1990); after prolonged isolation and sensory deprivation (Cromer *et al.* 1967); occasionally while carrying out their everyday activities; while dreaming; or after the administration of other drugs such as DMT (Strassman 2001).

5 I discussed this matter with Professor Yuasa at a meeting in Tokyo in October 2004.

7 Rethinking embodiment

1 In surveys carried out in Europe and North America, between 70–97 per cent of the participants reported that they were familiar with the feeling of 'being stared at' (Sheldrake 2003: 10).

2 See Chapter 1, note 7.

3 Merleau-Ponty's concept of the *body-scheme* was not influenced by Asian theories of the body. Such an intuition is given by the fact that he paid no attention to the somesthesis or to the third circuit of emotion-instinct. In contrast, Yuasa's theory

of the body places importance on these two circuits. Merleau-Ponty was led to postulate the body-scheme through the investigation of epistemology, an area that has interested philosophers greatly, that is, through the investigation of cognitive functions (Yuasa 1993: 121).

4 The meridian system is fundamental to the viewpoint of Eastern medicine. According to the Chinese medical system, every human body has eight or twelve 'lines' (*keiraku*) beneath the skin that connect with numerous points (*tsubo*) on the surface of the skin. It is assumed that 'qi' is always flowing through these lines and is closely related to human health and the life force. In Chinese medicine, therefore, a system of healing was developed that was aimed at controlling the flow of 'qi'. This is done by stimulating the various points (*tsubo*) and lines (*keiraku*) on the skin by acupuncture or moxibustion. This form of Chinese medicine has been practiced by many in Japan, even after the introduction of modern Western medicine (Shimazono 2004: 287).

5 For details of the AMI system and its data assessment, see Hiroshi Motoyama: *How to Measure and Diagnose the Functions of the Meridians and Their Corresponding Internal Organs*, Tokyo: The Institute for Religious Psychology, 1975; 'Electro-physiological and Preliminary Biochemical Studies of Skin Properties in Relation to the Acupuncture Meridian', *Research for Religion and Parapsychology*, June 1980, pp. 1–37; 'A Biophysical Elucidation of the Meridian and *Ki-Energy*', *Research for Religion and Parapsychology*, August, 1981; and 'Meridian and *Ki*', *Research for Religion and Parapsychology*, December 1986.

6 As a consequence of this belief, acupuncture therapy has been practiced for more than a thousand years, but has been largely ignored by Western medicine where it is regarded as unscientific.

7 This interview was held in Tokyo in April 2004.

Bibliography

Abe, M. (1985) *Zen and Western Thought*. Hong Kong: The Macmillan Press Ltd.

Abe, M. (1988) 'Nishida's philosophy of "Place"', *International Philosophical Quarterly* 28(4): 355–71.

Abram, D. (1997) *The Spell of the Sensuous*. New York: Vintage Books.

Achterberg, J., Cooke, K., Richards, T., Standish, L.J., Kozak, L. and Lake, J. (2005) 'Evidence for correlations between distant intentionality and brain function in recipients: a functional magnetic resonance imaging analysis', *The Journal of Alternative and Complementary Medicine* 11(6): 965–71.

AcKerman, D. (1999) *A Natural History of the Senses*. London: Random House.

Alvarado, C.S. (2005) 'Ernesto Bozzano on the phenomenon of bilocation', *Journal of Near-Death Studies* 23(4): 207–8.

Arnone, D. and Schifano, F. (2006) 'Psychedelics in psychiatry', *British Journal of Psychiatry*, 188: 88; author reply 89, http://www.ncbi.nlm.nih.gov (accessed 23 February 2006).

Aston, W.G. (1956) *Nihongi* (trans.). London: Allen & Unwin.

Atwater, P.M.H. (1995) *Beyond the Light*. New York: William Morrow.

Atwater, P.M.H. (1996) 'What is not being said about the near-death experience', in L.W. Bailey and J. Yates (eds) *The Near-Death Experience*. New York: Routledge.

Atwater, P.M.H. (2003) *The New Children and Near-Death Experiences*. Rochester, VT: Bear and Company.

Austin, J. (1998) *Zen and the Brain*. Cambridge, MA: MIT Press.

Bachelard, G. (1969) *The Poetics of Space*. Boston: Beacon Press.

Badham, P. (1990) *Near-Death Experience, Beliefs about Life After Death, and the Tibetan Book of the Dead*, Lecture Series II, Tokyo Honganji, International Buddhist Study Center.

Badham, P. (1997) *Religious and Near-Death Experience in Relation to Belief in a Future Life*, Second Series Occasional Paper 13. Oxford: Religious Experience Research Centre.

Badham, P. (1998) *The Contemporary Challenge of Modernist Theology*. Lampeter: University of Wales Press.

Badham, P. (2003) 'Life after death: an overview on contemporary beliefs', *Dialogue* 21 (November): 41–5.

Badham, P. (2005a) 'The experiential grounds for believing in God and a future life', *Modern Believing* 46(1): 28–43.

Badham, P. (2005b) 'A contemporary defence of the concept of the soul', *The Christian Parapsychologist* June: 209–20.

Badham, P. and Badham, L. (1982) *Immortality or Extinction?* London: Macmillan.

Bailey, L.W. and Yates, J. (1996) *The Near-Death Experience.* New York: Routledge.

Bardy, A.H. (2002) 'Near-death experience' [letter], *The Lancet* 359: 2116.

Barrett, W. (1986) *Death-Bed Visions: The Psychical Experiences of the Dying*, 2nd edn. Northampton: Aquarian.

Basso, K. and Feld, S. (1995) *Senses of Place.* New York: Columbia University Press.

Becker, C.B. (1981) 'The centrality of near-death experiences in Chinese Pure Land Buddhism', *Anabiosis* 1: 154–71.

Becker, C.B. (1984a) 'The Pure Land revisited: Sino-Japanese meditations and near-death experiences of the next world', *Journal of Near-Death Studies* 4(1): 51–68.

Becker, C.B. (1984b) 'Religious visions: experiential grounds for the Pure Land tradition', *The Eastern Buddhist* XVII(1): 138–53.

Becker, C.B. (1992) 'Indian, Japanese and psychoanalytic research on meditation', *Area Studies Tsukuba* 10: 121–30.

Becker, C.B. (1993) *Paranormal Experience and Survival of Death.* Albany, NY: State University of New York Press.

Becker, C.B. (1997) 'The meaning of near-death experiences', paper presented to the twenty-first International Conference on the Unity of Science, Washington, DC.

Becker, C.B. (ed.) (2002) *Time for Healing: Integrating Traditional Therapies and Scientific Medical Practice.* St Paul, MN: Paragon House.

Bell, R., Dahl, J., Moore, R. and Kalso, E. (2006) 'Perioperative ketamine for acute postoperative pain', *Emerg Med Australas* 18(1): 37–44.

Bergson, H. (1911) *Creative Evolution*, trans. A. Mitchell. New York: Henry Holt.

Bernstein, E.M. and Putman, F.W. (1986) 'Development, reliability, and validity of a dissociation scale', *Journal of Nervous Mental Disease* 174: 727–35.

Blacking, J. (1977) 'Towards an anthropology of the body', in *The Anthropology of the Body.* London: Academic Press.

Blackmore, S.J. (1982) *Beyond the Body: An Investigation of Out-of-the-Body Experiences.* London: Heinemann.

Blackmore, S.J. (1991) 'Near-death experiences: in or out the body?' *Skeptical Inquirer* 16: 34–45.

Blackmore, S.J. (1993a) 'Near-death experiences in India: they have tunnels too', *Journal of Near-Death Studies*, 11: 205–17.

Blackmore, S.J. (1993b) *Dying to Live: Near-Death Experiences.* Buffalo, NY: Prometheus Books.

Blackmore, S.J. (1996a) 'Near-death experiences', *Journal of the Royal Society of Medicine* 89: 73–6.

Blackmore, S.J. (1996b) 'Near-death experiences', in L.W. Bailey and J. Yates (eds), *The Near-Death Experience.* New York: Routledge.

Blackmore, S.J. (2003) *Consciousness: An Introduction.* London: Hodder & Stoughton.

Blackmore, S.J. (2005) 'I take illegal drugs for inspiration', *Daily Telegraph*, 21 May, pp. 17–18.

Blackmore, S.J. and Troscianko, T. (1988) 'The physiology of the tunnel', *Journal of Near-Death Studies* 8: 15–28.

Blanke, O., Ortigue, S., Landis, T. and Seeck, M. (2002) 'Stimulating illusory own-body perceptions', *Nature* 419: 269–70.

Bocking, B. (1996) *A Popular Dictionary of Shinto*. Richmond, Surrey: Curzon Press.

Bohm, D. (1988) 'Beyond relativity and quantum theory', *Psychological Perspectives* 19(1): 25–43.

Bonta, I.L. (2004) 'Schizophrenia, dissociative anaesthesia and near-death experience: three events meeting at the NMDA receptor', *Medical Hypotheses* 62: 23–8.

Bozzano, E. (1934) ' "Corpo eterico" ed esistenza spirituale' [The 'etheric body' and spiritual existence], *La Ricerca Psichica* 34: 582–95.

Bucke, R.M. (1901) *Cosmic Consciousness*. Philadelphia, PA: Innes.

Carr, D. (1972) *The Forgotten Senses*. Garden City, NY: Doubleday.

Carr, D. (1982) 'Pathophysiology of stress-induced limbic lobe dysfunction: a hypothesis for NDEs', *Journal of Near-Death Studies* 2: 75–89.

Carroll, L. (1965) *Alice's Adventures in Wonderland*. New York: Airmont.

Carter, R. (1989) *The Nothingness Beyond God: An Introduction to the Philosophy of Nishida Kitaro*. New York: Paragon House, pp. 31–2.

Carter, R. (1996) 'Strands of influence', in Watsuji Tetsuro, *Watsuji Tetsuro's Ringrigaku: Ethics in Japan*, trans. Yamamoto Seisaku and Robert Carter. Albany: SUNY Press.

Carter, R. (1999) *Mapping the Mind*. Berkeley, CA: University of California Press.

Casey, E. (1982) *Getting Back into Place: Toward a Renewed Understanding of the Place-World*. Bloomington, IN: Indiana University Press.

Casey, E. (1998) *The Fate of Place*. Berkeley, CA: University of California Press.

Chalmers, D.J. (1995) 'Facing up to the problem of consciousness', *Journal of Consciousness Studies* 2: 200–19.

Chalmers, D.J. (1996) *The Conscious Mind*. New York: Oxford University Press.

Chevalier, J. and Gheerbrant, A. (1986) *Il Dizionario dei simboli*, vol. 1, Milan: Rizzoli, pp. 451–3.

Christ, C.P. (1992) 'Why women need the Goddess', in C.P. Christ and J. Plaskow, *Womanspirit Rising: A Feminist Reader in Religion*. San Francisco: HarperCollins, pp. 273–87.

Churchland, P.S. (1996) 'The Hornswoggle problem', *Journal of Consciousness Studies* 3(5–6): 402–8.

Church of England Doctrine Commission (1995) *The Mystery of Salvation*. London: Church House Publishing.

Clack, B. (2005) 'Embodiment and feminist philosophy of religion', paper presented at conference, Embodiment and the Environment, 5–8 July, Oxford Brookes University, Oxford.

Clack, C. (2005) 'The spirituality of the evolving earth', paper presented at conference, Revelation and Evolution, University of Lampeter, 15–18 September.

Clack, C. and Clack, B. (1998) *The Philosophy of Religion: A Critical Introduction*. Cambridge: Polity Press.

Clynes, M.E. and Kline, N.S. (1960) 'Cyborgs and space', *Astronautics*, September, pp. 26–7 and 74–5.

Collier, B.B. (1972) 'Ketamine and the conscious mind', *Anaesthesia* 27(2): 120–34.

Comer, N.L., Madow, L. and Dixon, J.L. (1967) 'Observation of sensory deprivation in a life-threatening situation', *American Journal of Psychiatry* 124(2): 164–9.

Corazza, O. (2002) 'Ketamine, NDE and non-ordinary states of consciousness: a medical-anthropological observation on dissociative phenomena', in United Nations Interregional Crime and Justice Research Institute (FAO), *Journal for Drug Addiction and Alcoholism* [*Bolletino per le Farmacodipendenze e l'Alcoolismo*], No. 4: 88–93.

Corazza, O. (2004) 'The varieties of the near-death experience: a study in Japan', in F. Cariglia, *Echi d'altrove*. San Marino: Repubblica di San Marino, pp. 33–8.

Corazza, O. (2005) 'Space and embodiment: a Japanese understanding of human beings', paper presented at conference, Embodiment and the Environment, 5–8 July, Oxford Brookes University, Oxford.

Corazza, O. (2007a) 'Consciousness and Japanese martial arts', in D. Meyer-Dinkgräfe (ed.) *Consciousness, Literature and the Arts*. Newcastle: Cambridge Scholars Publishing, pp. 110–17.

Corazza, O. (2007b) 'The spirit of place: visions of the afterlife in Japan', in F. Cariglia (ed.) *Sopravvivere. Il velato destino della personalita*, Proceedings of the 11th International Congress on Borderland Experiences, San Marino, pp. 23–8.

Corazza, O. (2007c) 'Extended bodies: how do we think and feel about the body in the 21st century?' in D. Janes (ed.), *Back to the Future of the Body*. Newcastle: Cambridge Scholars Publishing.

Corazza, O. (2007d) 'Rethinking embodiment: a Japanese contemporary perspective: a workshop in commemoration of Professor Yasuo Yuasa (1925–2005)', *CSJR Newsletter*, SOAS, 14–15 (January): 8–10.

Corazza, O. (2008) *The Japanese Philosophy of the Body*. Distance Learning educational material. Lampeter: University of Wales (forthcoming).

Corazza, O. and Terreni, F. (2005) 'NDE in music: an aesthetic-musical analysis of String-Trio by Arnold Schönberg', in F. Cariglia, *Life after Life, 1975–2005: 30 Years of NDE*, IX International Symposium of the Near-Death Experience (NDE), pp. 47–51.

Counts, D.A. (1983) 'Near-death and out-of-body experiences in a Melanesian society', *Anabiosis* 3: 115–35.

Crick, F. (1994) *The Astonishing Hypothesis*. New York: Scribner.

Cytowic, R. (1995) 'Synesthesia: phenomenology and neuropsychology', *Psyche* (10).

Dalgarno, P. and Shewan, D. (1996) 'Illicit use of ketamine in Scotland', *Journal of Psychoactive Drugs* 28: 191–9.

Damasio, A. (1994) *Descartes' Error: Emotion, Reason and the Human Brain*. New York: Avon Books.

Damasio, A. (1999) *The Feeling of What Happens: Body, Emotion and the Making of Consciousness*. London: Heinemann.

Damasio, A. (2000) 'A neurobiology for consciousness', in T. Metzinger, *Neural Correlates of Consciousness*, Cambridge, MA: MIT Press, pp. 111–20.

Damasio, A. (2003) 'Mental self: The person within', *Nature* 423: 227.

Davy, H. (1800) *Researches, Chemical and Philosophical: Chiefly Concerning Nitrous Oxide, or Dephlogisticated Nitrous Air, and Its Respiration*. London: J. Johnson.

Deane-Drummond, C. and Scott, P. (2006) *Future Perfect? God, Medicine and Human Identity*. London: T&T Clark.

Dennett, D.C. (1991) *Consciousness Explained*. Boston: Little, Brown and Co.

Depraz, N. *et al.* (2003) *On Becoming Aware*. Amsterdam: John Benjamins Press.

Descartes, R. (1937) *Meditations on the First Philosophy*, trans. J. Veitch. London: Dent and Dutton.

Descartes, R. (1954) 'The interrelation of soul and body', in *The Way of Philosophy*, ed. P. Wheelwright, New York: Odyssey.

Dilworth, D.A. (1973) 'Nishida Kitaro: nothingness as the negative space of experiential immediacy', *International Philosophical Quarterly* 13: 463–84.

Dōgen, K. (1970) *Dōgen zenji zenshū* [Complete Works of Zen Master Dōgen], vol. 1. Tokyo: Chikuma Hobō.

Doi, T. (1986) *The Anatomy of Self*. Tokyo: Kodansha International Ltd.

Domino, G. (1989) 'Synesthesia and creativity in fine arts students: an empirical look', *Creativity Research Journal* 2: 17–29.

Drazen, P. (2003) *Anime Explosion! The What? Why? & Wow! of Japanese Animation*. Berkeley, CA: Stone Bridge Press.

Drugscope (2005) *Annual Report*. London, available at: <http://www.drugscope.org.uk> (accessed 4 January 2006).

Ebersole, G. (1989) *Ritual Poetry and the Politics of Death in Early Japan*. Princeton, NJ: Princeton University Press.

Eliade, M. (1959) *The Sacred and the Profane: The Nature of Religion*, trans. W. Trask. London: Harcourt Brace Jovanovich.

Eliade, M. (1964) *Shamanism: Archaic Techniques of Ecstasy*. Princeton, NJ: Princeton University Press.

European Monitoring Centre for Drugs and Drug Addiction (EMCDDA) (2003) *Report on the Risk Assessment of Ketamine in the Framework of the Joint Action on New Synthetic Drugs*. Available at: <http://annualreport.emcdda.eu.int> (last accessed November 2005).

Evans-Wentz, W.Y. ([1927] 1957) *The Tibetan Book of the Dead*. London: Oxford University Press.

Fantz, R.L. and Miranda, S.B. (1975) 'Newborn infant attention to form of contour', *Child Development* 46: 224–8.

Fenwick, P. (1997) 'Is the near-death experience only N-methyl-D-aspartate blocking?' *Journal of Near-Death Studies* 16: 43–53.

Fenwick, P. and Fenwick, E. (1995) *The Truth in the Light: An Investigation of Over 300 Near-Death Experiences*. London: Hodder Headline.

Flohr, H. (2000) 'NMDA receptor-mediated computational processes and phenomenal consciousness', in T. Metzinger (ed.) *Neural Correlate of Consciousness*. Cambridge, MA: MIT Press, pp. 245–58.

Fontana, A. (1974) 'Terapia antidepressiva con Ci 581 (Ketamine)', *Acta Psiquiat. Psicol. America Latina*, 4: 20–32.

Fontana, D. (2005) *Is There an Afterlife? A Comprehensive Overview of the Evidence*. Ropley, Hants: O Books.

Fox, M. (2003) *Religion, Spirituality and the Near-Death Experience*. New York: Routledge.

Franklin, J. (2006) *Exploration into Spirit: A Power Greater Than . . . , A History of the Alister Hardy Religious Experience Research Centre & Society*. Lampeter: Alister Hardy Society.

French, C. (2001) Dying to know the truth: visions of a dying brain, or just false memories? *Lancet*, 15 December 2001, 358 (9298), 2010–2011.

French, C. (2005a) 'Near-death experiences in cardiac arrest survivors', *Progress in Brain Research* 150: 351–67.

French, C. (2005b) 'Fantastic memories: the relevance of research into eyewitness testimony and false memories for reports of anomalous experiences', in R. Wiseman and C. Watt (eds) *The International Library of Psychology: Parapsychology.* London: Ashgate Publishing.

Frith, C. (2002) 'How can we share experiences?' *Trends in Cognitive Sciences* 6: 374.

Fromm, E., Suzuki, D.T. and De Martino, R. (1960) *Zen Buddhism and Psychoanalysis.* New York: Harper & Row.

Gabbard, G.O., Twemlow, S.W. and Jones, F.C. (1981) 'Do "Near-Death Experiences" occur only near-death?' *Journal of Nervous and Mental Disease* 169: 374–7.

Gadamer, H.G. (1975) *Truth and Method.* London: Sheed and Ward.

Gallagher, S. (1997) 'Mutual enlightenment: recent phenomenology in cognitive science', *Journal of Consciousness Studies* 4(3): 195–214.

Gallagher, S. (2003) 'Phenomenology and experimental design', *Journal of Consciousness Study* 10(9–10): 85–99.

Gallup, G. (1982) *Adventures in Immortality: A Look Beyond the Threshold of Death.* New York: McGraw-Hill.

Gibson, J.J. (1966) *The Senses Considered as Perceptual Systems.* Boston: Houghton Mifflin.

Graves, R. (1966) *The White Goddess.* New York: Farrar, Straus & Giroux.

Green, C. (1968) *Lucid Dreams.* London: Hamish Hamilton.

Green, S.M., Clem, K.J. and Rothrock, S.G. (1996) 'Ketamine safety profile in the developing world: survey of practitioners', *Acad. Emergency Medicine* 3(6): 598–604.

Greyson, B. (1983) 'The near-death experience scale: construction, reliability, and validity', *Journal of Nervous and Mental Disease* 171: 369–75.

Greyson, B. (1987) 'The near-death experience as a focus of clinical attention', *Journal of Nervous and Mental Disease* 185: 327–34.

Greyson, B. (1993) 'Varieties of near-death experiences', *Psychiatry* 56: 390–9.

Greyson, B. (2000a) 'Dissociation in people who have near-death experiences: out of their bodies or out of their minds?' *The Lancet* 355: 460–3.

Greyson, B. (2000b) 'Dissociation in people who have near-death experiences: out of their bodies or out of their minds?' *The Lancet* 2000, 355: 460–3.

Greyson, B. and Bush, N.E. (1992) 'Distressing near-death experiences', *Psychiatry* 55: 95–110.

Greyson, B. and Stevenson, I. (1980) 'The phenomenology of near-death experiences', *American Journal of Psychiatry* 137: 1193–6.

Grinspoon, L. and Bakalar, J.B. (1979) *Psychedelic Drugs Reconsidered.* New York: Basic Books.

Grof, S. (1979) *Realms of the Human Unconscious.* London: Souvenir Press.

Grof, S. (1985) *Beyond the Brain.* Albany, NY: State University of New York Press.

Grof, S. and Grof, C. (1986) 'Spiritual emergency: understanding and treatment of transpersonal crises', *Re-Vision Journal* 8: 7.

Grof, S. and Halifax, J. (1977) *The Human Encounter with Death.* New York: E.P. Dutton.

Gupta, B. (1998) *The Disinterested Witness*. Evanston, IL: Northwestern University Press.

Hadfield, P. (1991) 'Japanese find death a depressing experience', *New Scientist*. 132(1797): 11.

Hall, E.T. (1959) *The Silent Language*. Garden City, NY: Doubleday.

Hall, E.T. (1969) *The Hidden Dimension*. Garden City, NY: Anchor Book.

Halligan, P.W. (2002) 'Phantom limbs: the body in mind', *Cognitive Neuropsychiatry* 7: 251–69.

Hameroff, S.R., Kaszniak, A. and Scott, A. (1996, 1997, 1998, 1999) *Towards a Science of Consciousness (Tucson I, II, III, IV, V)*. Cambridge, MA: MIT Press.

Hameroff, S.R. and Penrose, R. (1996) 'Conscious events as orchestrated space-time selections', *Journal of Consciousness Studies* 3(1): 36–53.

Hampe, J. (1979) *To Die Is Gain: The Experience of One's Own Death*. London: DLT.

Haraway, D. (1998) 'Mice into wormholes', in Gary Lee Downey and J. Dumit (eds) *Cyborg and Citadels*. Santa Fe, NM: School of American Research Press.

Hardo, T. (2000) *Children Who Have Lived Before: Reincarnation Today*. Saffron Walden: The C.W. Daniel Company Limited.

Hardy, A. (1966) *The Divine Flame: An Essay Towards a Natural History of Religion*. London: Collins.

Hardy, A. (1979) *The Spiritual Nature of Man: A Study of Contemporary Religious Experience*. Oxford: Clarendon Press.

Harner, M. (1980) *The Way of the Shaman*. New York: HarperCollins.

Hay, D. (1982) *Exploring Inner Space: Scientists and Religious Experience*. London: Penguin Books.

Hay, D. (1994) 'The biology of God: what is the current status of Hardy's hypothesis?' *International Journal for the Psychology of Religion* 4(1): 1–23.

Hay, D. and Hunt, K. (2000) *Understanding the Spirituality of People Who Don't Go to Church: A Report on the Findings of the Adults' Spirituality Project*. Nottingham: University of Nottingham.

Heidegger, M. (1962) *Being and Time*. New York: Harper & Row.

Herzog, D.B. and Herrin, J.T. (1985) 'Near-death experiences in the very young', *Critical Care Medicine* 13(12): 1074–5.

Hick, J. (2002) 'Science/Religion', a talk given at King Edward VI Camp Hill School, Birmingham, March 2002. Available at: http://www.johnhick.org.uk/article5.html (accessed 21 February 2006).

Hickman, T. (2002) *Death: A User's Guide*. London: Random House.

Hobson, J.A. (1999) *Consciousness*. New York: W.H. Freeman.

Hobson, J.A., Pace-Schott, E. and Stickgold, R. (2000) 'Dreaming and the brain: toward a cognitive neuroscience of conscious states', *Behavioural and Brain Sciences* 23(6): 793–842.

Honorton, C. (1985) 'Meta-analysis of psi Ganzfeld research: a response to Hyman', *Journal of Parapsychology* 49: 51–91.

Hopfer, C., Mendelson, B., Van Leeuwen, J.M., Kelly, S. and Hooks, S. (2006) 'Club drug use among youths in treatment for substance abuse', *Am J Addict* 15(1): 94–9.

Hugo, V. (1917) *Notre-Dame de Paris*, Book IV, Chapter 3. New York: P.F. Collier & Son.

Hume, D. (1739) *A Treatise of Human Nature*. London.

Husserl, E. (1973) *Experience and Judgment*, trans. J.S. Churchill and K. Ameriks. Evanston, IL: Northwestern University Press.

Husserl, E. (1991) *On the Phenomenology of the Consciousness of Internal Time* (1893–1917), trans. J.B. Brough. Dordrecht: Kluwer Academic Publishers.

Huxley, A. (1992) *Huxley and God. Essays on Religious Experience*. Edited by J.H. Bridgeman. San Francisco: HarperCollins Publishers.

Hyman, R. (1985) The Ganzfeld psi experiment: a critical appraisal', *Journal of Parapsychology* 49: 3–49.

Ichikawa, H. (1979) *Seishin toshite no Shintai* (The Body as the Spirit). Tokyo: Keisō shōbō.

Itoh, M., Sasaki, T., Duan, X., Watanabe, K., Seto, S., Yashushi, M., Kumagai, K. and Yamaguchi, K. (2004) 'A physiological study on the effects of lavender aroma', *Journal of International Society of Life Information Science* 22(1): 109–17.

Jack, A.I. and Roepstorff, A. (2002) 'Introspection and cognitive brain mapping: from stimulus response to script-report', *Trends in Cognitive Science* 6: 333–9.

Jack, A.I. and Shallice, T. (2001) 'Introspective physicalism as an approach to the science of consciousness', *Cognition* 79: 161–96.

Jackson, M. (1983) 'Knowledge of the body', *Man* 18: 327–45.

James, W. (1890) *The Principles of Psychology* (2 vols). London: Macmillan.

James, W. ([1902] 1997) *The Varieties of Religious Experience*. London: Fontana.

James, W. (1904a) 'Does consciousness exist?' *Journal of Philosophy, Psychology and Scientific Methods*, 1(18).

James, W. (1904b) 'A world of pure experience', *Journal of Philosophy, Psychology and Scientific Methods* 1(20/21).

Jansen, K.L.R. (1989) 'Near-Death Experiences and the NMDA receptor', *British Medical Journal* 298: 1708.

Jansen, K.L.R. (2001) *Ketamine: Dreams and Realities*. Sarasota, FL: MAPS.

Jantzen, G. (1998) *Becoming Divine: Towards a Feminist Philosophy of Religion*. Manchester: Manchester University Press.

Johnson, M. (1987) *The Body in the Mind: The Bodily Basis of Meaning, Imagination, and Reason*. Chicago: University of Chicago Press.

Jung, C.G. (1936) *The Concept of the Collective Unconscious* [1968] in *The Archetypes and the Collective Unconscious*, (Collected Works No. 9, Part 1). Princeton, NJ: Princeton University Press, pp. 42–53.

Jung, C.G. (1983) *Memories, Dreams, Reflections*. London: Flamingo Edition, pp. 322–5.

Kasulis, T.P. (1981) *Zen Action/Zen Person*. Honolulu: University of Hawaii Press.

Kasulis, T.P. (1998) *Intimacy or Integrity: Philosophy and Cultural Difference*. Honolulu: University of Hawaii Press.

Kasulis, T.P. (2004) *Shinto: The Way Home*. Honolulu: University of Hawaii Press.

Kellehear, A. (1993) 'Culture, biology, and the near-death experience', *Journal of Nervous and Mental Disease* 181: 148–56.

Kellehear, A. (1996) *Experiences Near-Death: Beyond Medicine and Religion*. Oxford: Oxford University Press.

Kennet, J. (1972) *Selling Water by the River*. London: Allen & Unwin.

Kesten, B. (1991) *Feeding the Body, Nourishing the Soul: Essentials of Eating for Physical, Emotional and Spiritual Well-Being*. Berkeley, CA: Publishers Group West.

Kingsley, R. (1998) *Japanese Gods and Myths*. London: Quantum Books.

Krupitsky, E.M. (1992) 'Ketamine psychedelic therapy (KPT) of alcoholism and neurosis', *Multidisciplinary Association for Psychedelic Studies Newsletter* 3: 24–8.

Krupitsky, E.M. and Grinenko, A.Y. (1997) 'Ketamine Psychedelic Therapy (KTP): a review of the results of ten years of research', *Journal of Psychoactive Drugs* 29(2): 165–83.

Krystal, J., Karper, L., Seibyl, J., Freeman, G., Delaney, R., Bremmer, J., Heninger, G., Bowers, M. and Charney, D. (1994) 'Subanaesthetic effects of the non-competitive NMDA antagonist, ketamine, in humans', *Archives of General Psychiatry* 51: 199–214.

Kübler-Ross, E. (1969) *On Death and Dying*. New York: Touchstone.

Kuratani, K. (2004) 'Life, spirituality and the body', *Motoyama Institute Newsletter*, November.

La Barre, W. (1955) *The Human Animal*. Chicago: University of Chicago Press.

LaBerge, S. (1985) *Lucid Dreaming*. Los Angeles, CA: Tarcher.

LaBerge, S. (1998) 'Dreaming and consciousness', in S. Hameroff, A. Kaszniak and A. Scott (eds), *Toward a Science of Consciousness II*. Cambridge, MA: MIT Press, pp. 494–504.

LaBerge, S. (2003) 'Lucid dreaming and the yoga of the dream state', in B.A. Wallace *Buddhism and Science: Breaking New Ground*. New York: Columbia University Press.

La Fleur, W. (1992) *Liquid Life: Abortion and Buddhism in Japan*. Princeton, NJ: Princeton University Press.

Laughlin, C.D. and McManus, E. (1995) 'The relevance of the radical empiricism of William James to the anthropology of consciousness', *Anthropology of Consciousness* 6(3): 34–46.

Laughlin, C.D., McManus, E. and D'Aquili, G. (1990) *Brain, Symbol and Experience*. New York: Columbia University Press.

Lawrence, D.H. ([1930] 1993) *A Propos of Lady Chatterley's Lover*. London: Penguin Books.

Leary, T. (1983) *Flashbacks: An Autobiography*. Los Angeles: J.P. Tarcher.

Leary, T. (1997) *Design for Dying*. London: HarperCollins Publishers.

Leder, D. (1990) *The Absent Body*. Chicago: University of Chicago Press.

Leder, D. (1998) 'A tale of two bodies: the Cartesian corpse and the lived body', in Donn Welton (ed.) *Body and Flesh: A Philosophical Reader*. Oxford: Blackwell.

Lee, Y. and Hu, P.C. (1993) 'The effect of Chinese Qi gong exercises and therapy on diseases and heath', *Journal of Indian Psychology* 11(1–2): 9–18.

Le Goff, J. (1981) *The Birth of the Purgatory*, trans. A. Goldhammer. Chicago: University of Chicago Press.

Lempert, T., Bauer, M. and Schmidt, D. (1994) 'Syncope and near-death experience', *The Lancet* 344: 829–30.

Levine, J. (1983) 'Materialism and qualia: the explanatory gap', *Pacific Philosophical Quarterly* 64: 354–61.

Lilly, J. (1978) *The Scientist: A Novel Autobiography*. New York: Bantam Books.

Lingis, A. (1983) *Excesses: Eros and Culture*. Albany, NY: State University of New York Press.

Lobettti, T. (2006) 'Personal and social dimensions of the Akinomine (Autumn Peak) practice on Haguro Mountain', in *CSJR Newsletter*, SOAS, Jan. 2006, Issue 12–13, pp. 28–33.

Lorimer, D. (ed.) (2004) *Science, Consciousness and Ultimate Reality.* Exeter: Imprint Academic.

Lutz, A. (2002) 'Toward a neurophenomenology as an account of generative passages: a first empirical case study', *Phenomenology and the Cognitive Sciences* 1: 133–67.

Lutz, A. (2003) 'Neurophenomenology: how to combine subjective experience with brain evidence', *Science and Consciousness Review*, March (4).

Lutz, A. and Thompson, E. (2003) 'Neurophenomenology: integrating subjective experience and brain dynamics in the neuroscience of consciousness', *Journal of Consciousness Studies* 10(9–10): 31–52.

Lutz, A. *et al.* (2002) 'Guiding the study of brain dynamics by using first-person data: synchrony patterns correlate with ongoing conscious states during a simple visual task', *Proceedings of the National Academy of Science USA*, 99: 1586–91.

Lyotard, J.-F. (1986) *La Phénoménologie.* Paris: Presses Universitaires de France.

Malhotra, A., Pinals, D., Weingartner, H., Sirocco, K., Missar, C.D., Pickar, D. and Breier, A. (1996) 'NMDA receptor function and human cognition: the effects of ketamine in healthy volunteers', *Neuropsychopharmacology* 14: 301–8.

Mann, T. (1949) *Die Entstehung des Doktors Faustus: Roman eines Romans.* Amsterdam.

Marks, D.F. and Kammann, R. (1980) *The Psychology of the Psychic.* Buffalo, NY: Prometheus.

Marshall, P. (1992) *The Living Mirror: Images of Reality in Science and Mysticism.* London: Samphire Press.

Marshall, P. (2005) *Mystical Encounters with the Natural World: Experiences and Explanations.* Oxford: Oxford University Press.

Martinez, P. (2004) *Identity and Ritual in a Japanese Diving Village: The Making and Becoming of Person and Place.* Honolulu: University of Hawaii Press.

Maruyama, M. (1952) *Nihon seiji shisō shi kenkyū*, trans. Mikiso Hane, Studies in the Intellectual History of Tokugawa Japan. Tokyo: University of Tokyo Press, 1974.

Masters, R.E.L. and Huston, J. (1967) *The Varieties of Psychedelic Experience.* London: Anthony Blond.

Mauss, M. (1979) *Sociology and Psychology: Essays.* London: Routledge & Kegan Paul Ltd.

Meduna, L.J. (1950) 'The effect of carbon dioxide upon the functions of the brain', in L.J. Meduna (ed.) *Carbon Dioxide Therapy.* Springfield, IL: Charles Thomas.

Meltzoff, A.N. and Moore, M.K. (1999) 'Imitation of facial and manual gestures by human neonates', in A. Slater and D. Muir (eds) *The Blackwell Reader in Developmental Psychology.* Oxford: Blackwell.

Merleau-Ponty, M. (1962) *The Phenomenology of Perception*, trans. C. Smith. New York: Humanities Press.

Merleau-Ponty, M. (1968) *The Visible and the Invisible.* Evanston, IL: Northwestern University Press.

Merrell-Wolff, F. (1973a) *The Philosophy of Consciousness Without-An-Object.* New York: Julian Press.

Merrell-Wolff, F. (1973b) *Pathways through to Space.* New York: Julian Press.

Metzinger, T. (ed.) (2000) *Neural Correlates of Consciousness.* Cambridge, MA: MIT Press.

Metzner, R. (ed.) (1999) *Ayahuasca: Human Consciousness and the Spirits of Nature.* New York: Thunder's Mouth Press.

Mills, I.H., Park, G.R., Manara, A.R. and Merriman, R.J. (1998) 'Treatment of compulsive behaviour in eating disorders with intermittent ketamine infusions', *Quarterly Journal of Medicine* 91(7): 493–503.

Mitchell, J. (1973) 'Out of the body vision', *Psychic*, March: 44–7.

Moody, R.A. (1975) *Life after Life.* Atlanta, GA: Mockingbird Books.

Moore, C.A. (ed.) (1967) *The Japanese Mind: Essentials of Japanese Philosophy and Culture.* Honolulu, HI: University of Hawaii Press.

Moore, M. and Alltounian, H. (1978) *Journeys into the Bright World.* Rockport, MA: Para Research Inc.

Morgan, C.J.A., Mofeez, A., Brandner, B., Bromley, L. and Curran, V. (2004a) 'Ketamine impairs response inhibition and is positively reinforcing in healthy volunteers: a dose-response study', *Psychopharmacology*, 172: 298–308.

Morgan, C.J.A., Mofeez, A., Brandner, B., Lesley, B. and Curran, V. (2004b) 'Acute effects of ketamine on memory systems and psychotic symptoms in healthy volunteers', *Neuropsychopharmacology* 29: 208–18.

Morgan, C.J.A., Monaghan, L. and Curran, V. (2004c) 'Beyond the K-hole: a 3-year longitudinal investigation of the cognitive and subjective effects of ketamine in recreational users who have substantially reduced their use of the drug', *Addiction* 99(11): 1450–61.

Morse, M.L. (1990) *Closer to the Light: Learning from the Near-Death Experiences of Children.* New York: Ivy Books.

Morse, M.L. (1994) 'Near-death experiences of children', *Journal of Pediatric Oncology Nursing* 11: 139–44.

Morse, M.L. Castillo, P., Venecia, D., Milstein, J. and Tyler, D.C. (1986) 'Childhood near-death experiences', *American Journal of Diseases of Children* 140: 1110–14.

Morse, M.L. and Perry, P. (1992) *Transformed by the Light.* New York: Villard Books.

Morse, M.L. and Perry, P. (1994) *Parting Visions: Uses and Meanings of Pre-Death, Psychic, and Spiritual Experiences.* New York: Villard Books.

Motoyama, H. (1991) *The Correlation between Psi Energy and Ki.* Tokyo: Human Science Press.

Motoyama, H. (2008) *Being and the logic of mutual function*, trans. S. Nagatomo and J. Krummel. Encinitas, CA: California Institute for Human Science (forthcoming).

Murphy, M. (1992) *The Future of the Body.* New York: Penguin Putnam Inc.

Nagatomo, S. (1992) *Attunement Through the Body.* Albany, NY: State University of New York Press.

Nagatomo, S. (2006) 'In praise of non-performance in the performing arts', keynote lecture at the International and Interdisciplinary Symposium on the Changing Body in Training and Performance, January 6–8, 2006, University of Exeter.

Nagel, T. (1974) 'What is it like to be a bat?', *Philosophical Review*, 83: 435–50.

Nakamura, H. (1964) *Ways of Thinking of Eastern Peoples: India-China-Tibet-Japan.* Honolulu: East-West Centre Press.

Nhat Hanh, T. (1975) *The Miracle of Mindfulness: A Manual of Meditation.* Boston: Beacon Press.

Nietzsche, F. (1994) *On the Genealogy of Morality.* Cambridge: Cambridge University Press.

Nishida, K. (1970) *Complete Works of Nishida Kitaro*, vol. 4. Tokyo: Iwanami Shoten, pp. 208–89.

Nishida, K. (1987) *Intuition and Reflection in Self-Consciousness*, trans. V.H. Viglielmo, T. Toshinori and J.S. O'Leary. Albany, NY: State University of New York Press.

Nishida, K. (1990) *An Inquiry into the Good*, trans. M. Abe and C. Ives. New Haven, CT: Yale University Press.

Nishida, K. (forthcoming) *Basho* [Place], trans. J. Krummel and S. Nagatomo.

Noyes, R. and Kletti, R. (1972) 'The experience of dying from falls', *Omega* 3: 45–52.

Noyes, R. and Kletti, R. (1976) 'Depersonalisation in the face of life-threatening danger: a description', *Psychiatry* 39: 19–27.

Noyes, R. and Slymen, D. (1971) 'The subjective response to life-threatening danger', *Omega* 9: 313–21.

O'Regan, J.K. and Noë, A. (2001) 'A sensorimotor account of vision and visual consciousness', *Behavioral and Brain Sciences* 24(5): 939–73.

Orne, R.M. (1995) 'The meaning of survival: the early aftermath of a near-death experience', *Research in Nursing and Health* 18(3): 239–47.

Osano, S. (2003) L'Inferno di *Genshin* e Dante: una proposta per una storia dell'arte comparata, in *Visioni dell'Aldila' in Oriente e Occidente: arte e pensiero*. Convegno di Studi, 21 March 2003, Loggiato degli Uffizi, Florence.

Osis, K. and Haraldsson, E. (1961) *Deathbed Observations of Physicians and Nurses*. New York: Parapsychology Foundation.

Osis, K. and Haraldsson, E. (1977) *At the Hour of Death*. New York: Avan Books.

Owen, R. (1980) *Footfalls on the Boundary of Another World*. London: Trubner.

Palmer, P. (1997) 'The grace of great things: reclaiming the sacred in knowing, teaching and learning', Keynote address, Boulder, Co. *Holistic Education Review* 10: 8–16.

Panksepp, J. (1998) 'The periconscious substrates of consciousness: affective states and the evolutionary origins of self', *Journal of Consciousness Studies* 5(5–6): 566–82.

Parke-Davis product information sheet (1999–2000) *Ketalar®, ABPI Compendium of Data Sheets and Summaries of Product Characteristics, 1999–2000*. Datapharm Publications, pp. 1120–2.

Parnia, S., Waller, D.G., Yeates, R. and Fenwick, P. (2001) 'A qualitative and quantitative study of the incidence, features and aetiology of near-death experiences in cardiac arrest survivors', *Resuscitation* 48: 149–56.

Parvizi, J. and Damasio, A.R. (2001) 'Consciousness and the brain stem', *Cognition* 79: 135–59.

Pasricha, S. and Stevenson, I. (1986) 'Near-death experiences in India: a preliminary report', *Journal of Nervous and Mental Diseases* 174: 165–70.

Persinger, M. (1983) 'Religious and mystical experiences as artefacts of temporal lobe function: a general hypothesis', *Perceptual and Motor Skills* 57: 1255–62.

Persinger, M. (1987) *Neuropsychological Bases of God Beliefs*. New York: Praeger.

Philippi, D. (trans.) (1968) *Kojiki*. Tokyo: University of Tokyo Press.

Piaget, J. (1962) *Play, Dreams and Imitation in Childhood*. New York: W.W. Norton.

Pinker, S. (1995) *The Language Instinct*. New York: Morrow.

Pinxten, R., van Dooren, I. and Harvey, F. (1983) *Anthropology of Space: Explorations into the Natural Philosophy and Semantics of the Navajo*. Philadelphia, PA: University of Pennsylvania Press, pp. 9–14.

Piovesana, G.K. (1969) *Contemporary Japanese Philosophical Thought*. New York: St John's University Press.

Plate, S. Brent (2002) *Religion, Art and Visual Culture: A Cross-Cultural Reader*. New York: Palgrave.

Plato (1925) *The Republic*. Book 10, trans. A.D. Lindsay. London: J.M. Dent.

Polhemus, T. (ed.) (1978) *The Body Reader: Social Aspects of the Human Body*. New York: Pantheon Books.

Poortman, J.J. (1978) *Vehicles of Consciousness: The Concept of Hylic Pluralism (Ochema)*. 4 vols. The Theosophical Society of the Netherlands.

Pupynin, O. and Brodbeck, S. (2001) *Religious Experience in London*, Second Series Occasional Paper 27. Oxford: Religious Experience Research Centre.

Rabil, A. (1967) *Merleau-Ponty: Existentialist of the Social World*. New York: Columbia University Press.

Radford, R.R. (1993) *Gaia and God: An Ecofeminist Theology of Earth Healing*. London: SCM.

Rechtschaffen, A. and Kales, A. (1968) *A Manual of Standardized Terminology, Techniques and Scoring System for Sleep Stages of Human Subjects*. Washington, DC: Public Health Service.

Reich, D.L. and Silvay, G. (1989) 'Ketamine: an update on the first twenty-five years of clinical experience', *Canadian Journal of Anesthesia* 36: 186–97.

Release (1997) *Release Drugs and Dance Safe*. London: Release Publications.

Ricoeur, P. (1966) *Freedom and Nature: The Voluntary and the Involuntary*. Evanston, IL: Northwestern University Press.

Ring, K. (1980) *Life at Death: A Scientific Investigation of the Near-Death Experience*. New York: Coward, McCann and Geoghegan.

Ring, K. and Cooper, S. (1997) 'Near-death and out-of-body experiences in the blind: a study of apparent eyeless vision', *Journal of Near-Death Studies* 16: 101–47.

Ring, K. and Elsaesser Valarino, E. (2000) *Lessons from the Light: What We Can Learn from the Near-Death Experience*. Cambridge, MA: Moment Point Press.

Rizzolatti, G., Fadiga, L., Fogassi, L. and Gallese, V. (1997) 'The space around us', *Science* 277: 190–1.

Rizzolatti, G., Riggio, L. and Sheliga, B.M. (1994) 'Space and selective attention', in C. Umiltà and M. Moscovitch (eds) *Attention and Performance*, vol. XV, *Conscious and Nonconscious Information Processing*. Cambridge, MA: MIT Press, pp. 231–65.

Roberts, G. and Owen, J. (1988) 'The near-death experience', *British Journal of Psychiatry* 153: 607–17.

Rogo, D.S. (1982) 'Ketamine and the near-death experience' *Anabiosis: The Journal for Near-Death Studies* 4: 87–96.

Rosen, D.H. (1975) 'Suicide survivors', *Western Journal of Medicine* 122: 289–94.

Roy, L. (2003) *Mystical Consciousness: Western Perspectives and Dialogue with Japanese Thinkers*. Albany, NY: State University of New York Press.

Sabom, M.B. (1982) *Recollections of Death: A Medical Investigation*. New York: Harper & Row.

Sagan, C. (1977) *The Dragons of Eden*. New York: Random House.

Sagan, C. (1979) *Broca's Brain*. New York: Random House.

Sartori, P. (2003) 'A prospective study of near-death experiences in an intensive therapy unit' *De Numine*, Newsletter of the Alister Hardy Society, No. 35, Sept.

Sartori, P. (2005) 'A prospective study to investigate the incidence and phenomenology of near-death experiences in a Welsh intensive therapy unit', University of
Wales, Lampeter, unpublished thesis.

Sartre, J.P. (1966) *Being and Nothingness*, trans. H.E. Barnes. New York: Washington
Square Press.

Saver, J.L. and Rabin, J. (1997) 'The neural substrates of religious experience', *Journal
of Neuropsychiatry and Clinical Neurosciences* 9: 498–510.

Scheper-Hughes, N. (1994) 'Embodied knowledge: thinking with the body in critical
medical anthropology', in R. Borofsky (ed.) *Assessing Cultural Anthropology.*
New York: McGraw-Hill, pp. 229–39.

Scheper-Hughes, N. and Lock, M. (1987) 'The mindful body', *Medical Anthropology
Quarterly* 1(1): 6–41.

Schooler, J.W. (2002) 'Re-representing consciousness: dissociation between experience and meta-consciousness', *Trends in Cognitive Sciences*, 6: 339–44.

Schulz, C. (1993) *Peanuts*, Summer.

Schwarz, B.E. (1971) *Parent-Child Telepathy*. New York: Garrett.

Searle, J. (1992) *The Rediscovery of the Mind*. Cambridge, MA: MIT Press.

Sehdev, R.S., Symmons, D.A.D. and Kindl, K. (2006) 'Ketamine for rapid sequence
induction in patients with head injury in the emergency department', *Emerg Med
Australas.* 18(1): 37–44.

Shaner, D.E. (1989) *Science and Comparative Philosophy: Introducing Yasuo Yuasa.*
Leiden: Brill.

Shaner, D.E. (1989) 'The Japanese experience of nature', in D.E. Shaner, S.
Nagatoma and Yuasa Yasuo, *Science and Comparative Philosophy: Introducing Yuasa
Yasuo.* Leiden: E.J. Brill.

Shapiro, A.K. and Shapiro, E. (1997) *The Powerful Placebo*. Baltimore, MD: Johns
Hopkins University Press.

Sheldrake, R. (2003) *The Sense of Being Stared at and Other Aspects of the Extended
Mind.* New York: Crown Publishers.

Sheldrake, R. and Fox, M. (1996) *Natural Grace: Dialogues on Science and Spirituality.* London: Bloomsbury Publishing.

Sheldrake, R. and Smart, P. (2005) 'Testing for telepathy in connection with e-mails',
Perceptual and Motor Skills 101: 771–86.

Shermer, M. (2002) *Why People Believe Weird Things: Pseudoscience, Superstition,
and Other Confusions of Our Time.* New York: Henry Holt Books.

Shimazono, S. (2004) *From Salvation to Spirituality*. Melbourne: Trans Pacific
Press.

Shimazono, S. (2005) 'Foreword: toward the construction of death and life studies',
Bulletin of Death and Life Studies 1, 21st Century COE Program DALS, The
University of Tokyo, pp. 7–10.

Siegal, R. (1978) 'Phencyclidine and ketamine intoxication: a study of four popula-
tions of recreational users', in R.C. Peterson and R.C. Stillman (eds) *Phencyclidine
Abuse: An Appraisal* (Natl. Inst. Drug Abuse Res. Monogr. 21). Rockville, MD:
National Institute of Drug Abuse.

Sogyal Rinpoche (1992) *The Tibetan Book of Living and Dying*. London: Rider,
pp. 330–6.

Solms, M. (2000) 'Dreaming and REM sleep are controlled by different brain mechanisms', *Behavioral and Brain Sciences* 23(6): 843–50.

Sotelo, J., Perez, R., Guevara, P. and Fernandez, A. (1995) 'Changes in brain, plasma and cerebrospinal fluid contents of B-endorphin in dogs at the moment of death', *Neurol Res* 17: 223.

Sproul, B. (1979) *Primal Myths: Creating the World.* New York: Harper & Row.

Stevens, R. (2000) 'Phenomenological approaches to the study of conscious awareness", in M. Velmans (ed.) *Investigating Phenomenal Consciousness.* Amsterdam: John Benjamins, pp. 99–120.

Stone, M. (1976) *When God Was a Woman.* New York: Dial Press.

Strassman, R. (1995) 'Hallucinogenic drugs in psychiatric research and treatment: perspectives and prospects', *Journal of Nervous and Mental Diseases* 183: 127–38.

Strassman, R. (1997) 'Endogenous ketamine-like compounds and the NDE: if so, what?' *Journal for Near-Death Studies* 16: 27–41.

Strassman, R. (2001) *DMT: The Spirit Molecule.* Rochester, VT: Park Street Press.

Sutherland, C. (1992) *Transformed by the Light: Life After Near-Death Experiences.* Sydney: Bantam Books. (US edition published in 1995: *Reborn in the Light: Life After Near-Death Experiences.* New York: Bantam Books).

Sutherland, C. (1993) *Within the Light.* Sydney: Bantam Books. (US edition published in 1995: *Within the Light.* New York: Bantam Books).

Sutherland, C. (1995) *Children of the Light: The Near-Death Experiences of Children.* Sydney: Bantam Books.

Sutherland, C. (2008) *Trailing Clouds of Glory: The Near-Death Experiences of Western Children and Teens* (forthcoming).

Suzuki, D.T. (1959a) *Zen and Japanese Culture.* Princeton, NJ: Princeton University Press.

Suzuki, D.T. (1959b) 'The sense of Zen', in William Barrett (ed.) *Zen Buddhism: Selected Writings of D.T. Suzuki.* New York: Doubleday Anchor Books.

Swinburne, R. (1979) *The Existence of God.* Oxford: Clarendon Press.

Tachibana, T. (1994) *Near-Death Experience.* Tokyo: Bungei Shunju (Japanese only).

Tachibana, T. (1988) *Uchū kara no kikan* ('Returning from Space'). Tokyo: Chūōkōron sha.

Takuan, S. (1986) *The Unfettered Mind: Writings of the Zen Master to the Sword Master*, trans. W.S. Wilson. Tokyo: Kodansha Press.

Tart, C. (1965) 'Reports to the Parapsychology Association Convention', *Journal of Parapsychology* 29(4): 281.

Tart, C.T. (ed.) (1975) *Altered States of Consciousness.* New York: E.P. Dutton.

Thompson, E. (2001) 'Empathy and consciousness', *Journal of Consciousness Studies* 8: 1–32.

Thompson, E. and Varela, F.J. (2001) 'Radical embodiment: neural dynamics and consciousness', *Trends in Cognitive Sciences* 5: 418–25.

Thompson, E. and Varela, F.J. (forthcoming) *Radical Embodiment: The Lived Body in Biology, Cognitive Science, and Human Experience.* Cambridge, MA: Harvard University Press.

Turner, B.S. (1992) *Regulating Bodies: Essays in Medical Sociology.* New York: Routledge.

van Gennep, A. (1960) *The Rites of Passage.* London: Routledge and Kegan Paul.

van Lommel, P., van Wees, R., Meyers, V. and Elfferich, I. (2001) 'Near-death experience in survivors of cardiac arrest: a prospective study in the Netherlands', *The Lancet* 358: 2039–45.

Varela, F.J. (1996) 'Neurophenomenology: a methodological remedy for the hard problem', *Journal of Consciousness Studies*, 3(4): 330–49.

Varela, F.J. (ed.) (1998) *Sleeping, Dreaming, and Dying: An Exploration of Consciousness with the Dalai Lama*. Boston: Wisdom Publications.

Varela, F.J. (2001) Interview: La coscienza nelle neuroscienze (in Italian). Multimedia
Encyclopedia of Philosophical Science. http://www.emsf.rai.it/interviste.asp?d=452
(RAI).

Varela, F.J. and Shear, J. (1999) *The View from Within: First-Person Approaches to
the Study of Consciousness*. Thorverton, Devon: Imprint Academic.

Varela, F.J., Thompson, E. and Rosch, E. (1991) *The Embodied Mind*. Cambridge,
MA: MIT Press.

Varela, F.J. *et al.* (2001) 'The brainweb: phase synchronization and large-scale integration', *Nature Reviews Neuroscience* 2: 229–39.

Velmans, M. (1996) *The Science of Consciousness*. London: Routledge.

Wallace, B.A. (2003) *Buddhism and Science: Breaking New Ground*. New York:
Columbia University Press.

Watson, G. (1996) 'A Buddhist inspiration for a contemporary psychotherapy', PhD
thesis, SOAS, London.

Watsuji, T. (1988) *Climate and Culture*, trans. G. Bownas. New York: Greenwood
Press, Inc.

Watsuji, T. (1996) *Watsuji Tetsurō's Rinrigaku: Ethics in Japan*, trans.Yamamoto
Seisaku and Robert Carter. Albany, NY: State University of New York Press.

Weightman, S.C.R. (2000) *Mysticism and the Metaphor of Energies*. The Louis Jordan
Monographs in Comparative Religion. London: SOAS, University of London.

Weil, A. (1997) *Eight Weeks to Optimum Health*. New York: Alfred A. Knopf.

Welfeld, R. (1997) *Your Body's Wisdom: A Body-Centered Approach to Transformation*.
Naperville, IL: Sourcebooks.

Weston, A. (ed.) (1990) *An Invitation to Environmental Philosophy*. Oxford: Oxford
University Press.

Whinnery, J.E. (1997) 'Psychophysiologic correlates of unconsciousness and the
near-death experience', *Journal of Near-Death Studies* 15: 231–58.

Whinnery, J.E. and Whinnery, A.M. (1990) 'Acceleration-induced loss of consciousness', *Arch Neurology* 47: 764–76.

Wilhelm, R. (1962) *The Secret of the Golden Flower*. London: Kegan Paul.

Wilhelm, R. and Baynes, C. (1967) *The I Ching or Book of Changes*, 3rd edn.
Bollingen Series XIX. Princeton, NJ: Princeton University Press.

Wilson, E.O. (1984) *Biophilia: The Human Bond with Other Species*. Cambridge, MA:
Harvard University Press.

Winkelman, M. (1994) 'Multidisciplinary perspectives on consciousness', *Anthropology of Consciousness* 5(2): 16–25.

Wyllie, T. (1984) *Dolphins, ETs and Angels*. Santa Fe, NM: Bear & Company, Inc.

Yuasa, Y. (1987) *The Body: Toward an Eastern Mind-Body Theory*, ed. T.P. Kasulis.
Albany, NY: State University of New York.

Yuasa, Y. (1989) 'Contemporary science and an Eastern mind-body theory', in D.E.
Shaner, S. Nagatomo and Yuasa Yasuo. *Science and Comparative Philosophy:
Introducing Yuasa Yasuo*. Leiden: E.J. Brill.

Yuasa, Y. (1993) *The Body, Self-Cultivation, and Ki-Energy*. Albany, NY: State
University of New York Press.

Zahavi, D. (1999) *Self-Awareness and Alterity: A Phenomenological Investigation*. Evanston IL: Northwestern University Press.

Zaner, R.M. (1964) *The Problem of Embodiment: Some Contributions to a Phenomenology of the Body*. The Hague: Martinus Nijhoff.

Zeer, D. (2004) *Office Feng Shui: Creating Harmony in Your Work Space*. San Francisco: Chronicle Books.

Zene, C. (2003a) Lecture note on Edmund Husserl (November 24, 2003).

Zene, C. (2003b) Lecture note on Martin Heidegger (December 1, 2003).

Zhi-ying, F. and Jian-xun, L. (1992) 'Near-death experiences among survivors of the 1976 Tangshan earthquake', *Journal of Near-Death Studies* 11(1): 39–48.

Index